Susie;

You are a light!
Shine brightly on
your dreams!
Inate One!

Love,
Robin

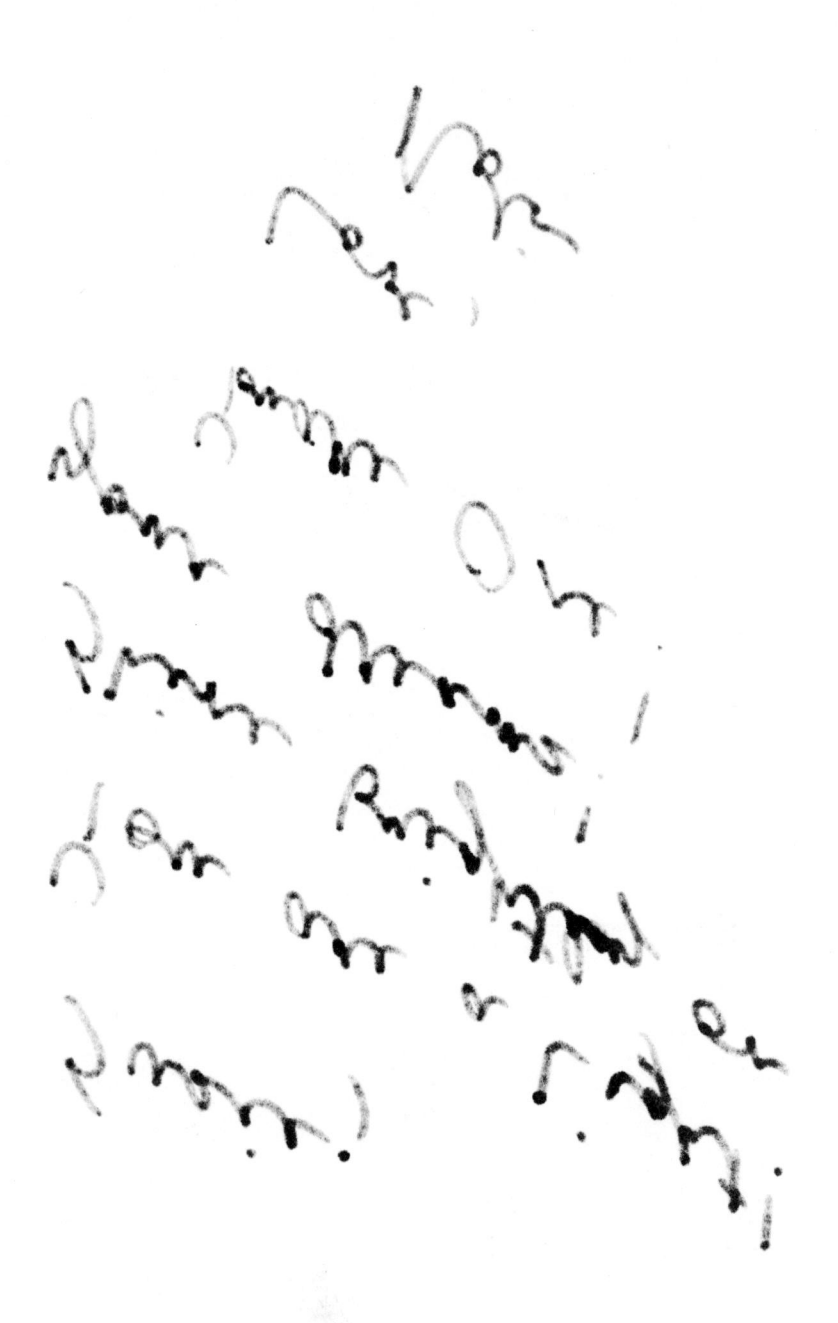

URANIUM WARRIOR

What I learned from Nunn

ROBIN M. DAVIS

BALBOA.PRESS

A DIVISION OF HAY HOUSE

Balboa Press books may be ordered through booksellers or by contacting:

Balboa Press
A Division of Hay House
1663 Liberty Drive
Bloomington, IN 47403
www.balboapress.com
844-682-1282

Because of the dynamic nature of the Internet, any web addresses or links contained in this book may have changed since publication and may no longer be valid. The views expressed in this work are solely those of the author and do not necessarily reflect the views of the publisher, and the publisher hereby disclaims any responsibility for them.

The author of this book does not dispense medical advice or prescribe the use of any technique as a form of treatment for physical, emotional, or medical problems without the advice of a physician, either directly or indirectly. The intent of the author is only to offer information of a general nature to help you in your quest for emotional and spiritual well-being. In the event you use any of the information in this book for yourself, which is your constitutional right, the author and the publisher assume no responsibility for your actions.

Any people depicted in stock imagery provided by Getty Images are models, and such images are being used for illustrative purposes only.
Certain stock imagery © Getty Images.

Print information available on the last page.

ISBN: 978-1-9822-6532-8 (sc)
ISBN: 978-1-9822-6533-5 (e)

Balboa Press rev. date: 04/23/2021

CONTENTS

DEDICATION

This book is dedicated to our beautiful planet Earth, Gaia.

FOREWORD

A story like this one is always important to be shared, however, in times of cultural crisis and chaos, this kind of story can help provide a map or at least signposts, for those struggling to respond with power to their own life challenges.

I envision that you find hope and inspiration in Robin's story of one woman's challenge when "life came knocking" in the form of a big international corporation intent on plundering her ranch and dreams of sanctuary and fulfilling work with the horses.

In addition to providing a story of empowerment and success of an individual, couple and community who stood up and said NO! to a big international corporation, this book helps us see the "uranium pits" in our own back yard and neighborhoods. It calls us to not look the other way, to think twice before we take the pitiful "payoff" for giving "them" permission to pillage our land and the "payoff" allows the plunderers into our back yards.

What does it take to Stand in Defense of Life? In Defense of the Earth? What does it take to react when we are threatened with assault from "big power," lied to about their intentions and the pollution and toxic residue from their presence? What does it take to be in integrity, and not be seduced by power and greed? What does it take to just say NO?

Robin's story gives the reader some hints and answers to these questions. This story provides examples of how each of us may respond to the challenges we face from every direction in which there is an assault. This assault may be on our own neighborhoods, or the assault may be on our personal sovereignty.

And sometimes there is an assault on the lands and waters upon which we live, as happens in the management of our public lands and industrial pollution clean-up sites. This story helps us see what is possible when collectively we are deceived— when there is a cover-up by the uranium industry of their grave poisoning on our most basic necessity—clean air and clean water.

This is also a story of what can happen where two or more are gathered together to fight for Life! Robin and Jay worked together to create a balanced team to face the assault; as a couple they were effective enough that they were able to attract a community of people and regional governance support to deal the "death blow" to the dangerous entity coming into their "neighborhood."

There is another layer to this story that in my own teachings I often see in people's lives. Many create a dream home, dream job, or dream company as a compensation for a wound that they are running from facing and integrating. There is a principle in Life that brings to us atonement—a reckoning experience that turns "our dream into becoming our worst nightmare". If this challenge is faced as an opportunity, it allows us to have to face our wound and redeem the gift in the challenge. We are then able to overcome the "nightmare" and to protect what we care about and walk in victory and redemption.

On a personal level, Robin was called to face her inner demons, her buried childhood pain and traumas in order to recover her strength and personal will to stand up to the oppressors. In this sense the uranium mine threat was a blessing as her gifts as a communicator and spiritual warrior were called forth. As she expressed her verbal gifts to politicians, public and the reporters, she was able to bear witness to her deeper purpose as an Earth Warrior and Water Protector.

I hope that this book calls you to step forth and meet the challenges all around you in your neighborhood, your city, your state and your country. Do not look the other way or accept the payoff of allowing the plunderers to take more innocence from the Web of Life that surrounds you.

Sharon Bringleson
Center for Horses and Healing
School of Earthkeeping

ACKNOWLEDGEMENTS

First and foremost I give deep appreciation and honor to my life partner, Jay. He saw things more clearly than I could and helped me open my eyes. I also want to thank my Mother for giving me life and offering me support and guidance through some very difficult times.

I offer honor and gratitude to those friends who made me question my view of reality enough to really look at what was setting up in my backyard. You know who you are and I am profoundly grateful for the fact that you would not allow me to sleepwalk my way into the destruction of our water supplies.

To the neighbors, community members and politicians that supported and stood by our need to protect water from corporate greed I can only say thank you, but it just doesn't ever feel like enough. You all blessed me with belief and commitment and energy. In turn I just want to offer you my blessing in return. Blessings of peace, justice and life to you all.

Our core group of CARD members, you all know who you are too. Let me just say, "YOU ROCK!" We did it. Yes, we did.

Those who helped this book become the reality that it needed to after many years of me poking at it and questioning myself in the very writing, Thank you. My terrific editor, Kris, my support and constant accountability partner, Sharon, and those of you I had read it to see if it was even something worth reading, Thank you!

And to you, the reader, thank you for finding enough value in this story to spend your precious time reading it.

INTRODUCTION

This is my story. A story of personal growth and a story of citizen success for the environment. This story is the story of my wake up call. I had many different internal scripts running and I had to wake up from them all in order to be functional as an activist.

The working title for this book was "What I learned from Nunn: How a Conservative Became an Apprehensive Activist" because of the many lessons I learned through my apprehension to waking up. I did not want to be an activist. I wanted to live my idealistic version of the 'American Dream.' One of the internal scripts that I ran was that, as an American, I was entitled to the dream promised to me. I deserved 'success' because I was a good girl who worked hard, paid her bills on time, was law abiding and church going.

When Powertech arrived, literally at our back door, I was certain that it would all work out for our highest good. I didn't want to look at the bigger picture, I just wanted to focus on my dream. After all, I felt that I was entitled because I had prayed about it and it was manifesting, or so I believed. I believed that God would take care of everything and I just had to passively focus on what it was that I wanted. The power of attraction, right?!? As a Christian I knew about the 'power of attraction' but it wasn't something that I was really focused on. My faith taught me that all I had to do was be a good Christian. THIS is how I would manifest my dreams. Through loving and praying and being nice. I believed that I didn't need to get dirty in a role of activism. This is what I believed. It is also how I remained in victimhood so that I could complain about my lot in life when things did not go my way.

I felt that we were in touch with God and following His Will because we were good Catholics who attended church every week and prayed for guidance most days. I was active within the Church by volunteering as a Eucharistic minister, lector and wedding coordinator. Before quitting in order to follow my dream of being a horse trainer and riding instructor, I had worked at Saint Joseph Catholic Church in the business office.

I remained active in the Pro-life movement from the perspective of attending Pro-life masses at the Church, writing to elected officials on a regular basis and always voting the Pro-life ticket. I was also a regular attendee at retreats at the Abbey of Saint Walburga and was even considering receiving oblation, which is a ceremony in which one promises to live the Benedictine Rule as a layperson. I am a Catholic Biblical School graduate and prayed the daily Missal.

I would describe myself as a Conservative Christian Republican. It was important to me to have those titles, just as it was also important to me to have the title of 4-H Leader and Natural Horsemanship Trainer. I didn't really realize it at the time but I needed something upon which I could hang my hat to prove that I was worthy.

I was always called emotional, but I used emotions more as a tool, as a way to get what I wanted. Not consciously, mind you, but certainly in the way I did things. I was often angry without really understanding what I was truly angry about. I'd project my anger onto Jay, my husband, or onto the political climate or society as a whole. It was easier than going within and learning about myself. I had some baggage that needed cleaning up but I couldn't clean it up without really looking at it first.

The lessons from the uranium mine battle were ones that forced my hand and forced me into really looking at what was driving me. I was 'content' living the lie that I was happy because I was married to a great guy and that my 'American dream' was coming true. I was content in not really learning about the intelligence in emotion but rather using that emotion in a dysfunctional way in order to defend the lie that I was telling myself.

It was much easier to project that emotion onto others in judgment and manipulation than to look at real truth.

I was good at making my own anger wrong. I wasn't yet at a place in my life where I could look at anger and ask the questions: What boundary has been violated? How can that boundary be restored? These are difficult questions for many of us and likely why anger as an emotion has become so demonized. It's tough to ask the tough questions. Making friends with anger in a healthy way is not something in which our society finds value. So I would take that internal anger, look for a place upon which to focus it and make the 'other' wrong for whatever thing I perceived as not being 'correct.'

The Truth is that when I turned within I'd find that I was truly broken and hurting inside. I'd find self-loathing. I'd find the source of pain and heartache.

I was seeking ways to truly get in touch with myself. I was attracting those things that would do that for me. Attracting those things that would make me see truth rather than being a person of the lie. The law of attraction is real and we can make ourselves buy into what is manifesting as the perfect life by ignoring what is happening outside of our own little bubble until our unconsciousness manifests something that requires us to go beyond the lie.

Living a lie does not mean that you will attract a uranium mine, or something outside of yourself, but it might mean you manifest acute or chronic physical or mental illness (dis-ease). It's all energy and the lessons will come as is best for your own personal growth. I am childless because I have dealt with endometriosis. I now know that I was at war with my uterus because I did not trust being female. This dis-ease was manifested by me to cover the lie that I was living. The body does not lie and will respond to the constant stress of living a lie.

The story of our quest to save the water from Uranium mining is also the story of what began my own looking into my story. Attracting a huge drama into my world, shattering my dreams of focusing on horses and youth and a nature retreat for both, I was put in a position to be a water warrior. Water, the element that represents emotion and the fluidity of life. Water which is LIFE!

I was thrust into a position where I really had to protect LIFE. Without water there is no life. I was thrust into a position of TRULY honoring all LIFE, including my own. When I speak of LIFE vs. life, I am referring to all of Creation and the Spark that makes it and connects it. I am referring to Love and how it is alive. I am referring to Divinity. LIFE is what we are a part of as well as what we live.

For this journey, I had to be willing to look within and love myself enough to step into an uncomfortable position in which I could have never imagined myself. I had to let go of titles and idealism and dreams and look hard and long into the face of reality AND I had to take action to address this reality. This is the real story. The story of personal growth and the action it took to begin that growth.

As you begin reading you will see places where I speak from a voice of a type of narration with the new found wisdom that I have as I write this. It feels important to add these reflections throughout as part of what I learned. The journey of fighting the uranium miners was a deep learning experience on many levels and I hope that this book can begin to help the reader drop into that depth. I recognize that the story is almost two stories in one, but they are truly inseparable. Without the challenges put in front of me as we had our hands forced into stepping into this role of activism, I may have not taken the deeper journey of learning about myself.

I hope you enjoy the read and find it helpful for you on your own personal journey through life as you navigate your own waters.

PROLOGUE

The black mare craned her neck downward until her whiskers touched the water inside the water tank. She drew back a little as her whiskers issued a dire warning. Something wasn't right. But, she was thirsty, so she pushed through the vibrational warnings.

As she touched her lips to the water, her sensitive tongue tasted that the water was "off."

She stopped drinking after only a few swallows and went searching for cleaner water.

After wandering the pasture for many hours, the sun beat down on her dark body and she knew she desperately needed water and there was only one source.

As she walked with purpose back to the water tank she felt a quickening in her uterus. The foal she was carrying needed water too.

She drank deeply, ignoring the alarm bells that were going off as she took in the heavy metals that were already killing off the new cell growth that her hair, her hooves, and especially the new baby needed for growth and survival.

As she lifted her head above the water a thin line dribbled from her lips back into the tank. Her thirst quenching had been interrupted by the movement she spotted not too far away from where she was standing. She watched as the strange men were doing what they do on occasion to check one of the well heads in her pasture.

She had a deep sense of foreboding whenever these men were around, but they had also become part of the scenery over the past several months so she chose to ignore them.

The mare, as all horses do, has a strong connection with all of life and the subtle energies. Some even call it a seventh sense because of its Spiritual nature.

She knew the water was contaminated. She knew that the men who now frequented her pasture did not have her highest good in mind. She knew that they were lost in greed and thoughtless domination of the land and the water.

Occasionally, the kinder of the two men might bring an apple or some carrots for the mare and her herd mates. The horses would gratefully accept this small gesture of generosity while holding space for this man to expand upon the emotion that guided him to do such things.

The horses would gather around him and move the energy they sensed and felt. They did this to reciprocate the kindness he offered. Moving this energy might help this man remember his own soul.

Occasionally, if the man's subconscious was open to it, one or more of the horses might visit him through the ethers in his dreamtime to share wisdom and connection.

In the end, it is his choice what he does with this support, but the horses know that they have knowledge to share for those with hearts open enough to hear.

At the water tank the black mare watched as she noticed the energy of the man today. He was closed off and hurried. She would not approach him this day.

She dipped her nose for another long drink that felt at once life giving and life taking. Lifting her head and turning away from the water tank, she gave her head and neck a big shake and several black hairs drifted to the ground. This was the price she paid for taking care of her needs for water.

As the months continued in this rhythm, she was no longer pregnant. The foal had come prematurely and had slipped from her body, dead and hairless. She and her herd mates were not feeling as good as they used to. Their ragged coats, thin manes and tails and sloughing hooves told the real story. It was only a matter of time...

CHAPTER 1

HORSES

"Robin! Robin! Where are you?"

Oh my God, Oh my God… Mom noticed the unlocked front screen door and peered out, her hand gripping the doorknob to steady herself. She felt nauseous, her heart pounding in her chest. Her ears filled with an internal *thump, thump.*

WHERE IS ROBIN! her mind screamed.

The distraught mother looked down the road, straining to hear police sirens. She hoped her panicked call had spurred them into coming fast. She needed help! She swallowed hard, bile burning her throat as she forced it back down by sheer willpower. *Where could she be?* My young mother had been busy with the laundry, her mind filled with the multitude of mundane things she had to get done that day, when she noticed I was gone.

The air pressure of the farm trucks driving by at high speed buffeted my two-year-old body. I closed my eyes and let the pulse of the pressure push me back onto my bare heels. I smiled, enjoying the warm moving air as it effortlessly shifted my torso forward and back.

The trucks whizzed by as I opened my eyes and immediately noticed the horses standing in the field across the street. *Oh yea…* that's where I had been headed. My toddler brain had been distracted by the pleasurable buffeting of air pressure from passing cars and trucks. The sensation helped me forget that my goal was elsewhere.

It was the horses that drew me. They had from my first experience as a baby, feeling the warm blow on my skin as my mom introduced her new infant to the muzzle of a friendly and curious gelding. While I have no conscious memory of this, my mom would say I had been touched by a horse before I could walk. Something about those big, lovely beasts made my heart fly open with joy like nothing else I'd experienced in my short life. I had bubbled over with excitement when I leaned on the front screen door and it swung wide open. Unafraid, I immediately tottered out the door and climbed on hands and knees up the five garden-level steps. My eyes focused on the big bay mare who was quietly grazing on the far side of a rusty barbed wire fence, well beyond the busy country road.

My mom dropped to her knees next to the bed and peered underneath. A drop of nervous sweat dripped down her nose and onto the floor. She wiped her face with the back of her trembling hand. She was running out of places to look. *Did someone take her? Had she been kidnapped?* Tears threatened. She was pulling herself up by the bedpost when she heard the short chirp of the siren. A police car had pulled in and parked under the tree. She flew to the door to let the man in, relieved that help had arrived.

I pulled as hard as I could at my dress. The spike in the barbed wire held tight to the hem, effectively holding me captive. The harder I fought the more entangled I became. My tiny hands fumbled ineffectively, creating a frustration that was new in my minimal life experience. I whimpered, teeth gritted, falling into the grass onto my back as I struggled with the sharp wire. Soon, a soft blow of air invited my attention. I turned my head to face a brown nostril that smelled like grass. Forgetting my predicament for a moment, I cooed into the mare's nose, reaching out to touch the silky muzzle with both hands. I squeezed the giant nose, a grin stretching across my little face. The gentle mare blew again, curious about the struggling creature who was trying to invade her pasture. Giggling replaced tears, the trapped dress forgotten in a moment of deep equine bliss.

Another quick search of the house revealed nothing. While child abductions were rare, they were not unheard of in the town of Arvada, just west of Denver, Colorado. The officer wasn't ready to accept that horrifying conclusion given all the places a toddler could hide, but concern was certainly growing. On a whim, he opened his trunk and pulled out a pair of binoculars. Scouring the area through the glass in a slow turn of his torso, he spotted an unusual flash of color in the field across the street.

"Mama, the fence got me," I muttered, my tear stained face pleading for rescue. My mom hugged me tight, tears streaming with relief as she forcefully tore the dress from the barbed fence.

My mom spent the next seven years trying to satisfy my need for horse-time. Finding her daughter safely across the busy road that harrowing morning, her dress tangled in the pasture fence's barbed wire, left her both relieved and concerned. Mom knew from that day forward that she had to keep an eye on her enterprising daughter whenever a horse was near. A new lock on the screen door and a new awareness of the necessity to constantly inspect that deterrent was only a partial fix. My mom was familiar with the addiction of horses, and was fully aware that her daughter was destined for a life with these special four-legged friends. Her goal was not to avoid equines, but to keep her intrepid daughter alive along the journey.

When I was 5, the fellow next door let me drive his ponies. I would come home from school, change my clothes, and head next door to hand feed the little horses the green grass I plucked from next to the fence. I would patiently wait for the owner to come home, see my pleading face at the fence, and hopefully wave me over. The owner enjoyed my company and enthusiasm, and taught me all he could about how to handle the spunky little beasts.

At 8 years old, I spent time at a nearby ranch that was owned by friends of my mother. While Mom was visiting the owner, I would follow one of the ranch hands around, watching and learning. I ate up everything and anything horse. The ranch soon became a favorite place for me to enjoy both riding and caring for equids of all kinds. I often got to ride

"Tony the Tiger," a little gelding who would buck and kick at other horses when they got too close. Instead of feeling fear, the thrill of the powerful gelding's bucking made me squeal and laugh with delight. What my mother didn't know was, eventually one of the ranch hands had other, more personal things to share with my young, naïve self. Things that were scary, inappropriate, and deeply traumatic. These covert and uninvited events would create profound emotional scars that I would have to deal with for the rest of my life.

At 10, I got a horse of my own. Our family and another family with kids bought three horses together, including a lovely mare for me. Arabesque was a dark buckskin, grade (unregistered), mare of unknown decent. And while she may not have had fancy papers, this mare was the most wonderful creature on the planet to me. Arabesque was my best friend. I laid on her back for hours, reading books, staring at the sky, or just dozing in the sun. Arabesque happily carried me all over the neighborhood as effectively as a car, instilling an intense appreciation for freedom that few children had the chance to enjoy. We played horseback Frisbee with the neighbor kids, and even raced the school bus down the street as it brought the elementary school children home. I would proudly announce to anyone who would listen that Arabesque had been clocked at a full 30 miles per hour by the bus driver.

Horses are in my blood. Horses feed my soul. Horses became my destiny. But it wasn't until adulthood that I discovered that a love of horses had put me in a position to be forced to take a stand and to do all I could to change how my community, and perhaps even the whole world, dealt with one of the most powerful and potentially toxic elements on the planet, Uranium.

CHAPTER 2

CHASING A DREAM

In November of 2005 Jay and I had decided it was time to take a look at larger properties where I could fulfill my dream of owning a horse ranch. I had an exciting vision of a place where I could train and board horses. I wanted it to be a safe place for others to come and to be in relationship with their horses in a more natural setting. I was enjoying success as a riding instructor on a small acreage in Masonville, but the neighbors were beginning to complain about the activity, and quite frankly I needed more room to operate a more sustainable business model. I also wanted to start a 4-H club and have the kids experience a day on the ranch as a part of their weekend activities.

Jay had a partnership in a civil engineering business which was thriving and offered us the additional support we needed in order to make such a move. Jay has never been a real 'horse' person, but he enjoys the animals and likes to be a part of protecting our natural world as much as he can. The conflict he feels working in the development world finds him continually seeking ways to follow his heart. He always found small ways to fulfill his passion for protecting the planet. Whenever a rough site plan for a new development hit his desk, he'd physically do a site visit so he could determine what features bore protecting as he developed his design. A 100 year cottonwood here, a natural wetland there. He'd do his best as he worked with the architects and others to help nature remain within a design.

Our Sundays after church quickly became the day for us to drive around and look at potential areas in which to move. If we spotted a place for sale, we'd spend time researching the neighborhood and anything that could be affecting the property and/or water rights before ever talking to a real estate agent about seeing the house. With Jay's background he knew many of the pitfalls that we needed to avoid, and the internet provided us the opportunity to view public records. We were thorough!

One of the hot topics in Colorado at the time was the Prairie Falcon Parkway Express, a proposed 210-mile long toll road along Colorado's eastern plains from Fort Collins to Pueblo. The project had become commonly known as Super Slab. As we looked at properties, we looked at all the information we could find on Super Slab. We certainly didn't want to buy property in an area with the potential of a superhighway coming through.

After intensive research and lots of time spent driving around and getting the feel for areas, we finally settled on the spot that was to become our current home. The land we were interested in had been part of the original land grant deal with Union Pacific Railroad that had been used to bring the railroad across the nation to the west coast. After the railroads had sold the surface rights, they generally retained the mineral rights.

"It doesn't look like there are any minerals that anyone might be interested in mining at this place," Jay said. "I checked oil, gas, coal, gold, you know the typical ones. I even checked for diamonds since we know they've found some of those deposits in northern Colorado and southern Wyoming."

Jay was more concerned about an easement that was on the property. With the rumblings regarding "Super Slab" this easement had him worried that the developers of Super Slab might use it to bring the highway right through our property, regardless of the fact that the original maps were showing it well to the south of where we were looking for property. Jay's experience with developers kept him on guard. He knew that until a project was in construction, all bets were off as to what the final project might look like.

We hired an attorney to research the easement. "Looks like the easement is just for the major power transmission lines. The Super

Slab developers would not have access to it," Jay told me after speaking with the attorney.

We finally felt that we had found our perfect place. It was a tidy, newly built home on 80 acres with lots of room to set up my boarding and training business. The location of the space was close enough to highways 85 and I-25 for relatively easy access for us to commute for shopping, Jay's work, as well as allowing clients to get to us easily. Yet, it was far enough away from these highways that we were truly out in the country and away from it all. We excitedly moved into our dream home in February of 2006.

We spent that Spring, Summer and into the Fall creating a safe and comfortable environment for the horses and the kids. Jay being very handy and with me helping him, we did most of the work ourselves with the occasional help from some good friends.

In the beginning, several of my students from southwest Fort Collins and the Masonville area followed me to our new location. The drive became too much for them, pretty quickly, though. I had expected that to happen so I was doing some networking to fill the void. We attracted two new boarded horses and I had three new riding students. Plus, I had started a Monday morning study group of adults with green(untrained) horses who wanted to learn right along with them.

The kids yelled as I heard another "SPLASH."

Another 4-H kid was dunked into the horse tank. I smiled and laughed and reveled at how this was exactly the type of pure and free experience of being in a natural location that I had dreamt of providing.

The kids enjoyed chasing each other and just creating as much chaos as they wanted until we organized into a hike through the pasture. Hiking along we'd watch as prairie dog tails waved goodbye in a chittering retreat. We'd see how close we could get and peer down their holes hoping to see a nose.

Jay and I were really beginning to love the prairie and all it has to offer. Moving from the foothills surrounding Masonville to the wide open prairie was a big change for both of us. The ecological system was so different. I had been used to mule deer and foxes who frequented our property. We had been blessed with a variety of songbirds and hummingbirds who had visited our bird feeders. It was difficult for me to leave this extended family behind, though, the prairie offered new and different wildlife to get to know. We were learning about the colony of burrowing owls who nest on the ranch every summer. We were enthralled by the little black and white lark buntings, who are the Colorado state bird and live in this area. The jackrabbits with those extra long legs and ears are amazing to watch as they walk and run. But the raptors are really the stars of the prairie. We've had the glorious opportunities of seeing golden eagles catch rabbits and have witnessed the stunning mating dives of these same incredible birds.

Our new home had been dubbed "the little house on the prairie" by many of our friends and family. We'd send them photos of rolling hills with nothing on them but prairie grass. Jay and I loved the panoramic sunrises and sunsets. We just couldn't take enough photos to share. In between working on improvements and building businesses, we'd spend time watching the storm clouds rolling in from miles away. We found ourselves learning which ones really meant we would get rain and which ones we could just enjoy watching as they rolled on by.

One storm in July gave us a pleasant surprise. "Look, that depression is filling with water," Jay said as we watched the monsoonal rains fall. After the rain stopped he quickly went exploring.

"We have at least 3 ponds out there," he said excitedly when he returned. We knew that we had an historical livestock well with a disintegrating tank and what looked like it could be a pond on the west half of our property, but these new ponds were a pleasant surprise.

We felt very blessed to have found the perfect place for us. We were living the dream.

CHAPTER 3

WE HAVE URANIUM

One day in October 2006 we received what we thought at first was a joke. The letter dated October 13, 2006 from Lone Tree Energy Associates proceeded to tell us about the Centennial project for uranium development that Powertech Uranium Corp plans to undertake on our land since they had just purchased the mineral rights from Anadarko. The plan was to do in-situ leaching (ISL). This technology is defined as being "new" and having very little, if any, surface impact while being a "controllable, safe, and environmentally benign method of mining which can operate under strict environmental controls."

Then, of course, the letter went on to lay out a proposed financial benefit to us as property owners. A $10 per acre "signing" bonus, a $2 per acre annual rental and the big benefit...... a 1% royalty based upon the "value" per pound of all U308 produced from the mines directly linked to our land.

We had already found out that our research regarding the location of Super Slab turned out to be unhelpful. Shortly after we had moved in and were getting settled we had received a certified letter that included the developers' NEW map. We were right in their new designed location. Being of generally good humor and not believing that the Super Slab would ever come to fruition, we joked about how we got caught anyway. Of course, Jay did get involved with the Super Slab opposition group on a small level and had even attended a few public hearings at the State Capitol by this point. So this uranium letter did seem like it could be a joke from one of our friends and/or family. How could so many things hit at once? (*Oh laws of attraction you can be so true...*)

We had had no idea that uranium was in this area. At the time of our research on the land, Colorado law had privacy statutes regarding the data acquired by a company who was prospecting for minerals. The prospecting that had been done in this area in the 1970s for uranium was not publicly recorded knowledge.

I had played the naïve role and the impact of the presence of uranium just wouldn't register in my brain. "Maybe this could be a nice source of income," I said, optimistically. I felt that we could use whatever we could get at the time since we still owned the house in Masonville. We were renting to a woman who planned to purchase the house, but we had set her rent lower than what our own monthly commitment to the mortgage was to make it affordable for her until her own house sold. Things were a bit tight.

If the letter was real, I did know that our rights as surface owners would be superceded by the mineral owners. We had purchased with eyes wide open to the split estate laws, and I am an advocate for property rights so I felt the need to allow the mineral rights owners their rights. Plus, they did say that the project would be unimpactful and regulated in all ways, I didn't figure there was any way the government would allow something toxic to happen where people lived. I also believed at that time that nuclear power could be the saving grace we needed to produce environmentally safe energy. Not to mention that being a good Conservative and therefore also a Capitalist, a part of me hoped that we might have just moved into some wealth.

"I think I'll check into this a bit," Jay replied as he looked at me with raised eyebrows. He already knew something about uranium and was a little disturbed by my lack of reaction. So, Jay began his research. In-situ leach mining (ISL) was new to him, he did a search on: 'in-situ leach mining for uranium.' Immediately, he saw page upon page that said "dangerous," "water pollution," "toxic" and other keywords that did not give him any feeling of comfort for the process. He began diving deeper. Jay read about ISL mines in the United States and abroad. He found clearing house sites for articles about the reality of uranium mining such as www.wise-uranium.org, and also spent a lot of time reading what the folks in the uranium mining industry were saying.

My idealism kept me firm in the belief that God wanted us here and since I always believed that things would work out as long as I had Faith I would just shrug and say to myself, 'it's all good.' Jay is more of a realist, even though he generally attempted to follow my idealistic view and prayed that this might be okay. He took the time to look very intently at both sides of the issue.

Our very full days of building the Ranch and its activities continued and turned into full weeks and months. Jay was still working 50-60 hours per week at his business. When he wasn't there, he was kept busy with physical labor building fence and other jobs. My horsewoman schedule was developing into a clear routine:

- Mondays: 9am - 1pm we had our adult horsemanship study group, every other Monday evening I had 4-H meetings for leaders;
- Tuesday and Wednesday: days to work on building, cleaning, riding, training, paperwork, etc.
- Thursday evening: 4-H meetings with the club.
- Friday: Lessons until dark, then a campfire that we had dubbed Friday Fire, a fun way for us and our boarders to relax under our incredible starry sky while we bonded around a campfire with hotdogs, marshmallows and general good fun.
- Saturday: 9am - noon, 4-H kids meet to work on 4-H projects. Some were riding and others would work on other project stuff; 1pm - dark; I would give lessons.
- Sunday: Church in the morning and lessons in the afternoon.

Any spare time was filled in by building the physical things needed to make the set-up a comfortable and safe place for horses and people alike. I was exhausted and would not allow myself to even think about uranium. Every time Jay brought it up, I brushed it off. "I'm sure there are plenty of protections and regulations in place," I'd blithely state.

Jay would look at me like I was from another planet, sigh, and say "You're gonna want to check this out." Then, not wishing to cause an argument, he'd let it drop.

Never one to want to really confront anything that might cause a disagreement between us, Jay would spend late nights reading about uranium and mining without discussing his findings with me. He kept hoping that he would find something we could do to protect our dream.

In December of 2006 we had a really warm day in which I was feeling very blessed to be doing what I love in such a beautiful place. We had decided to call the ranch Mustang Hollow. We had finally closed on the sale of our house in Masonville, much of the new fencing was done, and things were beginning to feel like we really had moved in. I felt that God was truly blessing us with His Grace.

I was watching a 6 year old student ride my best school horse and this student's dear horsey friend, Cherry. Today was one of his first rides in the new big arena.

"Just relax and allow her to have her head, she'll be alright," I coached. "Trust her and she'll be trustworthy."

As I watched this student ride, I had an opportunity to look out across the vast short grass prairie to the east. The sea of winter brown vegetation below the crystal blue sky was striking. The clear day allowed me to see the water tower in Nunn silhouetted in the distance. I felt really good.

This student's mother was relaxed and leaning on the fence while she watched her son. "He looks kind of nervous to be in the big arena, but Cherry is doing well."

I smiled and agreed. This was going well.

The rising dust and the sound of a vehicle coming from the west caught my attention. Living where you can see for many miles in most directions allows a person to watch many things at once. We had been here long enough to know all of our neighbor's vehicles and the common comings and goings of the area. I watched as an unfamiliar green van bounced down the dirt road toward the intersection at the corner of our property. The van skidded a bit on the loose dirt kicking up a cloud of dust as it ground to a brief stop at the intersection. Then it turned left and headed north toward our driveway.

As much as I wanted to believe that all things were good, I was beginning to be suspicious of any unfamiliar activity. The whole Super Slab, uranium mining, and who knew what other issues might be lurking, was starting to get to me on an unconscious level.

The van pulled up to our closed gate. A tall, well dressed, blonde gentleman got out. His bare head, slacks, and button front shirt told me he was not from the area. Keeping an eye on my young student, I watched from the corner of my eye as he opened the gate and drove on in. He never waved or called out a greeting to ask for permission as was typical of most of the people we had met so far. I was very curious because of the way this person just came on in with no hesitation. He paused to close the gate then continued to drive up our driveway.

I walked to the edge of the arena and stood near the fence. As the van approached us, I gave a small wave. My student and Cherry were my primary focus, but I had my head turned enough to watch what was playing out. The gentleman parked and quickly got out of his van. He began talking as soon as his feet hit the ground, "Hello," he said as he continued to approach with an outstretched hand and a big smile. "I'm a land guy working for Powertech Uranium Corporation. I used to be in the wrong lane with oil and gas, but now I'm in the right lane." He said with his slight southern accent.

I was very disturbed about the way he seemed to demand all of my attention rather than allowing me to finish my lesson before he began speaking, or even asking who he should be speaking to.

Out of curiosity, the student rode Cherry over to join us all at the fence, allowing me to focus on this person that was now in front of me.

"I'd like to tell you about the plans that we have for this area," he continued.

I recognized the business name because of the letter we had received in October. I did not want to deal with him nor his plans right then, or ever if the real truth be known. This interruption of a lesson of a beginner student on a horse was extremely bothersome to me.

His lack of awareness or concern for what I might have going on at the time was, as I was soon to learn, symptomatic of the way mineral rights owners treat surface owners. Their lack of concern for what the surface owner may be doing on the top of the land is a reflection of the reality that they really don't need to take the surface owner into too much consideration. They have their agenda and they will just push it forward by ignoring and running right over those who live on the property.

"I can't talk with you right now. Do you have a card?" I asked as I shook his extended hand. I just wanted to get rid of the guy and go back to my idealistic version of my life at the time. I was following my dream, dammit. Who was this guy to mess all that up!

"No, I'm new with the company and don't have cards yet," he replied.

He asked for our phone number. I gave him Jay's cell phone number since I certainly didn't want to be the one to deal with this issue. He got back in his van and drove away.

As we watched him bounce down the dirt road, the student's mother said to me, "That was certainly weird, wasn't it."

"Yeah, but I'm sure we as the property owners have enough rights and protections in place. I think it was just that guy." I really wanted to believe that. I was certain that we had been called to this location. That God had put us in this space so that I could fulfill my dream of helping people be more in touch with themselves and nature, all with the help of horses. I put on my Faith hat and promptly pushed this intruder and uranium aside for the rest of the day.

"Take Cherry down the fence line and stop her by that barrel," I told the rider as I jumped right back into lesson mode.

That evening I shared the experience with Jay. He wanted to talk a bit more about what he was finding out about ISL mining for uranium. "You do know that the owners of the mineral rights have precedent over the rights of the surface owner."

I had picked up the original letter with the information from Powertech regarding the Centennial project and was looking at their brochure with the verdant pastures with just a wellhead or two, "Okay, but it doesn't look like the mining operation would be too impactful. Maybe they will only take up a small portion of the acreage and we can continue to do our thing." From the drawings it looked like most everything would take place underground except for a couple of tanks on the surface. I was thinking of some of the natural gas wells I'd seen. I was hoping for something neat and tidy and small.

"From the photos of existing mines that I've been looking at, this type of mining is much more impactful to the surface than what they are sharing here," Jay replied

I had a good tired, the kind of tired where one just feels satisfied rather than exhausted from being outside all day on this beautiful day. I wanted to keep living 'Happily Ever After.' I didn't want to talk about uranium mining, no matter how much Powertech or Jay kept putting it in front of me.

"Well," I responded, "they own the mineral rights so there isn't anything we can do. I'm sure they will do it in a way to be able to work with us. We have rights of our own, I'm sure. Besides, we might be able to make a little money off of the deal."

Little did I realize that I was mentally encamped in a state of victimhood. I felt powerless to the ever pressing situation and wanted to just find the good in it so I could ignore the bigger picture. I had bought into this powerlessness by being a good consumer who recycled what I could, but missed the incongruence of how consuming and especially impulse buying was a big part of how I distracted myself from and yet participated in the destruction of LIFE, namely, the planet and its biodiversity. I fought the hopelessness fed by this sense of powerlessness by 'fighting' for the children through my Pro-life activities and felt I was making the impact that would make the biggest waves. My stance was that if we respected life at its most innocent and fragile that a deeper regard for LIFE as a whole would prevail. I knew about extinction of species and the toxification of nature, so I paid our dues to GreenPeace and The Nature Conservancy, but honestly felt that protecting the fetus is what would begin to tip our global awareness. I was a victim to Capitalism while I believed that I was doing all that I could to save the planet.

A few months later, in Early February of 2007, I found myself setting out to travel to Pasadena, California where I had been invited, as a peer, to be a part of an internationally known horse trainer's demonstration at the Equine Affaire. The invitation was also extended to a friend and local woman horse trainer. We both readily agreed and invited Laura, a mutual friend, to come along so we could make it a short vacation, as well.

We woke up to 10 degrees below zero and a fierce wind the day of our flight. Jay reassured me that he would be able to be home most of the day to continually break ice off the water tanks for the horses. We both have a deep regard for the value of water as life sustaining. Our ranch water transport consists of running water to the horses through 600 feet of garden hose attached to the spigot on the back of the house.

This was going to be a brutal day for Jay. I was torn between feeling guilty for leaving him behind with the horse responsibilities and being excited about escaping to a warmer climate and a break from the work on our new ranch. I stuffed the guilt while remembering that this trip was more than just pleasure. It would serve to build my dream of becoming a respected horsewoman.

While Jay was left at home to break ice on the water tanks and make sure all of the hoses were clear for the next water re-fill we three women were having a ball together. We laughed and carried on as the plane propelled us further from our regular responsibilities. Laura and I were just getting to know one another. She had joined our adult study group with her young filly recently and we had ridden our more seasoned horses together a couple of times. I was attracted to her open and fun-loving attitude. Laura could generally find fun in any situation, I loved her positive outlook on life.

We all were bouncing around from seat to seat on this nearly empty airplane to be able to see the best views of the landscape over which we were flying. We enjoyed pointing out the amazing natural features such as Lake Powell and the Grand Canyon.

At one point, as she was gazing out a window on a more desolate terrain, Laura turned serious and brought up the uranium mining issue in Utah. I casually said, "We have uranium at our place. There is a company that wants to take advantage of their mineral rights and mine it."

"WHAT?!?!?!," exclaimed Laura with a look of horror. A much different Laura from whom I was getting to know. She obviously had some opinions about uranium and uranium mining, and they were not good.

"They own the minerals and they say it's safe. I'm sure it will be fine," I replied. I didn't want our fun mood to be spoiled so early into the trip. I was all about by-passing any emotion that required depth. "They are doing it in lots of other places. How can it be all that bad anyway? I have faith that people will do the right thing."

"Robin," implores Laura, "I have seen so many issues with uranium mining. I cannot imagine this is safe. People do NOT always do the right thing. You are too much of an idealist."

Again with people wanting to burst my idealistic bubble, all I could think was that I just did not need the distraction of this whole uranium mining issue right now. I had my course plotted out and I was pursuing my dreams. "Laura, I am sure it's fine. Besides, what can I do? They own our mineral rights."

"All I'm saying is that you are going to want to check into this. It could be really bad."

I went on to tell her about the Super Slab politics in which we were already involved. I shared my confused state of mind on this issue. "The thing about Super Slab is that I've always been one who understands that the good of the many needs to outweigh the good of the few. I wonder how our country would be if everyone had fought against all of the existing highway system. I just hope that if it comes about we'll be compensated fairly," I expressed.

"Robin, Super Slab won't kill you! You need to really look at this uranium mining," she replied

Laura began sharing some of her history in the environmental consulting business that she and her husband used to own.

Though this was all interesting and I might have enjoyed listening to some of her stories at a different time, I didn't want to have to think about much more than having fun on this trip. This was my first opportunity in two years to travel, sleep in, and generally relax. I planned to take full advantage of it. I was putting on my Scarlett O'Hara-esque mask 'I'll think about that tomorrow. Tomorrow is another day.' Don't look at the bigger picture, let me just keep moving in the direction that I have in mind. I can't be bothered with what is really happening all around me while I follow my own dreams.

We spent the rest of the trip enjoying our time on and off "stage" at the Equine Affaire. When our portion of the Affaire was over, we three girls did a little sightseeing in Santa Barbara. I returned to Colorado after a long weekend of feeling warm and relaxed, but, also with a small voice niggling at me about the uranium mine.

Back at the ranch the seemingly ceaseless winter wind buffeted me as I hiked up the hill after another day of breaking ice and draining hoses. The winter was really dragging on with all of the wind and cold temperatures. We hadn't had a day that reached over 20 degrees F for several weeks. Getting water to the horses was taking up most of my energy so I was exhausted and very ready to come in for the evening. I had dinner on my mind and was wondering what time Jay might be home.

It was rare for him to be home for dinner those days. The civil engineering business was beginning to be a real drain on him. His partner had adopted a couple of special needs children within the past year. The medical appointments and the therapies that these kids needed was distracting this partner to such a degree that Jay was left to run the business virtually on his own.

That night, Jay got home before 10pm for a change. He set the mail from our PO Box on the kitchen island. I sorted through the junk mail and the bills before coming across a letter from Powertech Uranium Corporation. This particular letter was addressed just to Jay, convenient for me since I wanted him to be the rescuer in the situation while I stayed in victimhood and idealism.

Jay read the letter while I warmed up some of the spaghetti dinner I had cooked earlier. He didn't comment as he set the letter on the island. While he sat down with his dinner, I picked up the letter and joined him at the table.

The letter was dated February 13, 2007. They were writing to let us know about Colorado Revised Statute (24-65.5-101(3)) that required them to notify us that they intend to take advantage of their mineral rights. The letter included a press release showing Powertech's purchase of the mineral rights from Anadarko and closed by telling us we could call with any questions.

As much as I'd like to ignore the potential of a uranium mine I was starting to get the feeling that these guys were serious about taking advantage of their mineral rights.

This whole split estate issue was very difficult for me to reconcile with. Why do mineral owners get precedent over surface owners? I could see how the good of the many outweighs the good of the few, but, this was getting personal in so many ways. I was certain God had brought us to Mustang Hollow and so I held steadfast to the notion that God would take care of this situation too. All I had to do was pray about it, right?!?!

We didn't discuss the letter. I just put it back on the island. I wanted to talk about our other plans. It was rare that I was still up when Jay came home these days, so we had a few things to discuss. We had plans to purchase the adjacent 40 acres so that we could be stewards of our own little conservation area while creating a buffer between any additional neighbors who might move in to the north of us. Our second mortgage had been approved and we were getting ready to set the closing date. We discussed how we needed to coordinate dates between us and the seller.

When we straightened the kitchen before heading to bed the letter from Powertech Uranium Corporation hit the stack of other pieces of paper that should be dealt with some other day.

On March 12, 2007, we received another letter from Powertech. This letter was addressed to both Jay and I and said that he would like to meet with the both of us to discuss Powertech's mining plans.

I read this with a sigh. This issue just would not go away. I kept wishing and praying it away and maintained that if I ignored it long enough it would work out just the way I wanted it to.

"Jay," I said as he read the letter, "has he called you?"

"Nope, haven't heard a thing from them," he replied.

"Should we call them?" I asked.

"I don't know. All I do know is that this just doesn't seem good at all. They own our mineral rights and the way Colorado law is written, any rights we have as surface owners are secondary to the mineral owners rights."

"So maybe we need to sit down with them and work out whatever arrangements we need to."

"From what I'm seeing with existing ISL uranium mines, anything of this sort would virtually shut us down. Between the multitude of wells, the piping that may or may not be just laid upon the surface, the processing plant and the trucks that would be part of the operation, this location would not be safe for horses let alone the kids," Jay stated with sorrow in his eyes. "I haven't even really begun to tell you what might happen to our drinking water. This process tends to pollute the groundwater."

Our water?!?! Water is so important. I had been spending most of my winter figuring out how to get water to my horses. Water is truly life. Now, I was starting to have my eyes opened to the possibility of a threat since Jay was concerned about our water.

I finally sat and really thought about what could happen to our property, I began to feel utterly helpless and defeated. We had spent the last year draining so many of our financial and physical resources to set up what had the potential of being a beautiful and lasting gift to future generations. The vision I had was not to host a uranium mine, but to teach children and adults about horsemanship and to train young horses. I had hoped to create a sanctuary where people and their horses could come to get away from the mad dash of society. Where people could find themselves and connect with nature again. A space where horses are happy and healthy and productive in good jobs with their human friends. A uranium mine just did not fit with this vision. To be quite honest, I still did not know much about uranium, so that threat wasn't coming home so much yet. Only the potential threat to our home and livelihood because of the surface activity, the impact the miners would have on our property, and now the potential of our drinking water becoming toxic was becoming a reality.

The only course of action that I knew was to continue putting one foot in front of the other on the path to our dreams. The uranium mining issue was at least on my mind more, but I was feeling like there was nothing we could do anyway, so I'd just let things land where they may. I went into complete mental bypass of the present and handed my entire responsibility over to God. I prayed for Him to remove the uranium situation and by praying for what I wanted without really dropping into listening, then not only was I a victim of Powertech, but with this sort of attitude, I was also a victim of God and His will.

> Gentle reader, you may be asking yourself how was I being a victim to God in this scenario? I was taking the approach that I had no responsibility in regard to my actions. If this was to work out it would do so entirely through prayer. I didn't need to really pay that close of attention and DO something, if I prayed, lived a good life and asked for God to take this away from me, He would. And if He did not then I could rest in the fact that I needed to be better. I still had no intent at this time to do anything other than focus on my dreams and pray for God to remove any barriers to their achievement. I was looking to God to be my rescuer so that if He decided to not do what I asked I could remain in the victimhood that I was so used to being encamped. Heaven forbid that I might have to get 'dirty'.

> This is not to say that prayer is not valuable. It is highly valuable! And I'm not sure that without the aid of God/Spirit/The Universe/Creator/Jesus we would have been as successful as we were in the end. But at this time in the story I wasn't really seeking to hear my role or what might

need to happen. I was seeking for God to be my rescuer and to take this all away from me. I was not praying for the highest good from this situation, I was praying from a manipulative way with my ideas firmly embedded as to how this should be handled by Him.

The mental script I was running was that I was powerless and could only ask for help in the way that I visualized. Though my Spiritual practice was deep I wasn't trusting what I might be hearing from the inner voice. I wasn't trusting any voices other than the one I had in my head about my entitlement and my victimhood at this point. If I would have been asked by others, I would have said 'Yes, I'm listening. Can't you see that God brought us to this place? This is where He wants us to be. This is what he wants us to do. He is blessing my dreams and those who will benefit from them.' I couldn't see outside of that box yet. I couldn't consider the possibility that God had brought us to this location for different reasons. No, not yet. I had an agenda and that's all I could see.

Not too many days later we decided to host one of our Friday night fires, I needed a night of good humor and relaxation. We had not done Friday fires during the coldest months of winter, so I was really enjoying the feel of sitting under the stars with the wood smoke smells mixed with those of burning marshmallows. Our boarders seemed to enjoy this relaxing time as much as we were on this clear night.

One of our boarders, was a local real estate developer as well as being on the Colorado Land Trust Board. Jay began to ask him what he knew about surface rights vs. mineral rights. The discussion came down to essentially what Jay already knew to be true, mineral owners take precedent over surface owners. Jay then told him about the letters we had recently been getting from Powertech Uranium Corporation.

I shared my belief that everything would work out okay. "I'm sure they can't do anything without a fair agreement with us since we are sitting on the surface."

Our boarder disagreed. "Mineral rights take precedent over surface rights, Robin." He and Jay began talking more about what sort of options we might have. He encouraged us to talk to an attorney before we talked with Powertech, just so we knew what our options were. Jay agreed that that would be a good idea.

Another of our boarders started getting worried about how they would destroy the horse set up. "How can a company just come in and destroy an existing business? That's just not right," she vented.

Jay shared that they could show up with drill rigs any day and demand to access their minerals. "Oh come on," I put in, "surely they wouldn't do that." As I visualized a string of construction vehicles coming over the hill and demanding that we just stay out of their way. Jay agreed that that is not likely the way they would do things, but that technically, they could. The reality was that he was trying to get my attention and had hoped that by sharing in this group that I would begin to listen to the issue. His ploy was working.

> This is how my self-created lie would show up. I was in deep denial about anything really bad happening to me or around me. I did not want to feel that I was powerless so I would deny that such things could really happen. Even though my visualization went right to my perception of what might happen, I'd push that right out with the Scarlett O'Hara-esque "I won't think about that right now." And I'd plant myself more firmly into the belief that all things will work out for what is 'right' because I was willing it to be so.
>
> This is how a deep trauma of abuse can be covered up in the psyche. I had been in denial for 40 years. Just push it aside, have a cookie, or as we get older have a drink or

other mind altering substance, we'll just ignore that this happened or could happen and it will all be better. We can create our reality, right? Well, yes, yes we can until reality comes up and bites us in the butt and says "LOOK AT ME DAMMIT!" And we either choose to look at it or to manifest more drama/trauma or dis-ease.

Yes, dis-ease can be manifested by holding onto things. The body never lies and when we hold untruths and traumas the body cannot flow in a harmonious way, therefore stopping the flush of toxins in an area, or areas. Getting completely honest with ourselves in order to be in a good flow is not easy. We don't always recognize that we are not being honest with ourselves. This is possibly one reason why we attract the things we need in order to look at the lie we are living. God provides us with everything we need including our guides and angels who are there to help us see and to be really honest so that we can live a free and inspired life centered in reality.

This is why bad things happen to good people. Running a mental script about how one needs to just go along to get along is harmful in oh so many ways.

CHAPTER 4

A SHIFT IN FOCUS

Spring in Colorado often brings blizzards, so I was watching the weather closely as I planned a road trip to Kansas City, MO. I was accompanying one of my horsemanship friends and mentors to pick up her horse. We were going to bring her horse back to Mustang Hollow to board while she did some extensive traveling in the U.S. and abroad. As most road trips do, the hours of driving together over basically straight and flat terrain gave us plenty of time to talk about things we had never talked about before. We chatted about politics, religion, past experiences and future plans. We differed on many things, but we were also open enough to hear one another's beliefs and opinions.

The mile markers flew by as we chatted. Eventually, I mentioned the proposed uranium mine.

"They want to do WHAT on your land?" she gasped in disbelief, spilling her gas station coffee on her worn blue jeans.

"A company wants to mine for uranium. I don't think it will affect us too much. They say it's safe and unimpactful." I replied. There was still a part of me that trusted the government and I thought that the regulations would protect us and the water, regardless of what Jay was reading. Also, I believed that in being a good Christian, God would protect us. It would be some time before I realized that He had put me in the cab of the truck with this friend as His way of protecting us. I was still only open to asking Him to take this all away from us. And if He wasn't going to do that the government surely protects its loyal citizens. I believed that as a Christian-based country there was no way the government would allow us to be victims to a corporation.

"How can they come on YOUR land and mine? Don't you own your minerals?" she asked while dabbing at the wet coffee stain with a napkin. "Didn't you have an opportunity to purchase those at the time of your land purchase? Why would you purchase the land and not the minerals? Maybe you can go back and buy them now before this company comes in. No, I guess not since they are sure there is uranium there. Siggghhhh, You should have looked into this," she railed without pausing.

I interrupted her, "In Colorado it's pretty typical for people to not own their minerals. We didn't have an opportunity to purchase the mineral rights. We looked into things we believed might affect us. Uranium never occurred to us."

"Well, I cannot have my horse in a place that has uranium mining happening. I won't come there. It's not safe. All of the toxins, the heavy metals, it's just not safe." She went on with exasperation in her voice as she stuffed the now wet napkin into our traveling trash bag with more force than was required.

Startled, my foot eased up on the gas pedal. A semi sped by, rocking my truck in its wake. So, this mine could really impact what people think about coming to our ranch and especially keeping their horses there. I hadn't even considered that as an issue.

"I don't think there is anything we can do. They own the minerals, we own the surface. Colorado law gives precedent to the mineral rights owners. We will have to work with these guys." I replied with more resolve than I felt. I pressed hard on the gas pedal, lurching forward.

"You have to stop them. Uranium is used for nukes and nuclear power. I wish I could get a hold of some of my old friends still. They'd know how to help you. Robin, it's just not safe. All of the pollutants added to the air and the soil. The tailings will be so dangerous. They'll dig up your entire land."

"It's not that kind of mining. It's what they are calling in-situ leach mining. It's done underground in the aquifer. All that's on the surface are well heads." I reassured her. The speeding semi disappeared over a small hill. With a strange sense of urgency, I pushed the pedal to the floor.

"Oh great, even better. Your water will not be drinkable. I really cannot put my horse at risk by keeping her at your place. I'll have to find somewhere else to put her. I'll start making some calls once we get to Kansas City." She settled back into the seat, her mouth tight.

"What do you propose we do? This is a corporation and the laws are on their side. I'm sure the regulations and protections in place will protect us and the water." My voice cracked with worry.

At this point I began learning all about her history as an activist and political author. This friend shared some incredible and unbelievable experiences with me. It turns out that she had worked with Abbie Hoffman, the famous political activist. This friend shall remain anonymous here because it is a part of her life that she likes to keep relatively unknown. She described several scary moments when she knew her own life was in danger. One in which she was even staring into the open end of a gun while she was in a phone booth on the telephone doing the activist work in which she was involved. She was forced to hand over some key information that had "fallen into her hands" from the "enemy" to get out of that situation.

My conservative leaning brain was reeling as I listened to her stories. I just didn't know what to think. Part of me was emboldened by the fact that people can rally together and make a difference in the world, and part of me was very cynical about all of what I perceived as wackiness, not to mention the portion of me that was a bit frightened at the fact that she was relating some stories that showed a very real risk. Of course, her stories were from a different and more crazy time in the history of United

States politics, but not THAT long ago. What would I be getting into if we decided to fight this proposed uranium mine?

I had so many questions:

- How would we even get started?
- How does one go up against a big corporation who has rights of their own?
- What are the risks of uranium?
- Is this just a "not in my back yard" issue? As a conservative, the last thing I was interested in was being called a NIMBY when I began making noise about something that only affects me and my backyard.
- What would fighting this proposed mine mean to me personally?
- To Jay? To our marriage? To our reputation? To our plans?

The fact that Laura and now this woman who was a mentor and a friend were so concerned got me really thinking. Sure, they were people who would have my best interests at heart, but they were obviously concerned from a much bigger picture perspective than just it being our property at risk.

The rest of the trip allowed me to ask many of my questions and gave me plenty of time to really think about what it was we were up against. My heart knew the truth. Of course it always had. I believe God had been speaking to me and I had been choosing not to listen. Once I began to really listen I could not deny that truth. I had stayed in my head to remain distracted from what wanted to take me off my chosen, and quite frankly, what I felt was my entitled course. I was rattled and was being shaken out of my denial pattern by two good friends and a very loyal husband. Divine intervention was at work here for sure.

> When I say that my heart knew the truth, it goes to show just how deep of a denial pattern I had. My idealism overrode any good discernment that might allow me to tap into what my inner knowing might reveal. If I would have been able to get out of my head long enough to listen to what my body could tell me, I would have felt

the roiling of my stomach, the hesitation in my heart, the tightening of my diaphragm every time I thought about or spoke of the proposed uranium mine.

Instead, I made my body wrong and told it to shut up while overriding it with the thoughts that I had about what I wanted to believe. Again, this making the body wrong is a huge part of an unhealthy lifestyle. I had endometriosis and lived with intense pain because of how I refused to allow my body to speak. If I allowed my body to speak I might get into stories that I had no intention of hearing or telling. I was fine! I wasn't going to be anything but fine! I was determined to be fine and to make sure everyone else knew it. Until - I could no longer deny when my body said 'NO.' Those days would find me doing what I called 'mainlining' ibuprofen in order to deal with the pain. So, I just told the body to shut up with symptom controlling medicine that allowed me to ignore the root of why my uterus was yelling so loudly.

If I would have listened to the pain in my uterus I would have had to hear how much I didn't want to be a female. My femininity meant that I had a vulnerability that I didn't want to accept. Growing up in a patriarchal society meant that I was less-than. Even though I had bought into society's gender roles, I never wanted to be seen as less-than.

To really listen to my body and especially the signals of pain from my uterus I would have had to have developed the skills that I have learned since that time. I have learned how to practice somatic archeology through the help of a Medicine Woman trained in these types of explorations. Through practicing and learning how to reject my addiction to the mind and how to go into the body I have learned much about what my body was virtually screaming at me by creating dis-ease so that I had to listen. Through somatic archeology I have unearthed buried trauma that was rising to the surface in many ways that were asking me to go deeper.

Somatic archeology helped me learn to listen and to begin to look at the sexual abuse that I had endured when I was very young. To survive the trauma I got very good at stuffing my emotions and my memory so I would never have to look at it again I discovered that looking at the trauma and integrating it in a complete way helped me unwind many very unhealthy patterns.

But this is all stuff that I was unwilling to do before the Uranium Mine came my way. I had plans to remain in my denial and self-created idealistic reality. I was fine, wasn't I?!?! My heart, my husband, my friends of the time and my uterus were all yelling at me and now a potential uranium mine was making me stop and go deeper. I can see now that the threat of a toxic mine helped me mine for my own internal gold.

But, let's get on with the story.......

I called Jay from Kansas City.

"So, this proposed uranium mine, is it really a risk to more than just us and our plans?" I asked as I ran my fingers through my hair.

"It could really impact the groundwater," he replied.

"As in making it undrinkable?"

"Could," he answered.

"So are you wanting to fight this thing," I wondered?

"I'm not sure," he replied, "I don't think it would be right to allow them to do this."

"So we kind of have a moral obligation to get the word out about their plans," I mused while I stood up straighter.

"I guess we do," Jay admitted.

"We'd have to be all in. All or nothing," I stated, still remembering the stories that were ringing in my ears of past activism. "When I get home, let's meet with some of the neighbors and discuss what we should do."

The road trip home from Kansas City was much different from the road trip to Kansas City. My friend agreed to continue to keep her horse with us and she was excited by the fact that she could help me become a real activist.

"The first thing you need," she said, "is some political person and/or some big environmental group to get involved and really help you out."

"How do we do that?" I asked plaintively. I was still unsure about what I was getting into and falling easily right back into my victim role.

"I'd recommend a letter to the editor. Press releases. Anything that will put this information out so folks will pick it up and help you run with it," she replied. "Do your research. Know as much as you can about radioactivity, heavy metals, water movement, everything. Your horse career will have to be put on hold big time, this will demand all of your attention and reading."

This really disheartened me. I was on a roll with my career. I enjoyed the short bursts of "fame" that were being thrust upon me and felt like I was really going somewhere with my horse training. The 4-H club that we had formed was in its second year and was growing. I really enjoyed the kids and the horses. I couldn't put it all on hold. That was just too much to ask. Not to mention, I hoped to have a viable business to help us pay for the ranch we had just purchased, the additional 40 acres that we were still in the process of buying, plus all of the upgrades we were doing to the property to create a safe and comfortable place. I needed to think about this a little further. Truth be known, we had invested so much into the new ranch that I had to keep building the horse business to support what we had already done. Our debt was monumental.

"There IS no time," my activist friend said. "You're already way behind the ball. You've sat on this issue for over 6 months now. Who knows where Powertech is in their process. You must hit the ground running, and NOW."

Again, she related more stories of some of her past experiences. She began talking about getting the media involved. "I can see it now, Robin, you'll be doing an interview with the Powertech drilling rigs behind you and supporters surrounding you."

I had visions of an element of fame in my mind for sure, but it did not involve activist work. It involved only horses. Press conferences on a political or even a health and safety issue were not part of my agenda. I just sort of nodded and said, "I am no good at speaking."

"Trust yourself," she assured me. "Speak from the heart and it will work out fine."

After more of her stories and reassurances a fire was lit. I was committed to fighting uranium mining by the time we rolled back into Northern Colorado. I had just agreed to embarking upon the largest, and quite possibly the most dangerous marketing campaign of my life, and I still didn't know how to truly go about it. I was finally stepping into the voice from within that was telling me to get going and step out in Faith. The Divine had spoken through my friend.

We had driven through most of the night as we pulled the horse trailer into Mustang Hollow before noon that day. We unloaded her mare and got her settled with extra hay and plenty of water for her recovery from the long road trip. I gave my friend a hug as she climbed into her car to drive her last leg for the day. I thanked her for all of her advice and the fun trip we had just had. Then I tiredly walked up to the house for a much needed shower and a nap.

When Jay got home from work that evening, we sat down and started talking about what ISL mining for uranium entailed. He gave me several websites at which to look. The first thing I did was to look up uranium:

u-ra-ni-um. noun. Symbol U A heavy silvery-white metallic element, radioactive and toxic, easily oxidized, and having 14 known isotopes of which U 238 is the most abundant in nature. The element occurs in several minerals, including uraninite and carnotite, from which it is extracted and processed for use in research, nuclear fuels, and nuclear weapons. Atomic number 92; atomic weight 238.03; melting point 2,070F, 1132C; boiling point 7468F, 4131C; specific gravity 18.95;valence 2, 3, 4, 5, 6.[New Latin uranium, after Uranus, Uranus ; see Uranus.] Word History: Some chemical elements, such as ytterbium and berkelium, derive their names from the places they were discovered, but the element uranium owes its name to an earlier scientific discovery, that of the planet Uranus. Sir William Herschel, who discovered Uranus in 1781, wanted to name the planet Georgium sidus, "the Georgian planet,"; in honor of George III; others called it Herschel. Eventually convention prevailed and the planet came to be called Uranus, like Mercury and Pluto the name of a heavenly deity in classical mythology. This god, called Ouranos in Greek(Latinized as Uranus), was chosen because he was the father of Saturn (Greek Kronos), the deity of the planet next in line, who himself was the father of Jupiter (Greek Zeus), the deity of the next planet. The name of this new planet Uranus was then used in the name of a new chemical element discovered eight years later by M.H. Klaproth. Klaproth, a German scientist, gave it the Latin name uranium in honor of the discovery of Uranus. Uranium passed into English shortly thereafter, being first recorded in the third edition of the Encyclopedia Britannica, published in 1797.

Then I went further into the breakdown of uranium:
"Uranium is a naturally-occurring radioactive substance, very widespread in the earth's crust, but concentrated in certain hard rock formations. As the uranium atoms slowly disintegrate over billions of years, a host of radioactive

by-products are formed: thorium-230, radium-226, radon-222 and the infamous "radon daughters," including lead-210 and polonium-210.

As the miners dig the uranium-bearing ore, they inevitably release large quantities of radioactive radon gas into the mine atmosphere. Radon has a relatively short half-life (3.8 days); before long, the air in the mine is heavily contaminated with radon daughters. Adhering to microscopic dust particles, these tiny, pernicious particles are breathed into the miners' lungs where they lodge delivering a massive dose of alpha radiation to the sensitive lung tissue. The result is an extraordinarily high incidence of lung cancer, fibrosis of the lungs, and other lung diseases, all of which take decades to become manifest.[1]"

And more: *"The chart given below lists all of the decay products of uranium-238 in their order of appearance. Uranium-238 is also referred to as "depleted uranium".*

Each radioactive element on the list gives off either alpha radiation or beta radiation -- and sometimes gamma radiation too -- thereby transforming itself into the next element on the list. When uranium ore is extracted from the earth, most of the uranium is removed from the crushed rock during the milling process, but the radioactive decay products are left in the tailings. Thus 85 percent of the radioactivity of the original ore is discarded in the mill tailings.

Depleted uranium remains radioactive for literally billions of years, and over these long periods of time it will continue to produce all of its radioactive decay products; thus depleted uranium actually becomes more radioactive as the centuries and millennia go by because these decay products accumulate.

Lead-206, the last element on the list, is not radioactive. It does not decay, and therefore has no half-life."[2]

---

[1]   Uranium: "The Deadliest Metal", by Dr. Gordon Edwards, President of Canadian Coalition for Nuclear Responsibility, This article appeared in Perception magazine, v. 10 n. 2, 1992
[2]   www.ccnr.org/decay_U238.html

The chart of the breakdown looks like this:

Uranium 238 half-life of	4.5 billion years.	to
Thorium 234	24.1 days	to
Protactinium 234	1 minute	to
Uranium 234	245,000 years	to
Thorium 230	76,000 years	to
Radium 226	1600 years	to
Radon 222	3.8 days	to
Polonium 218	3 minutes	to
Lead 214	27 minutes	to
Bismuth 214	20 minutes	to
Polonium 214	160 microseconds	to
Lead 210	22 years	to
Bismuth 210	5 days	to
Polonium 210	138 days	to
Lead 206	stable	

Then I searched for polonium 210. Here I found a bunch of articles about the Russian KGB agent Mr. Alexander Litvinenko and how his death was attributed to the injection of polonium 210. Polonium 210 is also found in cigarette smoke and is always found with radon. It's extremely toxic, but the articles are quick to reassure that it's only toxic if ingested through inhalation, eating or drinking. Comforting, I thought sarcastically, especially since ISL mining is done within groundwater supplies. And radon, we in Colorado already know a lot about radon and the health risks associated. Many basements all along the Front Range have radon mitigation systems. In fact we had to put one in our Masonville home before the bank would give the new owner her loan.

I was not the scientific detail-oriented type. I loved to listen to and hang around these types of thinkers, but it's not my true nature. I operated from a total K.I.S.S. (Keep it simple stupid) mentality and allowed my faith that God would guide my intuitive nature more than needing to know the details and the big words that described the details. I was so idealistic that

I felt that I didn't need to know the details, God would take care of it, I didn't have to put too much effort into things if my faith was real. That was how I operated when it was something at which I just didn't want to look. Now, when it came to the horses, I was very detail oriented, so I had a huge duality here. I've learned that this phenomenon is a common result of a psychological split that unresolved trauma will create.

> This place of not really wanting to look into details was a reflection of my ungroundedness. The split that my unresolved trauma created is one that is a split between the 1st, 2nd, and 3rd chakras and the 5th, 6th and 7th. A disintegrated body. A disintegrated energy system. Truly looking at the trauma I had endured was the only way that I could integrate into a wholly functioning person. I needed alignment that allowed all of the chakras to communicate with one another before I could truly become detail oriented in all of life.

> The idealism that I functioned under by tossing off 'need to know' scenarios into God's lap was also a deeper reflection of the victimhood in which I was encamped.

Reading and learning about uranium had me REALLY out of my comfort zone now.

I went to bed that first night home from my pivotal road trip with big words swimming and panic brewing.

My activist friend called me early the next day. "Robin, I was up all night and I made a bunch of fliers that we need to distribute right away. I've already been out and put a bunch of these things all over town. I've had so much fun talking with people and doing what I used to do. Thanks for the opportunity to relive that part of myself. Anyway, I'm leaving town tomorrow and I do not want to be involved past getting you started. You go girl! Have fun with it."

I was happy to hear that she had been taking some action and was looking forward to seeing the fliers she had put together. "I'll bring you the copies I have left. Put them on cars in parking lots, get them to every realtor you know, just keep getting them out," she continued. "We can't let these guys walk in here from Canada and pollute our water."

As we hung up, I had agreed to follow through with her flier distribution, she had reminded me about the letter to the editor and press releases so I sat down to write my first letter. This was the beginning of the hours, days, weeks, months and even years, spent in front of a computer learning about and writing about uranium and uranium mining.

A couple of hours later, my activist friend pulled into the driveway and virtually leapt from her car with the excitement from her adventures in town. She showed me the fliers, as she shared some of the interactions she had with people she had handed them to. As I was listening to her tales while reading the fliers, it wasn't a wonder that she got some of the looks she was describing. I loved the effort to which she had gone, but I had to chuckle a bit at the almost elementary and frenetic energy these fliers seemed to proclaim. Still, I wondered, does this work? Do people respond to this kind of "yelling?" These fliers were all printed on astrobrite paper and were boldly handwritten in large block letters. Things such as "Send Powertech back to Canada," "Radiation without representation," "Over my dead body."

Inside I really questioned this sort of tactic. Since I didn't want to look at the emotions I was feeling, I assumed that others would feel the same way. What the fliers *didn't* do was give me any information about why I, or my neighbors, should be concerned about a proposed uranium mine. I didn't 'get' that uranium was incredibly dangerous when it was first presented to me. Of course, I was living in my own self-created reality where I felt that as long as I was a 'good girl' God and the government would take care of me and all of us citizens. I thanked her for the effort and the fliers as I sat them on the kitchen counter.

I wished my friend well on her latest journey and promised to keep her posted about our activities as well as how her horse was doing. We hugged our goodbyes and as we parted I enjoyed watching her virtually skip back to her car with the energy inspired from her productive day.

I really had intended to continue to distribute those fliers. But I kept thinking that yelling about death and pollution was not really the way to go. Sure some reactivity seemed called for, and as I said before, I have a tendency to use emotion to get what I wanted, but I felt like it would be better to empower people with information. We live in an area surrounded by universities. Tapping into the energy of intelligence and good decision making seemed like more of the way to go. We needed to leave the emotion out of it. Of course, I didn't want to have to tap into the real emotions that were stirring inside of me either, so that line of thinking fit well with my personal agenda.

> SPOILER ALERT! In the end our strategy of empowering people with information is truly what drove us forward with the success we had. The trick is to not stuff the emotions while doing so. To listen to the information gained from the emotions as they arise and take actions according to what the body needs to remain whole. Putting the emotion front and center without good information would be analogous to puking on someone and then hoping that they will join you as you both now seek ways to stop the puking.

Knowing Jay the way I do, I knew he would be appalled at the feel in those fliers. Emotion was not even a word he liked to utter let alone tap into as part of our intelligence. So I hid the fliers in my office for several weeks before I showed them to him. He only saw them when I began using them as recycled paper in our printer. His reaction assured me that I had made the right decision to keep them from him.

After further thought about how to get started on this project of fighting uranium mining, I called my friend Laura. "Okay, you've all convinced me that we need to do something about this proposed uranium mine. I'm looking for good ideas. Have any?"

"We need to let everyone in the area know what it being proposed," she replied.

"We need a public meeting," I brainstormed.

Laura liked the idea of a public meeting, but wondered how we could get the right kind of speakers to attend.

"I am not quite sure yet, but I feel like we just need to get started. Can you help me by finding a place?"

"Sure," she said, "but don't think I'm getting involved. I have too many things on my plate as it is. I can do this, cause it's easy, but that's all. I'll be happy to talk to you and share advice and information from our years in environmental consulting, but I just can't get involved beyond that."

Can't. Won't. Don't. Yeah but..... These were words I had tried, but weren't sticking. I knew about too many things being on my plate also. The difference was that I was being forced into this situation. At least that's what it felt like, I was now a victim to activism. "I understand," I sighed, "I think close to the area is good, maybe Wellington."

Enough activist stuff for me today. I needed to work on some 4-H stuff. The Larimer County Fair would be having their very first Musical Freestyle competition for the 4-H horse kids this year. I was excited because this was a personal suggestion of mine that had been well received.

Musical Freestyles are an artistic competition where the riders get to dance with their horses. I had been doing mini backyard Musical Freestyle shows for several years. I love the way they challenge the riders to excel in their riding as they create an artistic ridden routine to music. The horse and rider are generally in a costume that compliments and enhances the entire expression of the performance. It's always been a fun way to learn more about the personalities of the riders as they choose their music and costumes.

The Larimer County 4-H horse coordinator had asked me if I'd be willing to do a clinic for the 4-H youth to help them get started on creating their

Musical Freestyles. The clinic was coming up in just a few weeks. I needed to get some details worked out, handouts made and music CD's burned before then.

This was just the beginning of my split between impassioned activist and professional horsewoman. The split really boiled down to what it meant for me to participate in what was in front of me as a deeper connection to the web of life, and what I held as an idealistic vision of who I was and thought I wanted to be. My perceived reputation vs. a deeper calling to my life's purpose. At this point it was my intent to maintain a clear division so that I could maintain my mask without having to really expose myself to anyone else. Especially not to me.

> What was really at work here was my ego running the show instead of me stopping and listening to what my heart was saying. Part of my growth in this adventure was to learn just how damaging maintaining a split is to the psyche. It's hard work and a complete waste of energy. Looking back, I could have been so much more effective if I wasn't so invested in maintaining my fissured soul. The true chasm harkened back to the unresolved trauma. I was so used to just 'maintaining' that I didn't know how else to function.

> I couldn't allow myself to look too deeply at why the uranium mine was in my own back yard. I couldn't allow myself to see that the opportunity to teach at a deeper level was right in front of me. Don't get me wrong, it's not like I would just not talk about the uranium mine and what we were learning when I was amongst my horse groups, it's just that I had two hats that I would not allow to merge. If I had had good emotional intelligence and discernment at this point in my life I could have seen the way that I was holding back who I was truly becoming. I could have been more WHOLE by integrating what activism looks like while still functioning effectively in a job or career.

The emotional intelligence that I lacked at this time kept me from being okay with feeling angry over the boundary violation of Powertech and recognizing that I was in the process of restoring that boundary through my activist activities. The emotional intelligence that I lacked also kept me from being okay with the sadness that was constantly lurking because I was experiencing a deep loss of many of my previously held beliefs. Instead I worked hard to maintain composure and to keep a clear separation between who I just 'knew' I was meant to be, a well known and respected horsewoman, and what I was needing to do right now in order to allow myself to get back to that trajectory.

Spring really seemed to be taking a hold in northern Colorado. A nice break since the winter had been a very long, snowy and windy one. Laura had an appointment to bring her young horse Magic over for some extra help. I was looking forward to working with Laura and her beautiful filly. After a morning of horse chores, I worked with a horse that I had in training and then rode one of my own before Laura arrived.

"Hey, Robin, how are you today?" Laura asked as she led her palomino filly over to the round pen.

"It's a good day for horsin' around," I replied with a grin.

I helped Laura and Magic develop a partnership in the round pen while we worked on refining some of Laura's skills based upon Magic's responses.

When it was time for a break, Laura and I leaned against the round pen fence for a chat. "I booked the Leeper Center in Wellington for your meeting. Two weeks from now, that should give you enough time to develop a presentation and advertise so people can come." Laura said.

"Thank you," I answered, wondering how we could pull this off so fast, but feeling the need to catch up to Powertech. "I sure don't know what it is that we are getting into, but we seem to be running with it. I wish I could just concentrate on the horses and the kids instead of all this uranium stuff. I am learning so much about something I never even knew I'd need to know."

"I know what you mean." Laura went on to share how she had been speaking with former peers of her husband's from their time with the environmental consulting business. She was also talking with a friend of hers who had done socio-impact studies for the Federal Government. She told me how she was finding out that many of the environmental protection laws that had been put in place during the '80s had been eroded by preceding administrations.

As she was talking, I could feel my entire body begin to freeze. I was taken aback by how shallow my breath was becoming. Magic drifted over. She stuck her head right in between us and blew out a huge snort. Whew! Just what I needed help with! Releasing and Breathing! What a relief that horse gave me in that moment! She knew exactly what she was doing and what was needed. We laughed as we brushed off the horse boogies.

"Magic and I would rather that we have our attention on horses," I said. "Let's do just a little bit more round pen work then see how she wants to load into the horse trailer."

After a good horsey day, the switch back to activism began. Jay was coming home 'early' so we could meet with our nearest neighbors, Carol and David, early that evening. Jay had already been communicating with them often about the topic and I needed to catch up. The first thing I learned is just how much time they had each spent researching the topic. They began by telling me about all of the ISL mining operations they were finding that had violations of toxic spillage. One of the biggest was The Smith Ranch in Wyoming. Some of the players in Powertech had been involved in the Smith Ranch mine in the past. We sat down and looked at www. wise-uranium.org and the list of violations poured forth.

"Oh great," I reacted. "Are they in our aquifer too?"

"We don't really know what is going on underground," Jay replied. "There is plenty of conjecture and the uranium mining companies will tell you that they know EXACTLY what is happening. I keep going back to my days of college with a Geology professor. He always said we can never know exactly what is going on underground. It's too hidden, unknown and unpredictable." Jay went on to share that his research had taken him to looking into the groundwater quality standards through the Environmental Protection Agency (EPA). One of the things he found to be occurring was that the EPA would relax some of the drinking water standards in an area so that a mine site could be termed 'reclaimed.' He had found this in more than one U.S. location.

Realizing the already global nature of the impacts of uranium mining really solidified my thoughts on how we needed to get the information about the Powertech plans out right away. I was beginning to see how our local issue was not a NIMBY one, but one with much deeper and broader impacts. I also was feeling a great amount of fear about whether we would have a chance of stopping this.

I finally heeded the nudge to speak up about what I was thinking and what actions I had already taken to just make this issue go away.

"Laura has already booked the Leeper Center in Wellington. We need to share what Powertech wants to do with the public. Once people know about this issue, they'll help us stop it." I continued, "We live in an area surrounded by universities. There are a lot of educated people in the Fort Collins/Loveland/Greeley area. I don't know if we could get some of the local professors to talk at a meeting, or if we just do an open house set up where we could have a few computers up upon which we could show people these sites and maybe some posters showing what ISL is and where they plan to do it? I just feel that if we build on the educated community by sharing the information, it might shut down this project."

Everyone agreed that we are lucky to be in such an educated area, and felt that once people understood what it is that Powertech wants to do that people will get involved. Carol went on to share their experience of a meeting they had had with their land man that past December. He had told them that he was in the area to 'survey the mine sites.' They vividly recalled him saying that the land would be 'completely ruined as it's used as a pincushion' and that he stated that all livestock will need to be removed during the mining process which would take several years. She also shared that he had mentioned plans for an open pit uranium mine on a 640 acre area of land just a few miles to the south of us.

While digesting this shocking information, we turned the topic to maybe we could get some professionals to speak at our meeting at the Leeper Center. We thought that if we had speakers who have published research papers we would have credibility. Jay and Carol both knew some people they could ask. They both felt that they had either contacts through work or old professors that would be willing to come speak. Our budget was virtually non-existent, so we planned to ask for volunteers.

"I think we also need a website to share all of this information," I said. I hadn't worked in the computer field since Jay and I had married 12 years earlier. At that time I had quit my career to be able to stay home with any children we might have. I still feel comfortable just 'hacking around' on a computer to get a job done and had already built a couple of simple websites using existing 'point and click' interfaces. This was a job I could manage.

"Great idea, what should we put on it?"

"I don't know, but I think it's about just sharing the information we already have and is already out there," I replied.

"We can put all of our letters on it", David said. By this time we had already received three mailings from Powertech.

Jay and I showed them our letter to the editor that was poised to go out:

"Uranium Mining on the Front Range

Fort Collins now enjoys the distinction of being nationally recognized for its quality of life, featured as one of the top 15 healthiest cities in October of 2003 in the Organic Style Magazine and also named the 2006 Number One place to live in America by Money Magazine.

Soon, unless immediate action is taken, the less than honorable mention of Fort Collins' proximity to toxic uranium mining and contaminated underground water supplies could be added to those kudos. This dismal forecast will be a result of Powertech Uranium Corporation's recent mineral rights purchases in Weld County. The Canadian firm informed local residents via certified letter last October that it intends to mine uranium U308 utilizing in-situ (in place) mining technology to extract the radioactive component. This process is and will be occurring in a number of other states (Texas, South Dakota and New Mexico) and will be depending on our most precious and limited water supply.

The in-situ leaching process is a cheap and claimed environmentally benign method of extracting uranium from low grade ore deposits. This method works by injecting chemically charged native ground water into the element bearing porous sandstone aquifer causing the uranium to dissolve in the ground water. This solution is then pumped to a centralized facility to extract the uranium from the solution, stripped of uranium, the groundwater is then recharged and reinjected starting the process over.

The known dangers of the in-situ leaching technology are:
the risk that deadly, radioactive leaching compounds will spread outside of the uranium deposit and contaminate Front Range water supplies, (as has been the case in other areas where uranium is mined);
the unpredictable impact of the leaching solution on the rock formations; releases considerable amounts of radon;
the bonus of extracting other toxic heavy metals needing disposal; the impossibility of restoring natural groundwater conditions; disposal of radioactive waste water and slurries.

Right now, Weld County residents need technical, political, legal and environmentalist support. We also need courageous elected officials to invest themselves candidly, bravely and immediately in the defense of the physical and emotional health and fiscal welfare of their constituents.

Were you asked if you'd like to take the risk of having deadly uranium mined in your area? Contact your representatives and ask them if they will help us to defend what is left of our precious natural resources and the outstanding reputation of quality of life. Mining in Nunn is moving forward. As volunteer leaders of a 4-H club and hosting children and livestock on our property we are very concerned about this.

Jay and Robin Davis
Nunn, Colorado"

We agreed that this letter should be on the opening page of the website and that we should add the website address to our signature line.

"What about the links from all of the sites that are already out there," Jay added. "Why should we reinvent the wheel when all the information is there, we just have to guide people to it."

"We need to get elected officials involved," I added. "Let's make sure we have all of the contact info for our local, state and federal representatives so that people can just get busy writing or calling without even thinking about it."

"We already know all of the committee members from the Transportation & Energy committee from our time at the Capitol for the Super Slab issue," Jay put in. "In fact I think I have all of the e-mail addresses on my computer already."

David had already been in touch with some people at the DRMS (Division of Reclamation, Mining and Safety) and the EPA(Environmental Protection Agency) and felt we should add their contact information to the website too.

We began to make light of our situation in small ways and started joking about names and slogans. Nunn, Colorado has an historical water tower with the words "Watch Nunn Grow." This has been an inside joke all in and of itself for many years already. Nunn had seemingly plateaued at its population of ~500 people many years ago. Most of the town roads are still dirt and are lined with empty store fronts. In fact, someone had even scratched the word 'Weeds' under the word Grow on one side of the water tower.

Our joking lead to how we did not want to "Watch Nunn Glow" and our website domain www.nunnglow.com was born.

The meeting was productive and energizing. We were beginning to feel mobilized since we had come up with several good ideas that would allow us to take some action and start moving forward. Aside from the website, one of the most pivotally good ideas was to produce yard signs. We needed ways to raise money for this local cause and signs would give us a way to keep the issue in front of people as well as give us something to "sell." We decided that the signs should be bright yellow with black lettering. We also decided that we would place the standard radioactive tre-fold in the middle since it might draw attention. With the radioactive symbol placed prominently in the middle, we had to keep our wording to a minimum. The typeface would have been much smaller with "No Uranium Mining in Northern Colorado www.nunnglow.com", so we settled on "No Uranium Mining in Colorado www.nunnglow.com." These signs can still be seen all over Colorado. This seemingly small decision immediately made our movement a statewide one rather than just a local one.

We had also decided to do a neighborhood meeting of folks who had property within the proposed mining area. This information was easy to find through the Weld County Parcel Mapping site, so we set a date a few days away and penned a letter of invitation while including our letter to the editor. Jay and I agreed to have the meeting in our living room.

After our neighbors left, Jay and I sat down for a heart to heart. This was becoming very real! We both knew that we were not embarking on a simple project in which we could just dabble with in our spare time. If we decided to fight the uranium miners it would be challenging in many ways. We needed to really look at these challenges and see if it was risk we were willing to take.

First off, we knew that it would likely be expensive. We had already put ourselves at risk financially with all of the work we had done and were still doing on the horse set up. This risk would increase if I would not be able to focus on building our horse business.

As we talked of the very real financial risk involved, we spoke of what it would mean to lose. What if Powertech won and they were allowed to proceed with this mine? We would not be able to ethically ask people to bring their horses to board where the water had the possibility of being tainted with heavy metals and/or uranium. We would never put children at risk by bringing them into an area where big trucks were running up and down the road carrying hazardous materials. Neither we, nor our horses, nor our clients could drink the water coming from our well. We could end up living in a toxic area with no chance of selling. We could be left with nothing.

We talked of just selling out and walking away from the whole issue. As we examined this option, we talked about the fact that this was not just an issue about us. IF we were able to sell the place, how could we ethically sell it to another family? How could we sell it without being totally honest about the threat of the uranium mine? Not to mention the cloud our title already had on it from the Super Slab possibility. Who would buy it then?

Then we talked about asking Powertech to buy us out. This felt very wrong to us for so many reasons. This proposed ISL mining for uranium has the potential of polluting the aquifer. Would we be able to look ourselves in the mirror if we did not stand up for clean water? What happens when good people turn a blind eye and walk away from things that are just plain wrong? Could we do that?

We decided that we could not ignore the fact that water pollution was wrong. We talked a little about how the uranium would be used for nuclear power, which we both believed to be a cleaner energy source. We kept coming back to the fact that we could live without power, but could not live without water. No matter how we felt about nuclear power, good or bad, water is a finite resource.

We had to cut to the bare bones and decide that we were willing to risk it all. All of our money was already wrapped up into Jay's business, the property we were sitting on and the business we were building. We were prepared for and had considered these risks. We had never taken into consideration the possible threat of a proposed uranium mine. We had to ask ourselves together and separately if we were willing to lose it all to stand up for what was right.

We talked about our reputations as business owners. Jay's world was filled with developers who had a strong dislike for environmental protections that were in place. Those protections negatively affected their bottom-line when attempting to develop an area. As an example, the preble's meadow jumping mouse was often discussed as a disdainful creature by these types of clients because of the protections for this species and the studies they had to do before developing so as not to impact it further. Wetland protections made it more expensive to develop a piece of land too. Jay never would share his truth in how he felt about environment protections with most of these clients because it was not popular. How would becoming an environmental activist impact his client base?

My world was filled with clients who were both liberal and conservative, but I knew that the area into which we moved was made up of long generations of farmers and ranchers who were generally ultra conservative when it came to property and water rights. If I was speaking out against what many perceived as a property rights issue how would I then appeal to these local clients if I was an environmental activist? My family has always been strong Republicans who spoke of environmental organizations such as Sierra Club with disdain. How could I reconcile these entrenched beliefs with what I felt in my heart to be the right course of action, to become an environmental activist? Sure, I had developed a business mission that stated we were about connecting humans to nature through the help of horses, but I didn't want to appear too radical. I wanted a business that would make money, so staying to the right of the middle line between capitalism and conservationism, leaning more towards capitalism felt like the better place to be in order to be successful. How could I integrate these issues?

We decided that we..... for now..... at this moment in time... were going to do the right thing. We made the decision to move forward to fight Powertech on that day. Of course, we also knew that the further we got into it, the less likely it would be that we would be able to back out, ever. It really was a decision of all or nothing.

At this time, Jay's business was surviving, but he was still putting in many hours to make this a reality. His partner was becoming more and more distracted with his family obligations. Jay had to fill in a lot of gaps to keep the business flowing. How could we invest a significant amount of time in fighting uranium miners?

We talked of the pros and cons and risks for hours. We even slept on it and continued talking about it the next morning. We had to take this gamble by being "all in," otherwise, we would not have the level of commitment we would need for this kind of effort. Once we put ourselves on the front lines, we would have to remain there. It was daunting.

We discussed running. We discussed walking away from everything and starting fresh somewhere else. This had a lot of appeal to me. I was all about sticking my head in the sand again, walking away from anything too serious and just hiding out on the woods somewhere we could live off the land. Visions of taking my horses to some secluded place and living a simple life which required hunting and gathering for survival and living off the grid while using the horses for transportation still hold a LOT of appeal to me. Running felt like the much easier course of action.

We decided again to fight. We had to do what was right, we agreed. We simply had no real choice. Our inner guidance would not allow us to just walk or run away. The very real fact is that there really is no - away. Wherever we go, there we are. Always. I had spent a lifetime of running from things. I'd always find myself in some sort of drama, regardless. As I mentioned before, the universe was bringing to me exactly what I needed at the time to become a whole person.

I had spent my lifetime operating from a space of idealism and denial. I would put on a happy face to the world while harboring this constant underlying anger. People always commented on my smile and would encourage me to keep that smile. So, because that's what people liked, I'd continue to smile. I've actually found that smiling is an act which can change one's mood from a dour one to a more light one. So, I'd smile and believe that everything is right with the world because I was smiling. I'd make others wrong for not seeing the world through the same rose-colored glasses I wore. I truly believed that humans are inherently good and will eventually do the right thing. politically, I actually aligned more completely with the Libertarian party than any others, personal freedom was and is very important to me, though I was registered and voted Republican because I voted Pro-Life.

I had no intention of getting more in touch with my emotions as a form of intelligence. My intelligence was purely brain-powered and faith-filled. I was at a point in my life where I fully believed that God had brought us to our ranch because we needed to make a difference in the future generation through our horse business. My mask of a smile was my way of not needing to get in touch with my emotions. I could just put on a happy face and stay in my head. This uranium mine was not something I could just smile through. I was pissed off! How could these characters come into my dream and wreck it for their own goals? The paradigm of capitalism being all about he who has the most money wins was not working for me. We were the less resourced contender in this fight. We were the underdogs. I had to tap into my anger and use it effectively if we were to be successful. My mask was becoming cracked.

CHAPTER 5

GETTING IN TOUCH WITH MY INNER WARRIOR

Okay, the decision was made, the shift in focus was decided, mask firmly in place, I began right away. The morning following our meeting with our neighbors, I got busy developing my activist/warrior archetype. Since we wished to include our roles as 4-H leaders in our letter to the editor, the first thing I did was to send our letter to the local 4-H office for approval. I asked if they would allow me to go public with my role as a 4-H leader as we fought this issue. After reading it, they liked how we were approaching it in such a professional manner. They liked the way we refrained from mounting a personal attack and gave me a few guidelines regarding maintaining a high moral code whenever I used my 4-H leadership role for this fight. No problem since it fit right with my ideas of how this opposition to the proposed uranium mine would play out. We had every intent of using just the facts in all of our dealings with Powertech and this mine.

Letting out a big sigh, I knew that underneath this Spock-like public persona my emotions were roiling. But falling back into my Scarlett O'Hara-esque ways, I would not look at them too close. I would put them on the 'tomorrow' list.

Truly the teacher within me was beginning to come out. I was already a teacher to horses and horse loving people. Now I had to teach about water, mining and uranium. Honestly, this was a fairly easy role for me.

Next, with the "watch Nunn glow" catch phrase, I created a website that opened with a bright red background and yellow lettering. People still ask me, "Whatever happened to the red and yellow site?" Even though it was obnoxious and difficult to read, it really left an impression. The red with the yellow represented the glow of the uranium, danger, and the anger that I was feeling.

I began adding several of the things we had discussed the previous evening. I wanted to just get something up so that as the letter went out people would have a place to find more information. It wasn't fancy, just pages with links, scanned letters, and names and phone numbers where people could contact elected officials. I put a live link to my e-mail address and my phone number since Jay had his office job and our neighbors worked during the day as well. My schedule, though overfull already, was the most flexible of them all.

That done I wanted to get our letters of invitation to the local area landowners into that day's mail. Off to the Post Office I went.

Upon returning home, I decided to send out an e-mail to most everybody in my e-mail address book. My e-mail address book included family, close friends, some local and abroad horse friends, a few old high school buddies, horse clients and my 4-H contacts. I wrote a short note about the proposed ISL mining and our fears about water contamination. I included our letter to the editor and the website address and asked them to read what we were discovering and to help me spread the word. I also asked them to please contact the people on the list of elected officials to express their concerns.

The night was getting long and I was no longer seeing straight. Jay was still not home, but I needed to sleep. I had another restless night of big words and panic reeling through my mind and body.

The next morning I decided to make my own phone calls to the elected officials and to the Division of Reclamation, Mining and Safety (DRMS). I expressed my concern regarding the proposed ISL mining for our property. The DRMS informed me that their job is to protect the public, miners, and the environment during current mining operations, sharing that since there had been no permit application as of yet, they could not do anything to help me. I told them about all of the violations that we were seeing in other ISL operations and expressed my desire that they do the right thing if Powertech applied for a permit. I hung up from each of my phone calls feeling very brushed off and disheartened. Since this project was not already in operation, not a one of them could give me any help. I wondered why we had to be so reactive rather than proactive.

I had to stay busy, or my emotions might demand my attention.

> Writing this now from a place of emotional intelligence, I can share that, at this point, the emotions of fear and anger were driving me. Though, I knew that I was angry at the time, I also would not allow myself to find the message of boundary violations to drive a healthy relationship with the situation. I stuffed the anger and made it wrong which only made me more driven to set those boundaries however I could. Fortunately, I was sane and intelligent enough to not do irrational things. But the shadow (that side of your being that you don't want to admit having) drove me to not be in good relationship with a more whole lifestyle. The shadow made me simply remain as busy on this fight for as long as I could each day. I could recognize no time for self care or rest. Slowing my activity would mean slowing myself into a more reflective place… a place where I could not go because I'd have to look at the emotions and honor them.

> With emotional intelligence I would have been able to be effective as well as to have balance in my work, activism, and play time.

I moved on to contacting all of the newspapers I could find in Colorado. I submitted our letter to the editor and a press release, which was essentially our letter to the editor. Then I sent press releases to all of the TV and radio stations I could find.

Meanwhile, Jay and Carol kept sending me links of articles to post on the new website. I spent a lot of time reading these and getting the links posted. In just a couple of days we had a website upon which a person could spend hours learning about In Situ Leach (ISL) mining for uranium. We linked to sites in opposition, the Powertech Uranium Corporation and other sites from the uranium mining industry, sites from government regulating organizations, newspapers, etc.

We really felt that if people had all of the information in one easy to find location, they would come to the same conclusion as we had.

One of the most impactful and informative pieces of information we found in the beginning was a paper by Dr. Gavin Mudd from Australia: *An Environmental Critique of In Situ Leach Mining: The Case Against Uranium Solution Mining by Gavin Mudd, Victoria University of Technology. A Research Report for Friends of the Earth (Fitzroy) with the Australian Conservation Foundation, July 1998.*

This is a very thorough paper on the nature of groundwater, the technique of ISL mining with its potential problems, and the experiences of ISL around the world. The paper thoroughly explores the technological failings of ISL mining from the failure of the well casings, to leaking pipes, to failed mud pit liners. I began wondering what sort of "NEW" technology Powertech would be using. They continued to talk about how their ISL process would work because of current technology being better than technology from 30 years before. As long as this new technology that Powertech promised to put into place was proven, maybe their process would not produce the same historical results.

Then this paragraph caught my attention:

"There is simply no human endeavor that is without the possibility of accidents or problems due to human error. The occurrence of a massive reactor explosion at the Chernobyl nuclear power plant in the former Soviet Union, the accident at Three mile island in the USA, the tailings dam breach at Church Rock in New Mexico and other nuclear related accidents serves as a powerful reminder of the consequences of any failure. The operation of an ISL mine site is not immune to such failure, as is no industrial enterprise undertaken."[3]

Even though I was the idealist with a faith in humanity, there was that split where the realist would pop in and I could see our imperfection and the risk inherent in our technology. The human ego, too often, gets in the way of being in touch with what is real world. I could readily see where humans tend to have tunnel vision rather than whole picture view when it comes to designing, building and producing. Chasing the goal, especially when money was involved, commonly ignored the risks. Often these ways take advantage of the gifts our Earth offers in a way that does not take into account a true model of the Whole. This lack of being in touch with all of the elements, and the need to push through an agenda based upon computer models that suite ones purposes, is a recipe for disaster.

> The computer models will show a perfect picture based upon the agenda of those who provide the data. This computer model does not look at LIFE and its perfect imperfection. LIFE is a combination of the elements of fire, water, spirit and air and the way they all blend together to create a wholeness. Just like how I would not allow myself to find a balanced approach to the activism in which we were involved, Powertech would not allow themselves to look at the bigger picture of how their development project would affect the planet.

---

[3]   An Environmental Critique of In Situ Leach Mining: The Case Against Uranium Solution Mining by Gavin Mudd, Victoria University of Technology. A Research Report for Friends of the Earth (Fitzroy) with the Australian Conservation Foundation, July 1998.

Powertech and all miners should take into consideration that the technology they are using must take into account human error, as well as the way the earth is full of its own life. The earthen layers interact in a beautiful way because of the way there is life in soil, rock, sand and water. Maybe not the way we as humans generally think of life, but from a more connected way to the wholeness of the planet and how we are a part of this wholeness. If Powertech could have seen through the eyes of a more indigenous thought process rather than a imperial dominating one, they might have approached the idea of uranium extraction much more differently.

Instead, as most corporations do, they were not looking to ask permission, they were much more interested in taking through domination and entitlement. Exactly the same way a sexual abuser takes their pleasure from their victim. There is no conversation or seeking of real consent.

The next section drew my attention because of what Jay had already said about geology being an imperfect science.

"Although mining is often presented with idealized diagrams and figures outlining the geologic strata and essential processes involved, the basic concepts are always based on simplified theory and the reality of geological and hydrogeological systems are that they are inherently complex and often difficult to interpret and predict. Some of the principal concerns could be the small scale variability present within a palaeochannel leading to undetected excursions or problems in leaching, the behavior of faults in regional groundwater flow, and the presence of fractures (or dolines in limestone or karstic terrain) causing unpredictable contaminant migration away from a site.[4]

All I could think about then was that Nature, in its perfect glory, does not present a clean and perfect venue upon which to overlay our human-created

---

[4] ibid

clean theories and models. What kind of new technology could Powertech have that could alleviate some or all of these things?

I hoped that everyone would read this document. I downloaded the PDF file and then posted the entire thing on www.nunnglow.com. I e-mailed the document to everyone in my e-mail list, I e-mailed the document to the DRMS and attached it in a note to all of our elected officials. I didn't realize it at the time but I was being guided by my emotional response to this document and prayed that other intelligent people would feel the same way.

I spent hours organizing links of information and incidents of spills, leaks, excursions, etc. by state: Texas, Wyoming, South Dakota and more. I separated pertinent information by regulating agency as well, Nuclear Regulatory Committee (NRC), Environmental Protection Agency (EPA), the Colorado Division of Reclamation, Mining and Safety (DRMS), the Colorado Department of Health and Environment (CDPHE). There were many links for each page. All of this was very heady but one could learn as much as they wanted by clicking around from link to link. I just couldn't see any value in writing original stuff with all of this information out there already.

After a few days of website building, I realized that I had not done anything other than feed and water the horses for the past few days. I had one horse here for training and 6 horses being boarded. I needed to keep my agreements and maintain this growing business alongside of my activism. Not to mention that springtime in Colorado is a glorious time. The new grass growth, the birds returning and singing to find mates and build nests, everything was warming up and coming to life. It was time for me to take off my warrior hat and spend a day as a horsewoman.

The next morning dawned cool and sunny. I dressed in layers for the day to warm up and headed outside for my day with the horses. The horse I had in training was a horse that one of my boarders had just recently purchased. After a couple of "rides" on this fellow, this boarder approached me for help. He knew that his rides had not been safe.

"Hi boy, how are you today?"

He approached the fence to say hello.

After petting his neck over the fence for a bit, I slid into his paddock with the halter. This horse high-tailed it away from me and my agenda just as fast as he could. My method of training is to remove as much as possible of that which is domination tactics, and instead ask for what I want. I used many different Natural Horsemanship techniques to draw this horse to me and to gain his trust. He would have nothing to do with getting close enough to be haltered. At the time, I felt I sure had a lot of work to do with this horse. Knowing what I know now, I know that I was incongruent emotionally. I had fear, anger, sadness and grief all welling up inside of me, wishing to be expressed. I approached this horse without even recognizing all my own emotions, let alone allowing them to be heard. He felt this incongruence as a dangerous place to be. He was right, of course, but I just couldn't and wouldn't listen. I had been trained to 'leave my problems at the gate' when it came to working with horses. I was doing my best to do just that.

I had to walk away after more than an hour of just trying to touch him.

> Horses see incongruence of emotion in humans as a serious threat to their survival. When a person is stuffing emotions, rather than leaning into them and really owning their current experience, they are lying to themselves. The horses know that when we lie to ourselves then we cannot be completely honest with them. It's impossible.

> When put in relationship with a human, the horse is asked to listen to the human as their leader. If their leader is not honest they cannot be trusted to make good decisions. This threatens their survival. Horses are prey animals and rely on good leadership to keep them alive when danger threatens.

I decided, instead, to ride my mare Auris Cordis. As I rode, my mind was continually drawn to uranium, property rights, water, science, protection of life, the new conflict we were thrust into. I was mentally absorbed by all of this. When I was typing into the computer, it felt like I was doing something that would get us out of the situation into which we were thrust, front and center. I was taking action. But here in front of the horses, my mind and emotions were getting out of control.

Auris was on alert under me. I could feel her jump at any slightest noise. She was picking up on my stress and tension too. I knew that I would have to have a better handle on myself to be effective with the horses. It just seemed that the harder I tried to dismiss the turmoil raging in my mind and heart, the more the horses became reactive and the less they were interested in being with me. Even this experienced, solid mare was difficult to handle this morning.

With horses, bolting and shutting down are both just as dangerous to a rider because of their unpredictability. A shut down horse can begin bucking or bolting at any time. Just the smallest of stimuli can shock that kind of horse back into a present state just enough for them go directly into self-preservation mode and their fight or flight reflexes. I didn't realize it but I was the shut down horse. These horses knew it, and didn't wish to be around when I began acting out upon what was going on inside of me.

The anger I felt towards being dominated by others had infiltrated all parts of my life, conscious and subconscious. I decided to call it quits for the day with the horses and get busy on driving uranium miners away so maybe I could be right with my horses again.

I marched back to my office and the computer with the ever growing website and email list. I learned more and more about why we could never allow this uranium mining to take place. We just cannot live without water. A respectful relationship with water is important to all of life.

> The element of water represents our emotions. Water is fluid and flows just as we need to allow our emotions to flow. While I understood about the physical connection

we have to water as life, I didn't recognize the connection to the emotions. I was stuffing my emotions and was not in a respectful relationship with this part of myself. The horses were trying to teach me, but I couldn't hear the lesson at the time.

If I had not found a way to a respectful relationship with my emotions, I shudder to think where I may be right now. I was dominating them just as Powertech was attempting to dominate the water we rely upon. This toxic relationship with the emotions may have manifested in many, many ways. As you'll see as this story progresses, I was already busy manifesting dis-ease from without and within because of this inauthentic way of living.

My e-mailing was paying off in huge ways. As my e-mails were forwarded by my initial contact, then forwarded by their contacts, then forwarded by those contacts, we were virtually going viral. Initially, it would surprise me when I would get an e-mail from some unknown person who didn't live in our area and was really upset about the proposed uranium mine. Of course, I kept getting free advice on how to proceed with our battle. Much of it good, much of it repetitive and all of it dropped back into my lap, with the comments.... "You need to....." I kept hoping folks would begin to volunteer to help in meaningful ways. The thing that I couldn't see was that I was not good at asking for help. It was much easier for me to fall into my victim role and take on their "You need to…" suggestions as things that 'I' personally had to do.

As a victim I could not healthily take suggestions and then delegate. I felt like I had to do it all. Then I could project my anger right back at those who were attempting to be helpful. I'd fall into a dance around the trauma/drama triangle. They might suggest an idea, I would internalize that it was my responsibility to act upon the idea, then feel like I had no control over my life because I had so much to do. That would then make me feel angry that others just didn't see how hard I was working. A complete victim. To complete the triangle I would whine to someone about how hard I had it, and how bad these others were because 'they' couldn't just do something to help. Now I'm a persecutor to the 'others'. The person to whom I might be whining might then offer to take some stuff off my plate so they would then be the rescuer.

I would also take the rescuer role within our neighborhood. "Oh, don't worry, I have time, I can get that done." I'd say in a meeting or phone conversation. Then I'd become the perpetrator by talking about how nobody was doing anything, and find myself angry with everybody.

Sure, getting the word out was meaningful in oh so many ways, but how would that stop this dangerous project? We needed action of some sort. I wasn't sure what the action looked like. What more could I do? I kept e-mailing, researching and building our website.

The view through my office window shows any activity for a mile in any direction from which a vehicle can approach. A car came bouncing down our dirt road. As I idly gazed at it, I was suddenly shocked by recognizing the vehicle. Oh no, I had forgotten about a riding lesson.

I quickly logged off of the computer, pulled my boots on and jogged down the hill to meet my clients. This activism role was becoming all-consuming very rapidly. While I was helping this child with their horse, my mind kept being drawn back to the uranium issue. All I could think about was my ever growing list of things to do. I was very conflicted about where I should be and so was not present at all for this rider or the parents.

Once the lesson was over and the rider left, I allowed my mind to freely drift into the uranium issue while I did my horse chores. I kept wondering what action we could take in order to stop this potential mine. I was still not quite convinced that we COULD stop them. I couldn't see any other options, but to try. I looked around me at the horses, the wildlife, the prairie grasses. *How could anyone see all of this and want to destroy it?* I wondered.

The peace and beauty of the quiet evening filtered in as I sat on a fence rail to pray about our situation. I asked for God's guidance, but as I started to ask for guidance, I wondered why God had brought us to this place. Was it just to be put into turmoil? I asked why we have these things to deal with. My frustration was bubbling up. I thought we were brought to this place to build a safe place for the kids. This is what I had prayed for as we were looking for our new property. The purchase of this property had gone smoothly. The sale of our house in Masonville, though not quick, had proceeded without any major hurdles.

The ease of the purchase, the move and the way the business was progressing had seemed like all the right signs for being in the right place and doing the right things. I yelled to the heavens. "Why?!?! Why us?!?!? What are we supposed to do?!? Am I not doing enough to follow Your will?!?!"

The sounds of the horses munching hay and the birds singing their spring songs were the only answers I received. I started to cry. My confusion was overwhelming. I thought I always did my best to be a servant to God and His people. It is important to me to not go against His will. I walk and work in prayer constantly, my relationship with God is very deep. I always wanted to know what it was that He asked of me.

> Projection, manipulation, externalizing my personal power, victimization. All of this was who and what I was doing at this time of my life.

This uranium issue was something I had never imagined would come my way. I had believed that my main mission in life was to work with the children. My prayer life and the actions I always took from the prayer time drove me towards the kids and working to teach them. I taught more than horsemanship. Just getting on the horse and learning how to kick hard to go fast and pull back hard to stop was not my way of doing things. I used the horses to help the kids learn self-respect through respect of the horse. My analogies would even go as far as pointing out how the way we respect a horses' personal space is what we should also demand of others in our lives towards us. I wanted to empower the kids to love themselves as God loves them. It was my intent to help these kids build life skills through their relationship with the horses.

My faith always bled into my lessons. Not in a way that would offend people on different paths, but in a loving way that opened up deep dialogue between me and my students. I wanted them to know that it was safe to talk to me about anything they wanted or needed to. I was blessed to have many of these kinds of relationships with my students over the years. The students kept journals about our lessons in which I was allowed to read and to write comments back. It never surprised me to see personal notes to me about family issues, school issues or friendship issues. I would encourage the students the best I could and help them see solutions through their horsemanship. I really loved working with the children. And now I was already forgetting about appointments with the very people I was committed to.

I used to joke about how I was a riding teacher who was an underpaid psychologist. I asked God about all of these things and how it fit with uranium mining. I just didn't get it. I sat in silence for quite some time, hoping to hear the answers that were beyond my understanding. The sun was setting and the temperature was dropping. I was beginning to get cold.

I asked for guidance again and went back up the hill to my computer to keep doing what I knew needed to be done. Drive uranium miners as far away as I could. Protect our property and our dreams. Protect the water supplies for us and future generations.

I went to bed again that night before Jay got home. I still wondered why this task was being set before us. My thoughts and feelings of frustration and panic would not allow me to sleep well, but at least I was able to doze a little bit before getting up early the next morning.

As I kissed Jay good-bye for the day, I considered what needed to be done. As was becoming very normal by now, I logged on to check my e-mail first thing. While considering some of the replies I was getting I looked out my office window where a flash of activity had caught my eye.

A golden eagle that had been circling overhead dropped onto a rabbit right on the property we were hoping to buy. The hungry eagle hopped around on the ground with the violently struggling bunny in his tenuous grasp. I wasn't sure which one to root for, the majestic eagle or the cute cottontail. This was a battle of life or death for both.

The eagle was struggling to hang onto his active prey but finally got it pinned to the ground. Suddenly, from a nearby bush another rabbit bolted towards the eagle. He ran right at the eagle and kick-jumped at his head. The eagle jumped back, but did not release his grip on his hoped for meal. This bold bunny circled the dramatic scene and then jumped at the head of the eagle again.

The tenacity of the attack bunny was something to behold. The very pure struggle of life and death for each species was palpable.

The attack bunny circled each time before he'd jump-kick at the eagle. The eagle must have been feeling the brunt of those kicks. He'd jump back some with each one but kept a grip on his prey until finally, he just couldn't take it any longer. One well-landed kick finally sent the eagle on a short wing-spread jump out of the range of his attacker. Leaving his prey behind as he settled on the mound nearby.

The injured rabbit lay still for what felt like an eternity. The attack bunny stood nearby watching both the eagle and his friend. Suddenly, the injured bunny jumped straight up and shook all over. Quickly the two bunnies hopped into the safety of a nearby bush, leaving both the eagle and I stupefied over what had just happened. The eagle sat in the grass with a dazed look. Then he lifted off into an aerial circle over the land looking for new prey.

The ringing telephone jarred me from my revery of what I had just witnessed. "Hello?"

"Hey Robin, it's Shawn. So you guys are gonna fight this uranium mine?" he asked. Shawn was the developer who owned quite a bit of land near us, including the piece we were actively attempting to purchase for our conservation area. We hadn't really spoken with him about the uranium issue as we had been discussing the details on the property purchase. He had received one of our letters since he was an adjacent land owner. Our 2nd mortgage was due to close in a couple of days and we had begun to discuss dates for our closing with him on the adjacent property. We had a handshake deal with him regarding this property. We trusted him because of the several conversations we had already had with him, plus the fact that he was talking to me about having his kids join the 4-H club. He and his kids had come to our 4-H club Christmas party last December.

"I don't think we have any choice, Shawn," I replied. "This operation could pollute our drinking water. We moved out here to work with the kids and teach them about respect for themselves and nature. Uranium mining doesn't fit with that. Not to mention our entire financial future is tied up here."

"Hmmmmmm," he mused, "I don't think this ISL process is as damaging as you think it is. Besides we need the uranium for nuclear power. I've been talking with Powertech about buying the property adjacent to the piece you guys are gonna buy. It's pretty much a done deal."

"WHAT?!?!?!" I felt like I had just been kicked in the gut. "You would do that to us? What about the kids? What about the other families who moved out here because you built houses in which they could raise their families and build their dreams? You don't have to sell to Powertech! It only gives them more power and a better foothold in making this uranium mine a reality. We need to stand strong to fight this."

"Oh, I don't know, Robin. I believe in protecting the environment, but I just don't see how they will be polluting the water," he said.

"I think you need to talk to Jay," I replied. "He can tell you the details that I cannot. He's really looked into this and with his background he doesn't like what they're proposing."

"I don't think there's time for that. I close with them in a couple of days," he stated without much thought. He then changed the subject, "Anyway, when do you want to schedule the closing on our deal?"

"You are selling to Powertech and you want me to buy MORE property from YOU! Not in a million years." I was nearly hyperventilating at this point. Who did this guy think he was?!?! Selling us out to a uranium mining company and asking us to give him more money while we would be put at even greater risk. I hung up the phone without saying goodbye.

I looked out the window again as I tried to regain emotional control. My mind drifted to the bunnies standing up to the eagle who was clearly a very powerful force to reckon with. I don't know how much an eagle outweighs a cottontail rabbit but they are easily two to three times larger without the wingspan. This eagle had his wings out and had a cottontail pinned to the ground in his sharp talons. The little helper bunny saw his friend in trouble and went right to doing what it needed to do to protect its friends life.

I felt the answer from God in what I had been shown. Regardless of how small and helpless I felt, I needed to do what I could to protect life.

I called Jay to share this latest development with Shawn. He was very disappointed about the way I had spoken to him. Jay still wanted to purchase the extra land. He felt like if we held it we might have more control over our situation. I was afraid of getting in deeper.

"Go ahead and call him if you want," I told him. "But I just don't feel good about it at all."

Jay did try to call Shawn, but he never returned Jay's calls. Shawn sold the land we wanted along with the other piece to Powertech Uranium Corporation without ever speaking to us again.

By this time some of the media had started contacting us about our press releases. ABC News Channel 7 out of Denver, Colorado was the first news station who asked us if they could come out to report. Since they wanted to come at mid-day, I was the only one around. I could hear my activist friend's words echoing about my new fame. Yet again, I was doing something about which I had no idea. I was nervous about the filming and had never felt good about speaking in public, let alone on TV. The reporter, James Hucks, was a young and friendly man who put me at ease right away. We talked a little about the issue and found what he felt like was a good location from which to film. He wanted the horses in the background. He started asking questions about my concerns. As soon as I mentioned the children we had in our lives, I began to cry. I cannot find that old footage and don't remember all that he asked me, but I know most of my television debut was one of tear-filled answers. I was scared. Scared of what our future looked like, scared for the water beneath my feet, scared for the land and the animals, scared for the people, just flat scared. It all just flooded out of my eyes with the nerves of being in front of the camera.

After he finished the interview, he began packing up his camera and equipment. I was still having trouble gaining control of my emotions. He said quietly, "You have a huge fight in front of you."

"I know," I replied through the tears.

"What is your plan?"

"I don't really know yet. This helps, you being here and getting the word out. I don't know if we even have a chance, but we have no options."

"Good luck," he said with a sympathetic smile. "I don't think this is gonna be an easy issue."

"Thank you. Thank you for being here and thanks for the kind words."

As he drove away, I heard his question over and over..... "what's your plan?" We really didn't have a plan yet. We just kept putting one foot in front of the other and the "plan" seemed to be just sort of evolving right in front of us. The "plan" seemed to me to be one of information and numbers of people. The rest was just details that would work itself out as they needed to. These were my thoughts, and I had no idea how realistic and yet unrealistic they were at the same time. I was also thinking, I DO NOT want to see myself on TV. Especially looking like a crying idiot. I thought that I needed to keep emotion out of this.

I spent the rest of that day staying busy preparing for our neighborhood meeting and developing some ideas for our upcoming public meeting. We had the letters out for our neighbors and classified ads ordered, as well as community calendar announcements that were already being published. I had to stay busy for survival, so that I could keep my emotions under lock and key, so I could keep my home, so I could just not think about the reality of our situation too deeply. I sent more e-mails and added more information to our website until I could not see straight any longer. I didn't watch the news because I was so embarrassed by my performance, so I wasn't sure if they had run it or not.

The next morning I got a call from my mom. "Hey, we saw you on TV."

"Oh, so you saw me cry," I answered.

"Yeah, my sister called, she saw it last night and then they aired it again this morning so I got to see it."

I was torn between being excited that the word was getting out, no matter how bad I looked, and feeling like a real jerk for my performance. Oh well, time to keep putting one foot in front of the other.

My mom and my stepdad, Jerry, are also very conservative. They both stay informed and are politically active. When I shared with them how we planned to fight the proposed uranium mine, they were not quite sure what to think. My mom could see that we really didn't have any choice, but Jerry believes that nuclear power is the answer to energy independence. I hadn't called them about my embarrassing TV debut, so my mom was surprised to find me crying on her TV that morning. Mom reassured me that the story was a good start. It truly was just the start.

Jerry and I started having disagreements about what we should do. He was looking at the Powertech technical data and figuring it would be no big deal. "And you might make some money off of this. Did you know that uranium prices are quite high right now?"

I told him that I was more concerned for the water. "Why should we be polluting what we all know is a finite resource just for power?"

"I'm not sure it will be as impactful as you think," he replied. "They talk about success in other areas."

"Jerry, please take a look at our website and some of the information we've found. I have to warn you, I am probably gonna turn into a real Greenpeace kind of activist over this issue." Something totally out of character for me, and I said it to help him see just how important this issue is.

"Don't get too reactive," he warned. "You don't want to lose any respect in the community as business owners. Jay needs to be very careful with the kind of business he's in."

All I could think at the time was, what respect? What is respect in the community if you cannot look yourself in the mirror and say that you are doing the right thing? Self respect and living as God would want me were number 1 in my mind. Not to mention, I was also approaching a very interesting state of panic over the entire situation. I was feeling very trapped. Couldn't move forward with our dreams and plans, couldn't go backward by selling out to a uranium mining company, didn't know if we would make it financially if we weren't moving forward with the business plan for our property, didn't really know how to be an effective activist anyway. All of this welling up inside of me and Jerry being a relatively safe place for me to vent in that space and time, created a perfect storm in which I unleashed some very hurtful things which I projected directly at him. I yelled about the way he was not protecting us, I yelled about the way he was putting money ahead of our lives, I yelled about how much of a victim I was and how badly I needed a rescuer and none could be found. Another phone call that I ended without a goodbye...

I said some very hurtful things to Jerry. To this day I wish I could take them back. We've always been close and he has forgiven me since then, and I thank him for that, but it still hurts me to know that I hurt him with my angry words. I really wanted to be lashing out at Powertech for their injustice.

> As I think back about how I handled this relationship during this tumultuous time, I can see that I was speaking Truth for the planet but from a damaged place where I did not feel that I had the right to speak to a father figure that way. I said some things that he really needed to hear but the energy behind those words lacked impact because I was living as a person of the lie. I had a story that I was living, my own reality that I felt was true. I could not and would not look at my own personal trauma so that made me susceptible to other stories that were in part true but not totally true. I could not see the whole picture because of the way I would not look at my own whole picture.

> So rather than having a conversation in which I could stand in a place of personal power about the truth of the situation, I felt that I just had to get angry and lash out with things that were not completely true but instead, half-truths. Things that felt like needed to be said but energetically were unclean.

The underlying story of where most of my anger was coming from was really the core of the issue. Yes, I had very real reason to be angry with Powertech because of their violation of the boundary around our lives and livelihood. I also had a very real reason for being frustration with Jerry for not attempting to understand the situation we were in. What I didn't have a good reason for was the way I allowed my rage to take over and allow it to puke its vitriol all over another human. It wasn't just the anger of the present situation that was driving this rage. It was also deep wounding from previously unresolved trauma. At the time, I had no idea about such things, so I just blamed it on emotions as being bad. I kept telling myself that I just had to get a handle on my emotions.

I didn't realize the irony of presenting myself to be a water protector while at the same time making the emotional waters wrong. My disrespect for my own emotional body was disrespect and pollution of water in its own way just like the ISL uranium mining process was a deep disrespect and pollution of the waters of the body of our planet. This lack of respect for the waters within was setting me, personally, up for the need to clean up some toxic waste of my own.

CHAPTER 6

BUILDING THE TEAM OF URANIUM WARRIORS

The same day I saw my debut on Channel 7 News, Fox 31 News from Denver contacted me and hoped for an early evening interview. I had a conflict because of a 4-H meeting so I called Carol to see if she and David could meet with them. They agreed and met the mobile unit with the reporter at a relatively busy intersection about 2 miles away from our homes. It's not too common to see a news van in the area, so some of the local folks stopped to inquire. One of whom was on his way home from work in Denver at HDNET. It was the first he had heard of the potential uranium mine.

"We are not yet positive, but we think Powertech might be planning an open pit uranium mine in section 35," they told him. "The representative we spoke to last December made a brief mention of it. We don't have any documented proof yet, though."

"OPEN PIT URANIUM MINING!" This gentleman nearly yelled. "Where is section 35?"

Carol brushed aside some of her long brown hair as she pointed to an open field nearby.

Dumbfounded, this man slowly lifted his hand and pointed in almost the same direction at a house within view.

"That sure is close to my home," he answered with concern in his voice.

Carol gave this man the website address and invited him to join our neighborhood meeting in a couple of days. He readily agreed and got back in his van with a determined walk.

Arriving home from the 4-H meeting of that evening, I sat down to check my e-mail. At this point I had to stay on top of it or the numbers would grow to be far too many for me to handle. I found a note from another neighbor who had just heard about the proposed uranium mining. Ralph is a water quality engineer for the City of Fort Collins, his wife is a hydrologist. He expressed his concern and said he wanted to know everything there was to know. He also wanted to know what he could do to help. I happily added him to my e-mail list and sent him back a note that invited him to the landowners meeting the next day.

I answered a few more e-mails. *These e-mails are getting out of hand,* I thought. I needed a way that folks could stay in touch without me sitting at the computer to forward everything. People were sending me articles, news reports, personal accounts, responses from elected officials and more. That night I started a Yahoo! Group and invited everyone in my address book to join. *Hopefully this will relieve some of the pressure,* I thought tiredly. I hoped they would be able to share their information without me being the middle person.

I fell into bed thinking of the progress we were already making.

Our website was up. We were building a large list of folks who were e-mailing one another. Two television stories had run on two different stations. We still had two meetings scheduled, one with landowners and one in Wellington for the public. The uranium cat was slowly coming out of the bag. And all of this had happened in less than one week. This progress was helping to still my roiling emotions, somewhat.... I still felt this need to stay super busy, or it would all come crashing down on me. So I did...

Jay and I knew from the start that we were the proverbial David up against a well-funded and organized Goliath. We would have to have all of our facts correct and tight in order to stand tall against them. So we decided we needed to have good devices upon which to record all conversations amongst ourselves and with Powertech. I went to town and bought a digital voice recorder, a digital video recorder and the software needed to work with both. We also purchased a new laptop to be sure we had the best technology available. I called this our "up-armoring." We were officially redirecting any spending to the uranium fight rather than our planned improvements for my horse business.

David and Carol had paid for the first order of yard signs and we were making the copies of the letters, paying for postage and the website hosting. When you live in the middle of a proposed uranium mine and there are things that need to be done to fight it and protect your lifestyle and livelihood, and the money is not otherwise available, you open your wallet and make it happen. Happily. Don't even slow down the energy by hedging on spending on the project. That is what we believed. This was before the time of crowd funding sites and we didn't know how to ask people for donations, so we just did it.

April 11, 2007 the day of our first neighborhood landowners meeting was a cool spring day with no wind. Since I wanted to have some light snacks available for our guests, I decided to run in for some groceries. The previous week I had purchased a 5 subject spiral bound notebook in which I began to keep my jumbled thoughts and any important notes organized. I collected this, a good working pen, my purse and my cell phone, and headed for the door. I enjoy driving time because it's always a good time for me to consider our latest strategy. I had already written my grocery list into the notebook. Today, when I look back through the pages of this notebook, I see lists of errand stops, grocery lists, 4-H notes all interspersed in the middle of uranium notes and contacts with phone numbers as well as notes jotted during phone conversations regarding permitting processes and more.

I had one hand on the door knob ready to exit when the phone rang. I paused, "Hello?"

"Hi, this is Lisa, I saw the article in the Coloradoan and your website on the proposed uranium mine. I've been active in this sort of issue in the past. I'd like to help."

The article she was referring to was by Kevin Duggan of the Fort Collins Coloradoan, *"Uranium Mine's Impact Worries Property Owners"* that had come out this morning. The two things in this article that had my attention were some quotes by Richard Blubaugh:

"The sharp rise in uranium prices in recent years kindled the company's interest in mining the Weld County site, Blubaugh said. Demand for uranium is growing around the world, he said, with countries such as China and India planning to build more nuclear power plants.

Coal-fired power plants are out of favor because of the greenhouse gases they emit, he said.

"Nuclear is back on the front burner," Blubaugh said.

The article also quoted both David and I. Me, regarding my fears of water contamination where we were hosting a 4-H club, while David brought the attention to the fact that anyone who drinks water should be concerned. Then the article ended with a very interesting paragraph:

"If landowners do not cooperate, the company could go to court to gain access to its mineral holdings, 'but we really don't want to do that,' he (Blubaugh) said. The company will hold public meetings to discuss its plans with neighbors and surrounding communities and address their concerns."[5]

Lisa began to tell me about some of her experiences stopping proposed mining operations in South Dakota.

---

[5] April 11, 2007, *Fort Collins Coloradoan*, Uranium Mine's Impact Worries Property Owners by Kevin Duggan, April 11, 2007

Ah, finally someone who knows how to do this sort of thing, I thought. I had no idea who this person was, but I knew that I had no idea what I was doing so I asked her, "We are having a meeting with all of the landowners tonight. Can you come?"

"Wow, that's pretty short notice, um, I have a commitment already tonight, but this is an important issue. Let me see if I can rearrange some things. I'll do what I can," she answered.

She sounded so sure of herself. This felt very good to me. I gave her directions to our house and hoped that she would show up. I hung up the phone and got out the door this time. I drove with my mind on uranium and the incredibly long list of things I should be doing. I would drive with my notebook open and jot down chicken scratch notes to look at later.

My mind turned to the response that one of my e-mails to the Sierra Club had received. This note contained the phone number of a woman in Denver who had been active in the cleanup efforts of Rocky Flats in Boulder, Co.. I had her name and phone number written in my notebook. While shopping, she kept coming to mind. So, after I loaded my groceries into the truck I called her before starting the truck. "Hi, my name is Robin Davis and I got your name and phone number through the Sierra Club. We are in the process of researching and opposing a uranium mine that is planned for our property and the surrounding area."

"Ummmm, I hadn't heard about this. What's going on?" She asked.

I proceeded to tell her about the ISL and open pit mine proposal. As I finished telling her about the proposed project and what we were currently doing, I realized I needed to at least start driving home to get the cold groceries put away before they spoiled.

My contact started to share some of her experiences with the Rocky Flats project. She encouraged me and told me that she would help wherever she could. No sooner were these words out of her mouth when she reconsidered. "I just started a new business, sigh, I really can't spend a lot of time helping you right now. Let's talk about what you can do to really fight this thing."

The Sierra Club, much like most environmental organizations as I was quickly finding out, is made up of mostly volunteers who share their valuable time as much as they are able. Adding this new project to their already overburdened list of things to work on was not a simple thing to ask. In general, they need the local residents to rise to the occasion rather than just hand it to them, as I had wanted to do. They will support with ideas as much as they are capable of, but coming in and working as the central force of opposition is rare. Once a local opposition is established, they will often support with grants and even go as far as legal counsel and in person help if needed. These types of emails and phone calls were becoming very regular to me and my frustration was rising. I sighed right along with her and continued to listen while she ran down the list of 'you need to's.'

Some of the best advice she gave me was to make sure I contacted the Colorado Department of Public Health and Environment, Radiological Division. "They have to protect the safety and welfare of the people of Colorado, Robin. Let them know about the risk being proposed here. I've never heard of ISL mining, but it sure doesn't seem like the CDPHE would want radioactivity in our precious resource of water. It's not like we have a lot of water in Colorado. Find out what their existing regulations are."

We chatted a bit more and I continued to tell her of the things we already had done and were doing. She replied, "It sounds like you guys are already on a roll and doing well. Call me anytime if I can help you." I thanked her and we hung up.

As I started down a dirt road that leads to our home I was feeling hopeless because I believed that the Sierra Club contact would just 'fix' this mess for us. A shock of blue in the road caught my attention. I tapped the brakes to get a better look. As the truck creeped closer, I was surrounded by a flock of mountain bluebirds sitting in the road, on the fence line and into the adjacent pasture. I stopped to drink in their presence. I counted well over 50. Having moved from Masonville, one of the things we missed was the wide variety of songbirds found in that area. Bluebirds were one of my favorites and we always had at least one nesting pair in one of the boxes at our old place. Since they don't nest in the prairie, I never imagined I would see them here. It turns out they were migrating through. God was continuing to give me signs of wonder whenever I was feeling small and victimized. I considered the bluebirds to be a good sign of life and new beginnings. I soaked it in and decided, yet again, to pull up my bootstraps and keep going.

As the hour of the meeting approached I set out lemonade, some nuts and some simple crackers and hoped folks would show up. David and Carol arrived early and we discussed how to proceed with this meeting. Since we had no idea what the general mood of the people would be we decided to just open up the topic and see how folks were feeling about it. We still didn't know if we were loners in our opposition.

Trucks and SUV's began to pull into the driveway. People began to come in and introduce themselves. The same emotions were showing on all of these faces. Not happy neighbors glad for an opportunity to meet one another and socialize, but looks of fear and sadness and uncertainty. I began to worry about Jay arriving on time.

A single woman pulled up in her teal Subaru, she got out of the car dressed, not in blue jeans and flannel, but a cotton top and pants with sandals. I thought to myself, well here is a real 'granola' type. Not the kind of person you expect to see living in an area like ours which is filled with ranchers who generally drive big vehicles built to haul livestock and the things they need. "Hi, I'm Lisa. You must be Robin." She introduced herself with an outstretched hand. I took notice of her sureness and academic presence. I felt a sense of relief and hoped that she would just take over at that point. I'm sure that my brewing panic showed in my eyes and my shallow breathing. I quickly asked her to run the meeting, but she said that since this was our first gathering it would be better if she just hung out and listened. "You'll do fine," she reassured me. I was still unable to just give this thing to someone else to deal with.

As we were all sitting down, I noticed Jay pull into the driveway. I grew edgy as he paused, like he always does, to give the dogs his full attention long enough for them to settle into the thorough petting he offered before continuing to the door. We made eye contact as he joined the room, I was feeling angry that he was so 'late' and hoped that he saw that.

I spoke, "We thought we would begin by everyone introducing ourselves and talking about why we moved out here. I'm Robin Davis and we are here to build a horse boarding and training facility. We have a fun and growing 4-H club. We currently have 13 horses here and we own 6 of them. We are just now getting used to the prairie. We moved here from Masonville, where we lived for 16 years." I looked at Jay.

Man of few words Jay said, "I'm her husband, Jay. I like the open spaces."

David and Carol went next, "We moved here to raise natural beef. We want to protect the water from this uranium issue."

As we went around the room every one of them had a similar story of dreams being destroyed by Powertech.

Families who purchased land to raise children with a respect for a more natural lifestyle, families who moved away from pollution and crime, families who invested everything, time, money, emotion as they designed and built their dream home. The poignant stories in the room were evidence of the emotional and physical costs as well as the financial costs. The surprising letter from Powertech Uranium Corporation had added stress to each and every one of them.

These were the types of stories, alongside of a couple of absentee raw land owners who were not living here yet, but were at the meeting because of wanting more information before they proceeded with their plans to build.

We all talked of our options. Some spoke of contacting Powertech and asking them to buy them out. We all realized that our homes did not have a value in the regular real estate market any longer. We discussed the realization that they own our mineral rights, but wanted to know why it's fair for them to be able to come in and do whatever they want to those of us who live on the surface. Those whose mineral rights are not owned by Powertech expressed the fact that it didn't really matter if the mining was taking place on their land, we are all still affected because of the aquifer that we are all connected to.

We discussed what sorts of rights the mineral rights owners do have in the long run. It was concluded that we all knew the same thing. The mineral owners have precedent over surface rights.

The conversation turned to the existing water quality in our wells. Most had already had their water tested for drinkability. Some wells had water that was qualified as undrinkable. The conversation then turned to the fact that the uranium ore bodies had already been stirred up with the prospecting that occurred in the late 70's early 80's. At that time during the previous uranium boom, over 3500 bore holes and wells had been drilled during core sampling and monitoring the potential of mining the uranium. When the market for uranium had crashed, the project was abandoned. Colorado law holds prospecting as a private/secret matter. This was why few of us had known about the uranium in the area before we purchased, nor before we had received our letters from Powertech Uranium Corporation.

Ann, one of our neighbors daughters, and Lisa began talking about the different elements that would be stirred up with ISL mining for uranium. Cadmium, Arsenic, Radium, Selenium, Lead. Ann stated quietly, "I have a PHD in biology. And my husband has a degree in radio-chemistry. So we have a background in this."

The conversation turned to the details of where the ore body might be. As a group we wondered if any permits were drawn yet. David had spoken with the EPA and they said no permits were drawn through them at this time.

A common theme was trust. "I don't trust them," was said over and over. Interjected in different phases of conversation, "I don't trust them," by different voices "I don't trust them." When your living situation is threatened, it's unrealistic to be asked to blindly trust those doing the threatening.

Talk turned to the surface land that Powertech was already buying. One neighbor, Steve, brought up the fact that when Powertech bought the house and land they were also buying the domestic well on the property. He wondered if this would give them water rights. He had spoken to Shawn, who had built their house as well, he was told of the sale to Powertech and that it included the closed in, yet unfinished house adjacent to the raw land we had had an interest in. Shawn had told him that the house would remain unfinished on the interior. Many of us had a fear that the house would then become a processing plant for Powertech, since they had a shell with which to work.

One of the absentee owners shared his experience of talking with the landman of Powertech. He told him that he had three options, to sell outright, lease the surface, or fight them, and he was pressuring him for an answer.

The man who had stopped to speak with David and Carol while being interviewed had in fact come to the meeting and brought his wife. They were very concerned especially since the threat of an open pit uranium mine was very close to their house. She spoke up to share her experiences: "I lived in Montrose for a couple of years. I noticed a pretty high rate of cancers in the children and the number of birth defects in the area. One of my horses lost its hooves. We learned that it was selenium poisoning. That's when I started to research this area. We moved here to get away from uranium mines. We thought the prairie was safe from this kind of threat."

Lisa talked about the global nature of this issue and encouraged us all to keep that at the fore front of our minds and our voices as we talk to people about this. She went on to share that she was already working with a group in South Dakota regarding a Powertech project up there.

The talk turned to uranium and how it would be used for nuclear power. We talked about the dangers of radionuclides. The risks associated with the transportation and processing that would take place outside of the mining area. We discussed the benefits of wind and solar power.

Talk again turned to the water we are all using to drink. Ann told those whose water already shows some uranium in it about the benefits of different filtration systems. David reminded everyone that once the mining begins, those small amounts of uranium in the water will sky rocket.

Ann continued to discuss how uranium breaks down, "All of the daughters of uranium have the same radioactive characteristics, it's just a matter of where they are in the breakdown process. The shorter the half life, the more radiation. The mined uranium is less radioactive than the daughters which the mining stirs up. Not to mention all of the toxic heavy metals they stir up. They will only be taking the uranium, leaving many other toxins behind."

One of the neighbors asked, "Well, OKAY. So if we have to allow them on our surface, and they say that they will not be disturbing it, and they are mining in our water, how can they not disturb our water well?"

A loud voice pretending to be Powertech piped in, "Trust us we know what we are doing." Everyone laughed to ease our own fears.

David brought up the fact that Powertech has to stay at least 600 feet away from a domestic well during their drilling.

Ann reminded everyone that this is not really protection because of the way the toxins will travel and contaminate the entire aquifer over time.

Lisa had printed out the map of the Dakota-Cheyenne aquifer that was covered with dots signifying the wells that are drawing water. Some people wanted copies of the map so I told them about the link on www.nunnglow. com. A few of the people had not yet seen the website.

The discussion turned to how many people had already been doing their own research by searching in-situ leach mining and looking at the Powertech Uranium website. Everyone who had looked at a multitude of websites, many of which were linked to from ours, agreed that www. wise_uranium.org is the best. "It's the most thorough and has a good reputation amongst the regulating agencies."

"I spoke to the Colorado Department of Public Health and Environment, the Radiological Division, today." I put in, "This project is the very first in-situ leach mining project that would be done in Colorado. They don't have any regulations specific to in-situ leach mining for uranium, yet. If we can prove that there is a history of violations by this company, they said that is when they will deny the company the permit."

"That should be easy," one of the absentee owners replied, "it's all over the web."

"Yes, it is," I agreed. "The thing is, it's not this particular company, but different companies with the same players."

"Yeah, here in the US, Australia, Germany and beyond," added Carol.

The same absentee owner piped in, "I wonder if the best place to be effective in stopping this is through Weld County and particularly through the water judge."

"We need the help of some already organized groups such as Colorado Peace and Justice," the woman who had lived in Montrose put in.

"They actually contacted me today," I answered. "They wanted to know if we'd like to speak at their Earth Day rally. I excitedly told them yes. I'm not yet sure who will speak, but we are on their agenda."

After the room settled down from this exciting news, Lisa jumped in. "We need to learn all we can about any regulations that may or may not exist regarding in-situ mining and we need to know the exact process for permitting that Powertech will have to go through."

David volunteered that he and Carol could do that kind of research with the State. David had already been in touch with the Weld County Department of Health and Environment. He had been told that Powertech has a meeting planned with them on April 26 to learn about the in-situ leach mining process. "I need to get back to him with a list of questions and any concerns we may have so they can address these in the meeting."

David passed around the name and e-mail address of the person with whom he had been in contact. "Please everyone e-mail him directly with your concerns. He told me that he's not an engineer so he doesn't know about the in-situ process itself, but he's not too concerned about any toxins going too far because the water in the aquifer only moves in any direction 2 or 3 feet per year. I'm not sure how that fits with our domestic well refill rates, but that's what he said."

The group erupted into small conversations ranging from concerns about property values to more action items regarding who else we should be contacting.

I spoke up to bring the group back together and David encouraged everyone to stay on track. It was agreed that the place to start right now was with the Weld County Department of Health. Since Powertech already had a meeting scheduled with them, we needed our voices to be heard any way we could at this scheduled meeting. David had been told that the public could not attend this meeting so we needed to e-mail or call with our concerns. As a group, our main concern was the water and we all agreed to send our questions.

Talk turned to security. Could the uranium be used by a terrorist group to make a dirty bomb? Would the area be at risk of the type of people who would consider stealing the uranium? Would we all be living within a chain link fenced area with guard dogs? We had no idea what would happen and we sure didn't feel that we could trust Powertech to give us honest answers to these types of questions.

"I talked to the EPA and recorded my conversation with them," David said, changing the subject. "Powertech has been in touch with them but has not filed any applications yet. I spent the entire day on the phone. I think I spoke to every organization with whom Powertech needs to get a permit, and they have all been contacted by Powertech, but no applications have been filed yet. Just conversations. I kept asking about groundwater contamination. I never got a guarantee from any agency that regulations will protect us, nor whether or not contamination will occur. I even spoke to the state veterinarian. Interestingly enough he's at a state homeland security conference right now. I was going to anyone I could think of and with the threat to our livestock he seemed like a logical contact. He is supposed to get back to me.

As far as permits, I know there are three permits that Powertech will have to get through the Federal Government. They will need a land permit, a water permit, and an injection well permit. Powertech still has a lot of hoops to get this done.

We are on top of them and the public is finding out about this project. I think Powertech is getting nervous already because they had hoped to slide this in without many people finding out."

"Powertech is already threatening to sue, according to the article I just read," I put in.

"They will force us, as surface owners, to allow access through the courts," a landowner replied.

The fear in the room was palpable.

"Without the permits they have no power to demand access." David replied. "They also have to get some permits from Weld County."

Lisa asked if she could share her experiences. She was asked before she could even begin, "Did you win in South Dakota?" "We won." She replied

The room felt lighter with that short reply.

Lisa went on: "In 1977 we went up against several major and large corporations as well as the Federal Government and the State of South Dakota. Consequently, a large uranium ore body is still in the ground up there. The way we stopped them was that they began mining before any permits were in place. One of the things you all who live within the mining area need to do is have a central location for information. Report any activity at all. You never know exactly what they are doing. Watch them, record them, video tape them. People on the land are the key to this thing.

We also have to remember that we cannot go at a battle like this by only talking about the people who live on the land in the proposed mining area. We have to talk about the size of the aquifer, the number of wells on it, the lack of clean water in the world, the risks of radioactivity and heavy metals at all stages of the mining, milling and nuclear power generation. We need to talk about the history of this company or at the very least the guys who are in the company. We need to be solution oriented and talk about alternatives to nuclear power. We have to make sure everyone understands the global nature of this issue. That's what wins.

Of course the personal stories are good and helpful, so keep them going, but keep the bigger picture in mind, always."

"Emotion draws people to your issue," Steve put in. "The facts and the law are what will win."

"Exactly," agreed Lisa, "We need to map out the entire permitting process and pin point the locations where we can have public input. We need to be on top of them every step of the way. What we are trying to do is to make it harder to mine uranium here than for them to pack up and go somewhere else. Then what you hope for is that the somewhere else people are working just as hard so that you both are stopping the miners. The hope is that the company goes bankrupt rather than proceeding. Remember, though, if you are not working as hard here as the group in the next location is working, you will be the point of least resistance and the company will end up mining here.

"It will be a long hard, nasty fight." She looked around the room of people who were just getting to know one another, "You'll all argue with one another, but you have to just keep focused on what the goal is. Keep moving forward no matter what. You'll be alright."

"Yep, that's right," David put in, "we need to remember that we are here to stop them."

"You are going to be here with us during this whole process, right?" someone asked. We already knew we really needed her help.

"I hope to be," answered Lisa with a chuckle, "if they don't take me out first." We all laughed heartily. I thought back to my activist friend and her stories and felt nauseous.

"I was just contacted yesterday by a woman by the name of Miss D," Carol put in, "she saw me on Fox news. She fought against a proposed in-situ leach mine in the Briggsdale area for 3 years in the late 70's. She won and she kept all of her information. Now she'd like to share it with us."

This was the first we had heard of any previously proposed ISL mining in Colorado. Briggsdale was not too far from us.

We began talking about what strengths we each had and who and what we could bring to a battle. "I did my thesis on the effects of uranium mining on plant life and how the heavy metals from the mining operations collect in the plants and harm livestock and wildlife," Ann replied. "We really don't want this project to move forward. I've seen some pretty nasty results." Ann volunteered her services as a speaker. I mentioned our scheduled public meeting as well as the Earth Day speaking opportunity. Even though both of these events were less than 2 weeks away, Ann agreed to be the speaker at both of them.

Lisa began sharing some of her expertise then. "My Ph.D. is in Political Science with an emphasis in Environmental Policy," she said. "I'm currently teaching at CSU and have a business set up to help non-profit groups get started and stay focused. I can help you by training folks on how to work with the media. I'm willing to do as much as needed and wanted. I also have a Master's in Public and Human Services Administration."

The neighbor from Montrose said that she and her husband were working to get the word out any way they could and she pulled out a couple of different fliers she had designed. "These are very rough drafts, and we'd like opinions. We have an industrial size printer and can make professional looking fliers easily and I can print them out by the 1000's."

Coincidence or Providence? Our band of neighbors included a scientist who specialty was the effects of uranium mining on plant life and someone who had an industrial printer we could use. And, a Fort Collins local had already defeated a potential uranium mine in South Dakota and was well educated in how to deal with the politics of the situation. All of these people were sitting in our living room just a few of weeks after I was sure I needed to stick my head in the sand and get as much money as I could from uranium mining in my backyard. WOW. Talk about the Lord working in mysterious ways. I marinated in the Truth that we were following God's will. How could there be any stronger signs.

We then began talking details of the organization we were forming and how we needed money. "We need a war chest," David said. "And we need to put people in a role so we know our jobs."

I volunteered to be the central location of information. I asked everyone to keep sending me links and information that could go on our website. "We just need to keep spreading the word."

David told us, "This website is turning up everywhere it seems. When I was talking to the EPA they already knew about it. Some of our legislators are going to it. Also, the EPA said that they will have to be sure to post all and any information between them and Powertech because of the media coverage and the public interest already so early on in this process"

So, we were already making ripples.

Steve said, "Powertech has been visiting the website. So be conscious that whatever you are putting on the website will be used against us also."

"It is a war we are embarking on," Lisa said, "Do not kid yourself on that. It could get nasty."

Regardless of this being a war or not, I had no concerns about what we were putting on our website. We were sticking to nothing but facts. We had no editorial comments other than those that placed emphasis on the facts. We had no personal opinions or personal attacks. It was just the facts. The facts were that Powertech approached us with their entitlement to their minerals, evident in their own words in their own letters, and that ISL uranium mining was contaminating water wherever it was being done.

Steve brought up how that while he was talking with a Powertech representative, he volunteered to give a presentation at our meeting on

April 21. We all agreed that Powertech should do their own public meeting. We would share both sides of the information we had found, not just the Powertech models.

As we continued discussing the meeting we brought up some of the reactions we were getting from legislators who are not in our district. This went to show how far reaching the effects of the water contamination were.

"I heard they use acid in these processes," someone said.

Jay responded, "The ore bearer in this area will not support the use of acid, they'll use sodium bicarbonate. In a different ore bearer acid works well. For this one they'd add oxygen to mobilize the uranium."

Many voices put in, "I heard it's just treated water." "They keep saying treated water." "Yeah, just water."

Lisa interrupted, "They will use verbiage that makes it all sound pretty and nice. They'll never say what it's treated with or what the harmful effects could be."

Jay added, "Yeah, they've already changed the terminology from in-situ leaching to in-situ recovery. They changed this on their website just last week.

One of the things that keeps bothering me is their terminology and how they change things or say things that aren't clear. With the open pit mine, they talk about selling the by-products. What are the by-products? Sand and gravel?"

Lisa said, "Or will they get a permit for a sand and gravel mine and the uranium is a by-product?"

Jay, "Yeah. And the other thing that keeps really bugging me is that uranium is an element, not a mineral. How can they extract an element with mineral rights. It was 1909 when the railroad obtained mineral rights through here. That's when Colorado started its split estate agreements. Uranium was listed as an element then and the railroad maintained the right to iron and coal according to the original agreement.

"Not to mention the whole way these small companies keep coming on line as uranium mining companies. They are selling stock and making money hand over fist without even mining anything all based on the supposition of future profits available.

"All of that aside, I had called the Powertech representative to ask him some specific questions about the process. We were supposed to get together in person tomorrow, but he called back after he had a chance to look at the website. He learned that I work in the field of civil engineering so he asked if we could reschedule to a time when he could have his chief hydrologist along. The meeting is Friday. We want to have this meeting in a neutral location. We don't trust inviting these guys into our home. I've been thinking about having it in the conference room at my office, but if several of us sitting here would like to attend we'd need a bigger location that was more central to us all.

"We plan to video the meeting. One thing that seems to keep happening is that people are asking specific questions and they aren't being answered in the same way from person to person. There seems to be a lot of misinformation. We want to get straight answers. Also, we know that some of the higher ups in Powertech have a history of going after the character of the people who are opposing them. We want to make sure we have record of every interaction with them.

"One specific example is how Richard Blubaugh told a TV reporter that there is not any recorded incident of water contamination. I got online right after I watched the interview and sent the reporter 2 and one-half pages of incidents. Some of the information directly from the NRC.

"Another thing that is inconsistent is that in one place they talk about owning over 5700 acres of mineral rights, but the letter that disclosed the property owners who are affected is only 3 sections. Where else do they own minerals?"

One of the absentee landowners had also been looking at the Powertech website and maps, "Well, I know the map that James Bonner mailed me showed the ore body south of my property, but the one online map shows it on my property."

"Misinformation, what is the truth?" Jay responded. "Is it because of the exploration process or are they hiding things. I hope to find out in our meeting with them."

Lisa was glad to hear that we would not be inviting Powertech to our house. She also reminded us that maintaining solidarity amongst all the local landowners would be key so that Powertech is slowed down in their studies of the area for the permitting process.

We talked about putting up "No Trespassing" signs. We also talked about creating a strong sense of community so that we would stand together.

Talk then turned to making sure all of the surrounding landowners knew about this project. We discussed the need to get letters to each landowner that laid out what their rights are so far as allowing access to the surface. If the landowners know what is at stake, namely their water, they will be less likely to just let Powertech have access without proper paperwork and some agreement about compensation and any limitations.

Steve quietly began talking, "We just need to let everyone know about uranium and ISL mining and what it really means. I know I spoke to a Powertech rep on the phone and he told me some things, but it sure is nothing like what I'm hearing here. Now, I'm just thinking.... Oh, man..... I'm not a scientist, so I didn't know what questions to ask. I just know I'd like my well water to stay as drinkable as it already is. If we let everyone know what this uranium mining can do to air, land, people, water, animals they will agree."

Carol presented a rough agenda that she had developed for the topics to cover at the Leeper Center meeting.

"Can we do something about the red and yellow website," Lisa asked? "It's very difficult to read."

The red and yellow Nunnglow website I'd put together in a day was already becoming a link for information to people outside of our landowners. I had to laugh inside at the reaction our little website was getting. People were finding it. People were reading it. I didn't have a counter, but I know I was even getting e-mails from as far away as Sweden by now. I don't know how folks were finding it, but I didn't care. The word was getting out. We recognized, with the battle building up, we needed to have something more professional to reach those outside our immediate area.

"I'm a web designer," Steve volunteered, "I'll be happy to work on it."

More Providence at work.

Lisa brought up the fact that we needed to have people trained in dealing with the media. "Who would like to be the people who are the primary media contacts? Remember, though, the media will begin to choose who they like and gravitate towards them."

This discussion went all the way around the room and people either felt okay about talking to the media or were too shy. I kept feeling the nudge to speak up. I had totally embarrassed myself in my TV debut, but I knew I had things that needed to be spoken. If I was trained maybe I could do that. Torn though I was when the discussion paused I said with passion in my voice, "I'd like to be able to talk to the media. I really want to give the kids a voice. This is about protecting the health, safety and welfare of our future generations and I want to be able to speak as a 4-H leader and teacher." I was surprised at my own intensity.

Everyone was focused on me because of the passion with which I had spoken. After a short silence (where I was looking directly at Lisa), she gave me a slight nod

Talk then turned back to brainstorming about what to put on a flier. "We need to make sure we don't scare people away, but incite them with enough concern to come learn more," Ann said. "A tough balance."

Some draft ideas that the woman from Montrose had brought had been making their way around the room. We decided to make a few changes to tone down the verbiage but we all liked the skull and crossbones overlaid on top of the aquifer at the proposed mining site.

It was agreed that most of the flier should be a picture so a person could get the concept quickly, so we decided to add a photo of mutated sheep. The verbiage was simple: "What's your new neighbor up to?!" "Toxic Waste" "Come learn what Powertech Uranium has planned for your water supplies." Then it stated the date, time and location for the public meeting.

As the topic changed back to the meeting with Powertech in just a couple of days, Jay suggested we meet at the Wellington Comfort Inn meeting room. He said we need to video and voice record the meeting. "It's protection for both us," Jay said, "If they are concerned that we are spreading misinformation, we can point at the recording."

"Will they let you record?" one of the absentee owners asked.

"If they don't, the meeting is over before it starts. If they have something to hide, there is no reason to sit down with them," I replied.

As the meeting was wrapping up I felt some of the panic subsiding (for now) and a portion of the weight of our situation slowly lifting off my shoulders. This 2.5 hour meeting had been very educational and productive. I could see how some who had come with the idea that this proposed uranium mine might be okay to go forward had totally changed their minds while sitting here, and how those of us who had already decided that this mine was not okay were even more solidified. We were developing a team.

We set a date for our next landowners meeting to continue plans for our upcoming public meeting and ended the official part of this meeting. As we all drifted about while getting to know one another better, I noticed a common theme. Each and every one of us was expressing a faith in God. It was interesting how this group of people who hadn't known each other before tonight all went to our core beliefs. We were all in survival mode.

We needed to remember who we really were, and we did. We were all coming back to our most basest of instincts.

Here I had been wondering if anyone would show up and what the mood would be. It turned out that we had faith filled, highly educated and specialized people within our own neighborhood who were ready to fight uranium mining near Nunn, Colorado. We were officially rolling.

I walked up behind Jay as he and David were talking. "This is insane," Jay ran his hands through his hair. "Boy, don't I know it," David replied.

"I thought we had left this kind of stress and madness behind us in Masonville. Now we have to fight to keep our water unpolluted," Jay continued. "I just don't have time for this."

We had left our home in Masonville amidst a great amount of conflict within the community. The riding lessons I was giving suddenly had become an issue with our next door neighbor. They had previously been supportive, and I never really understood what had changed. They became quite belligerent about the 'business' I was hosting on our property. Our community was a covenanted community and one of the covenants did specify that businesses were not allowed. This never was an issue through the many years that we had lived there. We knew of several of the homeowners who hosted businesses out of their homes. Piano teachers, psychologists, paint studios, landscape designers, accountants, etc. Each of these businesses used their homes as their 'store fronts' and it was not unusual to see clients parked in front of their homes. A very interesting fact is that the neighbor who began making the noise hosted two businesses in their home and had a steady stream of vehicles in and out of their property.

We did what we could to lessen any impact from the lessons. The neighbors were not complaining about dust, manure or flies. These were things that we were very conscious of keeping to as much of a minimum as we could. Their main complaint was the fact that they could see the lessons. After talking with them about solutions, we spent a lot of money on over a dozen 12 foot evergreen trees to line the property line and therefore, hide their view of the lessons. We were interested in staying out of conflict.

We thought we had dealt with the issue and things were fine. That is, until one day, we received a certified letter from our homeowners association inviting us to a meeting to discuss our business practices. Since the community was a close community and we thought we knew everyone on this board relatively well, we were quite taken aback by the approach. This did not feel good at all. We went to the meeting and told them that we thought we had dealt with the issue. They agreed that we had done what the neighbors had asked, but that we were in violation of the covenants because of operating a business.

After this meeting we contacted an attorney. While we were doing our research and having meetings with the attorney, the community was being torn apart by the entire ordeal. Emotions ran high in every direction, phone calls were flying in support of us and disregard for the complainants. The same number of phone calls were flying in support of the sanctity of the covenants in order to protect the property values of the community. The business owners in the neighborhood were torn.

Our attorney advised us that we had a very strong case and could have won a case handily. We could have dismantled the existing covenants. The distress caused in the community and within ourselves had become too much. That is when we decided to not pursue the legal options and to make a change. We were looking forward to some peace and quiet in our new home and community after the long six months of neighborhood strife. This uranium mine was not the peace we had hoped to move to. Yes, I was still attracting those things I needed in order to go within and learn more about myself.

David, Carol, Jay and I, hugged one another in our mutual relegation to our current situation.

On her way out the door, Lisa said to me, "Be careful. Be aware of any strange vehicles going up and down your road. Lock your vehicles in the driveway. Keep your doors locked. You might even want to get a big dog."

"Why?"

"These guys stand to make a lot of money and they don't like to be opposed," she answered. "This could get dangerous. What sort of security do you have? Do you own a gun?"

"We have dogs," I told her.

"Those dogs are WAY too friendly to be a threat to anyone, especially this one," She was scratching the ears of our black lab as he was leaned almost entirely over onto her leg.

"I'm sure we'll be fine," I reassured her.

As everyone left, I closed the door behind them and told Jay what Lisa had said about security. We discussed how this was beginning to feel like war. "We're warriors," I quipped as I picked up after our meeting. Jay went to bed shortly after everyone left I could see that the long hours were wearing on him.

I needed to do some 4-H work that evening, so I sat down to plan our next 4-H gathering and to e-mail the club with the plans. I was thankful that it appeared that some of the stress of the uranium fight was leaving my shoulders because I needed to get back to working my horse business and staying on top of my responsibilities as a 4-H leader, a huge commitment in its own right.

I fell into bed exhausted and at last finding some peace of mind. We were warriors and we had additional warriors by our side. It felt good to know that we had support, and not just upset landowners, but upset landowners who had good educations and were ready to take on this gigantic venture.

Even though I felt peace when I dropped into bed, this is the night the soon to be repeating nightmare began. *"The black mare craned her neck downward until her whiskers touched the water inside the water tank. She drew back a little as her whiskers vibrated with the energy of knowing that they were in contact with something that is not for the highest good of the mare. But, she was thirsty, so she pushed through the vibrational warnings. ..."*

CHAPTER 7

THE MEETING

Things were really starting to flow. Not only was my e-mail box full to over-flowing, even with the Yahoo! Group, but I was starting to get phone calls from all sorts of different people, including the media. I started a habit of beginning and signing all of my e-mails with the phrase 'Uranium Warriors' after our last house meeting.

At the end of several of these days Jay and I would find ourselves sitting in our living room, each with a laptop on our laps doing activism work. We chuckled together about our "geekiness." We'd stay up until all hours, he'd get up early and go to his office, work until 7 or 8pm, then return home to work on uranium. I would get up and do some horse chores and maybe some training or riding or 4-H, but by now my days were primarily taken up by uranium. We thought we were busy before as we were building our new ranch and horse business, but now it was out of control. We always tried to find the humor and made dumb jokes about the situation as our way of dealing with the sticky emotions.

The Greeley Tribune had called and did a phone interview with me for their Saturday edition. I was really excited to be getting some attention in Weld County. I recall the reporter asking me several questions about the risks and what it is we were fighting to protect. Even though I was still learning how to really talk with the press, it felt like a very good and professional interview. I hadn't given much thought to how generally everything one says is "on the record." As the interview wound down and we were chatting about activism in general and I made a joke: "We are even going to get bumper stickers that say "Hell No We Won't Glow!" The reporter laughed and thanked me for my time. I hung up feeling good about the whole experience.

Jay had finalized our meeting with Powertech and the landowners, so we would have our first opportunity to look them in the eye and ask them questions.

We had developed a thorough list of questions for them. In fact we posted the list on our website and asked the public if they had any additional questions. As a water quality issue that had the potential of affecting many people it seemed like the right thing to do. Many of our questions were derived by just reading the Powertech proposed mining project and listening to what they said to the media. The questions were questions we had been asking ourselves, so we decided to just ask Powertech. They were the experts and the developer of the project so we thought it most logical to go straight to the source instead of settling for conjecture. We wanted the facts. We were hoping that they would honestly explain this new technology that they kept rejoicing about. The idealist part of me wanted them to still my fears and show us just how they planned to mine the uranium, protect our water and compensate us fairly, all with integrity.

April 13, 2007 - Friday the 13th, the day of our meeting with Powertech.

Sitting at my computer, I gazed longingly out the window into the beautiful Spring day. All I could think was that I'd much rather be outside enjoying Nature and the horses. Instead I spent another day inside on the computer as a uranium warrior.

As I went through my e-mails that morning, I noticed an e-mail back from Larimer County Commissioner, Karen Wagner. She was encouraging and asked to be kept in the loop because of the proposed mining proximity to

Larimer County and how it could impact them. She was also clear in how there was nothing she could do because of the jurisdiction.

Nice to know I was getting the attention of Larimer County. I still had not heard anything directly from our Weld County Commissioners. As I read her note, I hoped that the request Commissioner Wagner said she made for notification of any Powertech permitting action from Weld County would prompt some sort of action from the Weld County Commissioners.

I found it very interesting that Larimer County would respond before Weld County. I had lived in Larimer County for more than 20 years before this move to Weld County. Part of the reason we had moved into Weld County was the fact that Larimer County's land use code was making it very difficult for equine schools. The process for zoning a property as an equine school was very expensive and time intensive, no matter the size or impact on neighbors.

We thought that Weld County was more committed to maintaining an agriculturally friendly county. I had called the Planning and Zoning department before our move, told them of our plans and asked them about any special permits or anything we would need. They had told me that we had a "Use by Right" since we were zoned agriculture.

This commitment to agriculture encouraged us during our move. It surprised me that I had not yet heard from Weld County Commissioners in support of our agriculturally based business, especially since we were hosting a 4-H club. I had thought that the Weld County Commissioners would have at least expressed a desire to look into the impacts of mining on a residential and agricultural area. The silence from them was deafening.

The sun dipped lower in the sky, it was time for me to wrap things up and prepare to head into town.

The crunching of gravel alerted me as David and Carol drove in to pick me up for our meeting with Powertech. Jay was still working long hours so he was driving to the hotel directly from work. I was feeling a little lost and angry with Jay for leaving me to arrive and set up on my own at another important meeting. I knew we were in this together, but I was scared and wanted him by my side physically. Truth be known, I wanted him as my rescuer rather than having to stand on my own feet as an empowered individual.

This is another way that my dysfunctional relationship with myself showed up. Jay was truly doing as much as he possibly could to keep his business running, our new home moving forward with all the requirements we had for the horse business, and now researching and meeting and responding to a uranium mine. There was a part of me that could not recognize that because of my deep emotional wounds. I expected Jay to fill my emotional needs at all levels. I was not interested in having to be independent only because I truly did not know how to be independent and empowered in a healthy enough way to go up against something as big as this issue was. The fact that something as big as the uranium fight showed up to force me to really look at my wounds and learn how to heal them is interesting on many levels.

First, clearly I was very attached to the lie that my life was 'all good.' I had a positive outlook on life to the point of dangerous idealism. I needed to learn how to maintain a positive outlook as well as to see reality. I had a strong Faith but it was a Faith that relied on outside sources not one that was deep enough from within. My Faith was not a true love for self, but one that needed constant reassurance.

Second, as I sit back and look at the strength it took to really step into this battle, I can see that there was a valuable 'gold' that needed to be uncovered. It took something of this magnitude to be able to begin to see this gold.

Third, as I said before, sexual abuse is theft of the soul. Especially childhood sexual abuse when the psyche is developing. My soul was so fragmented that I needed something to genuinely rattle me to be willing to dive deep into the healing work that would bring those fragments back into a wholeness.

Opening the door, our eyes met as Carol and I both recognized the mutual fear we were feeling. She reached out and pulled me into a hug and said, "Put on the cloak of Christ, Robin," as much for herself as for me. "God will protect and guide," she reassured.

With our new digital recorders charged and ready to go we arrived at the Comfort Inn half an hour early. We moved tables around into a big square so we could all look the Powertech guys in the eye. We set the digital video recorder in one corner and chose the best location in which Powertech should sit so we could see them on film. We set our digital voice recorder in the center of the square. When Steve arrived, he added his digital voice recorder next to ours. We weren't going to miss recording any of this meeting.

I distributed the questions around the table to everyone present and placed a copy in front of the empty chairs we were reserving for Powertech.

Most of the neighbors from the meeting at our house a couple of days earlier were in attendance. We really didn't know one another well yet, the only thing we all knew we had in common was this fight to protect our water and our land. We were all very nervous and kept fussing with our printouts of the questions and making lame jokes as we got to know one another a little bit better while we waited.

One of the things we were unsure of was whether or not the Powertech representatives would be okay with us recording the meeting. We were all in agreement that we would discontinue the meeting if they were not honest enough to allow filming and recording.

Jay arrived right at the scheduled time of the meeting looking harried. We greeted and I handed him a printout of our compiled list of questions. He had scheduled the meeting so it made sense for him to run it. We were all looking forward to having many of these questions answered tonight:

Questions posed to Powertech Uranium Corporation on April 13, 2007
Can you please explain to us the difference between low-level radioactive waste materials and transuranics? How are these waste materials handled, and where are they legally disposed of?

Our research of the public records indicates that Powertech Uranium Corp has retained the services of Wallace Mayes as an expert on your panel of project managers; however, it appears that his lax oversight on previous projects has resulted in numerous spills of radioactive contaminants into the water, soil and air. With a documented track record like this, why is this man on your payroll?

In the likely event of a spill on our property, what federally licensed and bonded company is on retainer with Powertech Uranium Corp. to clean up the environment, how long will it take and what reporting, monitoring and site-safety verification process and guidelines do you follow to assure property/ homeowners that their home is safe enough to inhabit?

If the leach mining that you propose is not a threat to our environment, then why do we have to remove our livestock from the property, suspend youth activities and monitor our drinking water supplies for the duration of your mining operation on our property?

We are now aware that there is a significant risk of environmental contamination to the water and soil from in-situ leach mining, and yet you assure us that there is not a risk of airborne radioactive contamination. What technology does Powertech Uranium Corp. use to monitor air quality, how long has this technology been in use, and what company will be making these tests?
    How many monitoring stations will be in place for each property owner: spacing and locations?
    Will these stations continually track air quality for excursions of radon and radon progeny?
    Specifically lead-210 and polonium-210.
    What branch of the federal government oversees the test results?

To whom do you submit water, soil, and air quality reports during your work on our property, and what radiation levels/parameters are you required to follow?

Please reference the specific environmental guidelines that you are required to follow, and provide us with a copy.

How much money will Powertech Uranium Corp. put in escrow for the health care of local community members who are exposed to contaminated water, soil and air?

 What is the life of this escrow account and who will be the facilitator?

Which NRC approved waste facility will Powertech Uranium Corp. be using? What is the method of transport to this site?

Richard Clements, Jr. is listed as being retained by Powertech Uranium Corp. What is his continued role in the current litigation between Kleberg County of Kingsville, Texas and Uranium Resources, Inc.?

What market is the uranium mined by Powertech Uranium Corporation sold to?

Does this uranium stay in the United States or does it go overseas?

We understand that Powertech Uranium Corporation is actively seeking to and is currently pursuing purchasing real estate within section 15, T9N, R67W. To what end?

 Why is Powertech Uranium Corp interested in open and empty buildings?

Is Powertech Uranium Corp. still planning on doing an open-pit uranium mine in section 35, T9N, R67W?

In some documentation Powertech Uranium Corp refers to the uranium extraction process as in-situ leach and other in-situ recovery, why the difference in verbiage?

We see that the Centennial Project agreement allows Powertech Uranium Corp to retain by-products; from the uranium extraction process, what other valuable by-products do you expect to find?

Powertech Uranium Corp continually calls the water being re-injected into the aquifer "treated" what is your definition of this treatment process?

> *What will be added to the water during this treatment and reinjection of the water into the aquifer?*

Many in-situ leaching sites use hydrochloric acid in the process of uranium mining. Powertech Uranium Corp states they will use oxygenated water with sodium bicarbonate. Have you ever and do you plan to at some point, use hydrochloric acid on this or other projects?

> *Even if your yield of uranium is not quite what you expect from just this solution?*

What is your projected drilling date?

How deep will the wells be?

How many wells will there be?

Where, specifically, is the planned location of these wells?

What specific Homeland Security Rules must you follow to protect surrounding communities from terrorist activity?

Why would Mr. Blubaugh continue to say that he has never heard of any aquifers being contaminated from in-situ leaching processes of uranium extraction when there are MANY documented cases? Kingsville Dome is one. Just look at the links on our website, you'll see many other examples from around the world. A 2007 NRC report verifies these contaminated water supplies.

Do you know EXACTLY where the aquifers are in relation to the wells Powertech Uranium Corp will be drilling and using as injection and extraction wells?

Are you familiar with which aquifers may be affected by any leakage or spillage? Please name them.

Where will the drying and packaging of yellow cake occur? Uranium Mills or onsite?

What mill will receive the by-product tanks if not processed onsite?

What specifically has Powertech Uranium Corp learned from places where the aquifer has been damaged by this in-situ process?

What new technology will Powertech Uranium Corp be incorporating to avoid just such a tragedy?
Things such as updating the drilling process. Updating the type of casing used to line and protect our water supplies. Updating the monitoring and shut off system to limit the amount of hazardous and toxic elements being released into our water, soil and/or air. We want to see the plans of the wells, the manufacturers being used for the construction materials, all specifications on the construction materials, etc.

Most of us sat or stood where we could see the front door as the clock ticked past the time of our scheduled meeting. The Powertech representatives were late. Someone commented about how they must be lost. We all found this comment hilarious because of the way they kept promoting their local standing as part of how they were the good guys.

As we were all laughing about their tardiness and some of the reasons we thought this might be so: they were fearful of us; their car broke down; they got the date wrong; etc, the front door opened and in walked a tall blonde man decked out in a silk forest green suit followed by a shorter gray-haired man with a corduroy blazer over a simple cotton shirt.

We quieted down as we watched them inquire at the desk and the clerk pointed them to our private room. I felt the butterflies in my stomach quicken as I recognized the tall man as the one who had stopped by our place the day I was working with my student.

Entering the room, they introduced themselves, and I quickly told them that we would be recording the meeting. I wanted that out right away so they could refuse or continue forward before any more was said. They told us that they knew it was likely that we would be recording and how their manager had told them that if we were recording, then they had better be recording too.

With that a large shopping bag was produced that quickly revealed a small "boom box" still in its packaging, along with brand new audio cassettes and batteries. While looking for a place to put this now unpackaged and set up recorder, I was asked if what was in the middle of the table was cell phones.

"No, they are digital recorders," I replied, as I moved them a little to make room for the much more archaic technology.

"Oh, well your technology is much more advanced than ours," he jokes.

We laughed and rolled our eyes at one another and I answered, "Oh THAT makes us feel more comfortable."

As our journey was quick to show us, our entire experience with Powertech had this interesting comedic Wyle E. Coyote kind of feel to it. We found we really were one step ahead of them in so many ways. This created, within us, a serious mistrust for what they kept promising as their 'exciting and new ways of extracting uranium.' We kept asking 'what is this new technology?' and they kept pulling blunders such as using a boom box to record a professional meeting.

David directed the Powertech representatives to their seats and offered water. This was his way of keeping the topic of water right in front of them. David did a great job of constantly re-directing the meeting back to the topic of water in every way he could that night.

With everyone seated and water and coffee procured, Jay began the meeting by directing the attention to the list of questions, "We made copies for everyone so we can all be on the same track as we get these answered."

Jay's attempt at beginning a meeting with a clear agenda was ignored as the blonde gentleman began speaking about his family history in Colorado as a way to develop relationship and rapport. He then turned the topic to his journey through the energy industry, while focusing on pulling a book out of his briefcase.

I feel certain that he thought that would make us all feel a little more comfortable with him. He also talked about how he came to Powertech as a 'land guy' after long research into the company so that he could feel comfortable selling all of us on their project. He told us that he is not only the land guy but also the Project Manager for the Centennial project for Powertech Uranium, Corp. His entire presentation was punctuated with his slight southern drawl and folksy vernacular. He truly came across as someone who really believed in what he is doing and was committed to being our contact person. It felt like he wanted us to like him and to buy into this project just as wholeheartedly as he had.

Once the book was exhumed from the briefcase, we were all introduced to it: "*Investing in the Great Uranium Bull Market, A Practical Investor's Guide to Uranium Stocks*" From the Editors of Stock Interview; as a phenomenal resource into why nuclear power is the way to go for a more green future. This book was offered to us as a compilation of data that would be helpful in convincing us that uranium mining in our water aquifer would be a great idea. We were all told that this book would enlighten us and bring us to the side of the uranium miners because of its green ideology. (*Insert eye-roll here*)

While extolling the benefits of nuclear power the land man went on to share how he came to move from the oil and gas industry to uranium mining because of his belief in right livelihood. His definition of right livelihood was the way he saw himself as doing good or harm in his livelihood. We were encouraged to trust him and Powertech because of his belief that he was doing more good than harm by mining for uranium.

During this introduction both gentlemen discussed how we should trust their models because of the engineering principles and the regulators who monitor them. We were told that if we do not trust their models that we should not drive down a divided highway or enter a high-rise building because these are all based upon sound science and engineering. Since the nuclear industry is the most regulated industry in our society all of its phases must be safe, according to them.

This introduction seemed to go on forever, and it felt as though they took over the meeting right away rather than even attempting to begin to speak to our questions. I had the feeling that we were being talked into believing that not only were these guys who were in front of us the smartest guys in the room, but look, we were also supposed to defer to an even smarter bunch of 'regulators' who have "advanced degrees and deep training". We were encouraged to trust science well above and beyond what we had all been discovering to be the long-term reality shown at existing mining sites. We were encouraged to believe in the power of the money to be gained rather than our relationship with the water and the land.

So far as I'm concerned it doesn't take an advanced degree to look at the current records of the mining industry and see how they are contaminating aquifers all over the world. In fact, still today, any person can log into www. wise-uranium.org to see daily news with spills and violations from around the world. There are no opinions or tangents to follow on this site, just a compilation of facts. It doesn't take an advanced degree or deep training to read facts about spills, leaks and violations. It doesn't take deep training to have a relationship with water. By this time my anger was right on the surface as I felt as though I was being talked down to! I'm sure they could see it in my eyes.

Finally the introduction paused with him seeking to know how we envision the meeting going.

"First and foremost, let's go line item down the list of questions and see what can be answered and what can't be. Probably the quickest way to get through this." Jay proposed, as he attempted, again, to maintain a clear agenda.

We were immediately reassured that the questions we have are very "germane to the issue," and that they would all be addressed over time. I leaned back in my chair, I hadn't realized that I was perched on the edge in my frustration at this point, and I felt myself lighten a little as we were encouraged by the fact that we had good solid questions and that they would soon be answered. But then another soliloquy started about the nature of risk. How we live in a world of risk and risk taking and again how we needed to trust science. I started to lift out of my seat again. We were assured about how the risk to our air and the environment would be taken into consideration which led David to ask: "When you look at risks you are gonna look at risk to water too?"

This question was followed by a long dissertation about how they are in fact especially tuned into the water. The speakers cadence and constant inserting of the phrase 'gonna take a look at' was difficult to follow at best. While closing the speech with the fact that his take on the situation would most certainly be different from ours because of the very reason that we live on top of the aquifer, he then asked what it would take for us to feel okay.

"Buy all of our land," I replied a little too quickly.

I wasn't feeling anywhere close to okay with all of this talk about right livelihood from those whom I saw as the guys who felt entitled to just walk onto my land and tell me what they planned to do with it. I wasn't feeling okay about how these guys came in and just took over the meeting even though we presented them with an agenda of questions that we wanted answered. I wasn't feeling okay about how they both were rambling about the financial gains, impacts and commitments that they and the company had to their bottom-line, rather than the environment and especially our water. I wasn't feeling okay about being in this room after spending the last two weeks learning about all of the issues surrounding ISL mining for uranium and how it was contaminating water wherever it was done, and then how they were both telling me that it's for the greater good. I was frustrated with the web of words that revealed a love affair with science and a love affair with money over LIFE.

I was feeling trapped between a rock and a hard place because I too had the concept that nuclear power may be a solution for our energy needs. My mind and my emotions were on overload as I attempted to sort out 'right livelihood', the greater good, and why I was in the middle of all of this anyway. When they asked me: 'What do I need to do to make you feel okay?' I spouted out, "Buy all of our land." That is what bubbled up. The feeling that I had of being in a trap just spouted out in those few words. I still wanted to run away. I still didn't want to deal with this whole thing. I grasped for a straw that might still offer me a chance to follow my dreams of building a viable horse ranch. I lunged at a lifeline.

As soon as I said it, I knew it was unrealistic and that it wouldn't really solve anything because of the water supplies that are being contaminated. I couldn't turn a blind eye to this so I attempted a lame recovery, "It would have to be everyone on the aquifer, though," I added.

David continued doing an exceptional job by maintaining the focus on the water. "I'd really like that but, we have to go to the core issue here, water. Water. Water. Water. Water," he stated.

I felt small and selfish in that moment but was, thankfully, able to find my inner warrior resurface and begin to engage the real issue again.

We were told that the possibility of buying us all out MAY exist at some point since there was so much money available to be made from this mining operation. The price of uranium was at a record height. Of course, this was nothing they could do for us right then, but, we were all told that the possibility existed. It was even reiterated "The Possibility Exists" with emphasis. Along with this emphasis we were also warned that Powertech is not the only company who was seeking places to mine for uranium since the price was so high and the demand, "even need," existed. My feel was that they were dangling a carrot of buying us out just long enough to get us to agree to not fight the uranium mine.

We were encouraged to view Powertech as an ethical company who would take good care to do right by everyone while they rake in the money. We were told that they wanted to find ways to keep us 'whole.' I felt the audacity in this desire to keep us whole and how it pertained only to money. Wholeness is not created by a payoff. Wholeness is only accessed through a connection of mind, body, spirit and emotion. Money may be a tool that has the possibility of helping to achieve wholeness but it is not wholeness in its entirety. Most of us sitting in that room that night had come to live where we were because of our individual dreams. We each had a deep connection to the land that we were on, even if only for a brief time to date.

The very fact that we had gathered together showed that we were all wishing to remain whole by protecting the land, the water, and our lives, not by being paid off. To remain completely whole one must have a balanced relationship with all of the elements. Fire, Water, Earth, Air. These guys sounded like they wanted to pay us off while they contaminated water. Disrespecting one of the key elements does not achieve wholeness.

It felt like they were bent upon playing our emotions while at the same time telling us not to be emotional. The way we were given potential hope of gaining money by selling out a part of our soul felt like a power play of immense deceit.

In this meeting, I was the emotional one who spouted with things like "can we throw in a little justice here too?" (when the topic was framed around American ideals such as truth and liberty). I told them that we as the landowners sitting on a potential uranium mine felt naked and violated because we knew that we had no real power since the mineral owner's rights superseded ours. I would feel myself riding an emotional roller coaster as I kept hearing the love affair with science over life. I moved quickly between anger, fear, sadness and grief. My spouting allowed me to speak out in ways that helped me to move some of this emotion and to remain engaged, but it clearly was not suiting to the Powertech representatives as they peppered their statements with comments about how we as a group needed to remain level-headed and be willing to work with them rather than against them. I'd take a deep breath and attempt to listen with an open-mind, but would invariably find myself disgusted enough to spout again.

I reminded them that I had started the whole process with an open-mind when they would state how the modeling they could provide would give us confidence only if we remained open. I told them that my open-mind became a critical one once I saw the many failures. In fact we all kept asking them, in various ways, how they would be doing things differently with their proclaimed newer and better technology. We never got a good answer to this question, just more statements about trust and risk and how risk is in everything we do.

We were even told that we make daily choices that are risky, such as crossing a street and choosing to breathe air and to drink water. Yes, you read that correctly, we choose to breathe and to hydrate. Don't worry, both David and I said at the same time: "Those are necessary!" The fumbling and mumbling that followed was something to behold.

Steve attempted to pin them down on a percentage of risk this uranium mine would pose to us after we were told that risk is a part of life: "And make no mistake, it's a gamble. And we're the ones being asked to gamble. And it's not with pocket change, it's with our families. When I go to Vegas, I know the odds of blackjack. I can figure that out. Here, tell me the odds. I don't know what the odds are!"

None could be given. No odds could be given. Just the continued response about how we needed to trust science. From my perspective, science is not about trust. Science is about truth. Being asked to trust the science sounds like a revivalist preacher attempting to convert us to their beliefs. We didn't need trust, we needed data – hard data. We were getting hard data about existing mine sites and the historical contamination. I was not interested in a religious conversion based upon computer models.

The added assurance they gave was that Powertech would have to purchase bonds. Then seemingly in the same breath, we were told that they had to be triple-bonded and the representatives turned to one another and said that one of the things they intend to do was to address this triple bonding because it was too much.

David had already spoken to several regulators who had said that the bonding required for uranium miners was not enough to cover the clean-up costs of the left-over contamination. Tax-payers end up footing that bill. I still wonder why they would tell us that they believe that the bonding was too much and that they wanted to find ways around it when they were attempting to convince us that they are the good guys who stand to make a ton of money as well as do right by all of us landowners within the area of the mining.

While seeking to find places where they could sway us to see them as the good guys, they offered us the sand and gravel that would need to be removed in the open-pit area. Then they told us how lucky we were to be a part of the conversation about what happens to the sand and gravel as well as the raw land that Powertech had purchased. They excitedly told us that it could be turned into a golf course at Powertech's expense after the mining project was completed. A golf course in the middle of open prairie land and large acreages! A golf course that would draw people to our area, create a field of grass that was no longer native and requires a significant amount of water and chemicals to keep it green and lush. A golf course that would most certainly insist upon eradicating most of the wildlife such as the prairie dogs and all of the snake species.

In fact, around the topic of golf courses, we were told how our activities to date had interrupted golf games because of how they now needed to catch up to what we were already putting out to the public through our website and the media. This made me furious as I informed them that they had interrupted my horseback riding and business building because of THEIR activities.

They sought to assure us that our businesses and lives would not be impacted by the mining process. They kept speaking about how their socioeconomic studies would show job creation. They never thought to consider how just the perception of the danger around uranium would be enough to preclude anybody wanting to come to Mustang Hollow for lessons or boarding. They did not take into consideration that the Natural

Beef operation that David and Carol had would not look like a healthier option when the beef was raised within a uranium mining area.

Not to mention that the touted beauty of ISL mining is that the human resource requirement is minimal at best. It was our stance that more businesses would be impacted negatively than jobs would be created long-term.

This meeting went on and on. The Powertech representatives held the floor most of the time. They directed and re-directed the conversation based upon what they were willing to talk about. They wanted us to know the history of the project and the land. They wanted us to know that their models were based in science so they must be accurate and would surely give us confidence. They wanted us to know that they were the good guys and that the uranium is here, so if not them, others would be willing to take what would be rightfully theirs if Powertech left and sold the mineral rights. The implication was that only Powertech was ethical enough to take the current landowners into consideration.

Jay kept attempting to draw the meeting back to our list of questions and sought clear answers. He brought up the fact that the EPA relaxed regulations in order to accept that a mining site had been reclaimed because there had not been good baseline data. He also kept asking how they could call the aquifer 'contained' when there had clearly been several holes drilled for sampling in the area during the 80's uranium boom.

Jay brought up how lenient the inspection process was on abandoned bore holes in the late 70's and 80's and wondered if Powertech could assure us that these holes in the Centennial project area were abandoned appropriately. David added that his contact at the EPA even agreed that the likelihood of the over 3000 holes drilled at that time being abandoned properly was slim.

This line of questioning drew chuckles and head shakes as these two representatives appeared to be both entertained and surprised by this line of questioning because, as they admitted, this information would be important to their permitting process. When Jay asked these questions they also said that these were some of the same questions they were asking as they moved forward.

Carl and Ann, the two most experienced with how radioneucleides act in water and the long-term impacts of uranium mining were passing notes back and forth as certain things were brought up about the process.

When we were told that we ought to be grateful for the fact that Powertech will be coming to remove the uranium, Ann said that they would not be taking the selenium and instead would be disturbing it so it would then be mobile in the water. She also brought up the issue of the other heavy metals they would be mobilizing and leaving behind in the water. In fact, after a little more mumbling from the representatives, Ann got them to verbally admit that the selenium was an issue and that they were uncertain as to how they might address it.

Carl directed the conversation to the labs they were using to test the water quality as well as the timeframe required in order to get an accurate reading on radioneucleides. We had been told that they would be using a lab in Northern Wyoming or South Dakota. Using these labs would not allow for the short time frame required for accurate testing of the radioneucleides (rad). These rad deteriorate or even disappear quickly. As an example, Carl pointed out, polonium only has a 24 hour hold time and it would take that long to get to one of these labs.

More head shaking and mumbling and then a discussion about closer labs that could do this testing. Carl happened to work at one such lab that was local and federally accredited in testing rad. The Powertech representatives did ask for more information about this lab because, as they said, they were committed to keeping things local as much as possible to also show how they were committed to the socioeconomic health of our community during their mining operation.

Both Jay and Ann asked in two very different ways about how confident these representatives were that this project would move forward and be successful. Each answer indicated that they firmly believed that this was a viable project and they intended to push it as hard as possible. In fact, when Jay asked his question, the response was, "I haven't lost one yet."

Jay's work in the development field has put him in the position of doing public presentations that included opposition, as well. He had had many meetings in front of elected officials that included public input in which he had to defend the project. He looked this representative right back in the eye and said, "Neither have I."

I was so proud of Jay in this moment. He is usually very quiet and allows things to just slide off of him. He was taking this uranium mine opposition as a personal mission. His research had shown him that we had no choice other than to fight them because of the contamination of water. He let them and all of us at this meeting know that he was in it to win it! He now took this is a personal competition to see which one of them would finally lose their first project.

The meeting finally began to wind down. It began to break into a more disorganized feel as conversations began to overlap and small groups formed. We began shifting into standing groups and some even gathered stuff in preparation to leave.

Jay and I were beckoned into a private corner. David and Carol saw the movement and joined us. We were grilled about just how deep our concerns really were. He wanted to find out if we were emotionally driven purely because we owned property within the proposed mining site or if we had deeper concerns. After we expressed our deeper concerns for the water, for the entire aquifer, he reiterated that he is encouraging Powertech to buy out all the landowners in the area.

Jay told him that we would like to consider the idea, but that we would still fight the mine. We were told that we would have to sign a contract that said we would no longer oppose the mine. He then went into a long speech about how much Uranium is selling for and how much of a good thing that was for us because not only would it mean we would get appraised value, but potentially more. There was the possibility that we would be able to move comfortably with a profit.

We listened and I must say I had to seriously consider it. I still wanted to run.

FINALLY….. we all began to pack up and leave.

Walking out of that meeting in a daze, I felt like I had just been put through a misinformation campaign of monumental proportions. Keeping up with the mumbling and continued use of the phrase "take a look at" was very tiring. I was exhausted. I believe the meeting could have been cut in half had the mumbling and the repetition been cut out. Four hours! Four hours designed to make us feel as though they have everything under control, with the result of making us all feel much more distrustful.

Ann was essentially offered a job.

Jay and I were put on the hot spot and asked to take the money and run.

We all were told just how lucky we were to be a part of this project.

As we all gratefully left the building and stepped into the parking lot, there was a lot of joviality. We heard laughing and joking and building comradery. I got into the car with Jay where we both became silent.

As I watched the houses and mailboxes turn into fence posts and power poles I pondered what it might mean to take the money and run.

As we pulled into the driveway our silence was broken by me asking if Jay thought that Powertech would really buy us out.

"I'm not sure," he replied.

As we parked and entered the house we began a conversation about what that might look like. We even discussed that if Powertech offered a large amount, it would be difficult to say 'no.'

That night Jay and I spent another sleepless night of soul searching. I believe that if we would have agreed to just go away quietly, they would have followed through. We were quickly becoming key players in the resistance to this uranium mine. If we folded up camp and left it may have disheartened many people enough to have resulted in different results.

I often wonder if Powertech would be mining right now if we had sold out. Though, there were many good people who came together to oppose the mine, would our selling and leaving really have made that big a difference? Would they all then have asked to be bought out as well? Would Powertech have done that? We will never know.

What I do know is that Jay and I talked a lot about these same questions as we discussed the very real possibility of being bought out. We also then discussed that there is truly no where one can go to get away from this type of love affair with money and science over LIFE. We both agreed that we could not live with ourselves if we did sell out.

By the next morning we were discussing how the Powertech representatives spewed facts and figures that were meant to ease our fears or to make us feel silly even having any fear. We were implored to look at a bigger picture of how nuclear power is the way to save the planet. We felt that this form of communication was designed to confuse, obfuscate, and dishearten us so we would not fight them.

So we added to the questions based upon the meeting and the discussion we had been having:

Our meeting on Friday, April 13th leads us to understand that one of Powertech Uranium Corps goals is to change the negative face of uranium mining and especially the in-situ process. We are somewhat relieved to hear that, and yet still mistrusting. I'm sure you fully understand that we are very concerned about this type of operation and the risks to the quality of our water, soil and air. The likelihood of heavy metal poisoning and radiation poisoning are greatly heightened by having an in-situ uranium mining process in our aquifer. Powertech Uranium Corp has a great opportunity in meeting their goal of changing the negative face of uranium mining by working with the communities of the Centennial Project. The Northern Colorado area is filled with highly educated and interested people. The best thing Powertech Uranium

Corp can do is to honor our educated body by providing us with everything down to the minute detail of their in-situ leaching process.

I boldly suggest that all governing bodies involved with any of the permitting process ask that each and every one of these questions and more be answered in full and minute detail before granting any permit. We would be honored to have you begin to answer these questions and we will post them on our website for all to see.

Powertech Uranium Corp has a great opportunity to show good-will in regard to maintaining an environmentally clean in-situ uranium mining process by offering to double the bonds that the state of Colorado requires be posted. If Powertech Uranium Corp is confident about their work ethic, this will not be any bother to them. Once the mining operation is complete and the site is vacated in a reclaimed and restored manner, the bond could be returned. Is Powertech Uranium Corp willing to put their money where their mouth is?

According to a statement at our meeting with the Powertech representatives, the corporation stands to net around $900,000,000 (at 4/13/07 uranium prices) from the Centennial Project. Show us your good faith by helping us maintain the health of our water, soil and air here in Northern Colorado. The amount of profit available as well as the level of technology available really gives Powertech Uranium Corp an incredible opportunity to "clean up the act" of the uranium mining industry. Will you do that? Explain in detail how.

Mr. Blubaugh has expressed how Colorado is an agreement Environmental Impact Statement state and that this will ease the permitting process. What does this mean?
Is Powertech Uranium Corp working on their Environmental Impact Statement for the Centennial project?

We understand that one of the key factors in whether excursions of radioactive and heavy metal contaminated slurry enter into the aquifer greatly rely on the care taken in closing the Rocky Mountain Energy Corp bore holes. Please outline your plan to study Rocky Mountain Energy Corps bore holes. Will this study be completed and included in the permit applications?

What procedure would be used to close these bore holes properly?

What documentation is in place or will be produced that shows that all 3000 RMEC bore holes were closed properly?

Where exactly are these bore holes located? X, Y coordinates, please.

Powertech Uranium Corporation mentioned that they will need to have proper lighting at all ISL sites. How will you protect neighbors from the light pollution?

Please provide us with a copy of your emergency procedures in the event of leakage, spillage or other types of excursions of radioactive elements and/or heavy metals in our water, soil or air.

Even Powertech Uranium Corp representatives admit that selenium released during the ISL process is a problem. What specific way do you plan to deal with selenium?

We mailed these questions along with our original list to Powertech's snail mail address as well as their e-mail address.

Oh, and of course, they went up on the website immediately.

CHAPTER 8

GATHERING FORTITUDE

Saturday morning, the morning following our meeting with Powertech, both The Rocky Mountain News and the Greeley Tribune ran their promised articles. Included in the article were a couple of quotes by Richard Blubaugh, president of environment, health and safety at Powertech. One of which caught my eye *"...To date, there is no confirmed uranium in-situ operation contamination to drinking water supply. There are allegations, but that doesn't mean they're true."*[6]

Then I was quoted in the last paragraph: *"We are even going to get bumper stickers that say "Hell No We Won't Glow."* Egads, was all I could think. In the Greeley Tribune no less. Land of conservative farmers and ranchers. We look like a bunch of freaky hippies from the 60's spouting off about fear-based unknowns. Not to mention, this kind of verbiage was not upholding the high moral code that 4-H demanded of me. I felt like crawling under the bed and just not coming out. I didn't want to ever speak to the press again. This whole journey was such a rollercoaster ride of ups and downs and no one is harder on me than myself. After beating myself up for awhile, I put on my big girl pants and remembered that at least we are still getting the word out.

---

[6]   Greeley Tribune, "Uranium Mining raises concerns" by Roxye Arellano, April 14, 2007

This entire reaction to the Greeley Tribune article was a deep reflection of my own self-loathing. We had just had a four-hour meeting the night before, and with all of the soul searching that Jay and I had done afterwards, I was feeling empowered and committed to standing up against the uranium miners and all the regulators. Even with all of this, I still was concerned about my 'reputation.' I didn't want to come off as a radical for fear that people would look at me as though I was crazy. I wanted to be seen as an intelligent professional who kept her emotions in line rather than spouting them as a war cry.

I went into a dark place for as long as I could allow myself that day. I hit hopelessness in who I was and what I was presenting to the world. I hit hopelessness in being smart enough to take on these powerful people. I hit hopelessness in juggling my emotions and remaining stable. All from one quote that had appeared in the newspaper. I was struck by the fact that I had a serious lack of self-love and self-forgiveness.

The only thing that kept me going was that my schedule was so busy I had no time to really drop into the darkness for long. With that level of busyness I was able to carry on.

Since it was Saturday it's our 4-H club day. Snow was falling lightly and a good stiff breeze was blowing. We had invited the parents to meet with Jay while I worked with the kids. Given the weather, I decided to take the kids on a field trip to see the Budweiser Clydesdales. I was really looking forward to the outing. I loved having the laughter and energy of the kids around me when I could, especially these days.

As I herded the kids into the van I had borrowed to accommodate our numbers, one of the younger cloverbud kids asked why his mom wasn't coming with us to see the 'giant horses.' I told him that Jay had some things to share with all of the parents and his mom wanted to hear about it too.

"Is it about the bad men who want to come pollute your water?" He asked. I had already shared our plight with his mother over a week ago.

From the mouths of babes, I thought. "Yes, it is. We hope it doesn't happen," I answered.

"Don't worry, Robin," he replied. "Mommy and me pray for God to protect your water every night."

The tears stung my cheeks as my heart swelled from the support of the most innocent.

With the kids gone, the parents were able to focus entirely on what Jay had to show them. He just used our yellow and red website to give these people a brief tour about what was happening so far. He also used the Powertech Uranium Corporation website to add a bit more detail on in-situ leach mining for uranium. He answered all the questions as best he could. The one thing he was clear about is that as members of our 4-H club they were not required to help us at all or to even agree with our efforts. We just needed them to know what we were doing since we were mentoring their youth. Plus we were very clear on the fact that these parents needed to be aware that there may be potential health risks to the children if they continued to bring them to Mustang Hollow.

Opening the door upon our return, I heard the parents still in conversation but as soon as the kids ran in to share their excitement from the field trip the meeting wrapped up rather quickly. One couple who lives within 2 miles of us was really angry. They had not heard anything about this proposed uranium mine until now and it became quite clear that it would affect them as well. They owned their own mineral rights and as far as we know, there is no uranium ore body below their surface. But, they do have a domestic well. This couple vowed to participate in the opposition and left with the continued knowledge and dismay that they may have not known about a uranium mine within 2 miles of them if we had not shared the information with them. It brought to my mind just how often we all do not really speak with our neighbors, especially when you live on large acreages and moved to a place to be 'away' from people.

As the parents gathered their children and prepared to leave, most of them gave me a hug of support on their way out the door. I was feeling supported and ready to face our challenge with renewed faith. While saying my goodbye's I noticed that one of the more intense mothers stayed behind. As soon as I closed the door on the last family, I had this feeling of being cornered. She looked me in the eye with intensity and said, "You need to contact the legislators, Robin." The joy I had been feeling by spending time with the kids quickly faded.

"Yes, I know. We have," I replied.

"They need to know what is happening," she continued without pause. "They won't want a toxic uranium mine within the vicinity of Fort Collins and such a high population."

"I wouldn't think so," I answered while she continued to talk without taking a breath. I was starting to feel small and trapped as she continued.

"You need to get more people involved. You need to get organized. You need to get the Fort Collins City Council involved. You need to........ You need to........ You need to.......... You need to........." She went on without pause with her list of items that we needed to do.

I looked at her with hard eyes and abruptly interrupted her list, "I know what we need to do." I spoke loudly as I leaned forward, "This is a huge job, and I am only one person. This is not only our battle, it's everyone's. Water is a finite resource and we are doing everything WE can to protect it. Without water there is no life. I can't believe there are people out there who think it's okay to pollute water. We can live without power, but we cannot live without water. There is so much to be done. We need to help everyone see that we shouldn't be polluting water. This is killing us all. I can't save the World, I just cannot do it all." I ended by staring her down.

I could see this mother was taken aback by my energy. After a pause she looked at me very seriously and said "Robin, you are so angry." And she turned to walk away.

My stress and frustration came bubbling to the surface as I just couldn't take it any longer. In reality rather than allowing my inner little girl to feel further abused by her words and intensity, I responded in a way that was my little girl saying "stop!" Then my adult-self took over for a short time then I ended the speech as a victim. I really did not have strong emotional intelligence, but I had a strong desire to shut her up without angering her further and to remind her and myself that I knew what the challenges were.

Had I been in a better place emotionally I would have been okay with the anger, recognizing that her need to project her own anger onto me was a serious boundary violation. Instead I engaged in a dance where I allowed her to project her anger and then take the position of superiority over me. I see now how damaged I was. I allowed it. I did not claim my own space. Therefore, I ended as a victim.

If I had been strong enough to let her know that she could not do that and that I had every right to be angry about the situation, the relationship may have developed into a stronger and deeper one. Instead it was one in which she felt like she could tell me what I need to do and then to also tell me just how wrong I was for feeling the way that I was. The relationship/interaction was a parent–child one rather than adult-adult.

I don't remember exactly how I responded, even today. But I do know that I took her words to heart and had to reflect upon how I was presenting myself to others. Of course I was angry about our situation. I was also very scared. I knew we had a lot of work in front of us and that daunted me. I knew we could lose everything. I was feeling violated by Powertech and their way of telling us what THEY plan to do. I was overworked, losing sleep at night for oh so many reasons, and just plain mad at the world for putting us in such a difficult situation.

I was angry at God for placing these burdens upon us. We had prayed and prayed before we made the move to Nunn. We went into the decision with open eyes and an obedient heart. We asked God if this was where He wanted us. We kept hearing "Yes." The financing, the move, everything went smoothly. Yes, it was a TON of work to move and to get even partially set up with the horses and the facilities for the horse business, but we were getting it done and in good manner. So this proposed uranium mine on top of the stress that was already there, did much to push me right to the edge.

I felt that I had to fully consider this anger thing. I was completely immersed in the cultural trance that emotions were either positive or negative. At the time I believed Anger and Fear were definitely negative emotions and meant to be dealt with in a way to just 'Get Over It.' Sadness is another sticky emotion, according to my lack of emotional intelligence understanding! I believed one may be a little sad over sad events, but I thought I couldn't let that sadness go on too long (however long too long is perceived as being.... an hour, a day, a week...) because then, I believed, you must be depressed and need help. Only Joy and all the emotions surrounding it were okay. I had developed a mask of a smile. Oh, apparently I was very good at this smile because I often got complemented on it. No matter what was truly going on inside, I would smile. 'Smile and the whole world smiles with you' – it's true. 'Smile and you can change your mood' – this actually works, try it sometime. Smile. Smile. Smile. 'No one will ever know what is really going on inside.' Well, my smile was cracking and my anger was showing. My lack of emotional intelligence made me tell myself that it was time to pull up the boot straps, stuff that bad ol' anger, brighten up that smile and move on.

And so I did..... I stuffed the anger without hearing the message of boundary violations behind it. I stuffed the anger just as I'd been doing most of my life until it bubbled up in some of the most uncomfortable and often totally unrelated circumstances. I stuffed the anger until my body could not hold it any longer. I had a lot of anger that had been stuffed for a lifetime. I didn't know that I could tap into the energy of righteous anger and have a healthy relationship with that emotion. I didn't realize that stuffing the anger only made it fester and become blockages that really didn't serve me. I didn't realize that I had some really old wounds that deserved to be heard and felt. I didn't realize that I was a walking mess of violated boundaries that didn't allow me to really speak up for myself in a completely functional way. I just used the anger to keep me going in a dysfunctional way by pushing myself too hard, losing sleep, snapping at the most petty things and creating false relationships. Stuffing and pushing onward were what I knew, so I continued......

One of the things we were beginning to learn as we were reaching out and talking to more and more people was that not many find it necessary to get too involved. Maybe they were really thinking this uranium mine was going to be easy to put to rest - that all the folks living out by Nunn only needed to be informed, say 'Hell No' we don't want your stinking uranium mine, and the issue would be done. Much of the public really didn't think that a uranium mine so close to a large population could really happen. We were eternally hearing: "You need to do_____ (fill in the blank)." It seemed as though they felt like they thought the uranium mine was our issue to deal with. It appeared that they believed they had the good ideas, but we were to execute them. I cannot tell you how many times I've heard that message. It feels like nearly one million times. I know intentions were good, but it sure is painful to hear that over and over, especially when you are overworked and maxed out already. Gentle reader, if you are confronted with an issue and you can see an action step, ask the person to whom you are talking if they have done X and if they answer that they have, then ask if there is more that you can do to help. If they answer that they have not had a chance to do X, or even thought of doing X, then ask them if you can do it for them. This small gesture will go a long, long way in energizing the folks driving the issue and could be the one thing that actually takes out the keystone in the wall that has been blocking their success.

In the first days of our fight, the attitude voiced loudly by many of the folks who live in the Nunn area was 'here we go again.' This issue to them was just like the Super Slab developers trying to push the little guy around.

Many of the residents surrounding Nunn and the other small towns in the area were stuck in victimhood. They had been beaten up so many times, all they could see was their land being threatened yet again and that they would likely lose to rampant capitalism. Of course, I completely related to this state of victimhood and would fall back into it on a regular basis, until that "bad ol' anger" rose again and propelled me forward.

While many of the active voices were still crying out, "here we go again," the momentum with those coming on board at the first home owner's meeting was changing the tone of this fight with the awareness that could not be just a landowner's battle. To succeed it was going to be and had to be much bigger. It was about a shift in consciousness in the way we 'use' resources on a global level, especially water. It was also a shift in consciousness regarding victimhood on a local level. And a shift in consciousness on a personal level regarding emotional intelligence and how our emotions are one of God's greatest gifts.

With these shifts in consciousness as a driving force, we e-mailed large environmental organizations for help. We looked up folks like Erin Brokovich and Robert Kennedy, Jr. We tried every avenue possible to find help and to just share our plight. We could not win with this being a small-scale issue. We needed it to be big, and at the same time fully address it on the small scale. We had to look at the drop of water, then the pond, then look at the ocean, then act according to which needed to be addressed in the moment. It's the only way to keep the issue from becoming a NIMBY(Not In My Back Yard) issue, to gain support from the larger population, and to keep all of us motivated.

Sunday. I prayed for peace in dealing with this whole huge thing that had been put in front of us. And also that the help we needed would show up. As angry as I was at God for not protecting us from this situation, I still felt that prayer would help. God can handle my anger, He gave it to me so I could just offer it right back up to Him. I had no fear of being deserted by God by being angry with Him.

I left Church feeling supported and fed and ready to, again, put on the warrior hats.

Our meeting with the Powertech representatives had left many of the landowners with the need to gather again, so we invited a few of them over that afternoon. As our new friends and neighbors began to arrive, it was starting to feel like we were long-time friends, even though we had only known most of one another for a few days. Trauma will bring people together like that.

We began by talking about how we really didn't get any useful information from our meeting. We had our list of questions and they had said that the questions were 'germane' to the issue, yet they kept talking in circles to us. We agreed that they may not really know that information yet, but we felt that it's appropriate that they provide us with a timeline as to when they might be able to answer those questions.

The discussion went on to cover the details of heady topics such as zoning (and the agricultural 'use by right' many of us have), water and well refill rates (how Powertech's science doesn't jive with the actual), and our existing water quality.

We always came back to our fears about what could happen to our water quality if they did mine. We had all done enough research by now to understand that uranium was not the core issue. The heavy metals that are stirred up in this type of mining are more of a concern.

Carl reiterated his concerns about the water testing done during the mining operation, "Powertech is saying they will be using a Wyoming water testing lab, this is of great concern because uranium, as they pull out samples, depletes very rapidly. I believe that we need to make sure that Powertech uses a local lab when they are doing their testing, rather than taking the 24-48 hours that are potential when shipping out of state. We want the report to be its most accurate."

After talking from a logical and fact-based place, we dropped into our emotions and started to talk about our feelings from the meeting just a couple of nights ago. We found it interesting how after the formal portion of the meeting ended the Powertech representatives split our group up and cornered a couple of us as soon as they could. "Jay and I were taken aside and I noticed that Carl and Ann were with the other guy in another corner." I said.

I shared that we were quizzed about the possibility of selling out. Then I asked the couple, "I wonder if they were offering either or even both of you a job?"

"So they offered to buy your property?" Steve asked before Ann or Carl could answer.

"Yeah, but we were told that we'd have to sign some sort of 'no compete' agreement so that we would have to stop fighting them," I answered. "Jay said we'd fight them regardless. I had our digital recorder in my hand, so it's on tape."

Having the recorder in my hand reminded us of how prepared we were in this war. We all agreed that it's pretty amazing how organized we already were. David mentioned how he and Carol kept talking with Jay and looking into how many violations were out there. They were scared and felt like they were all alone. "Once we got Robin on board, LOOK OUT!" he quipped.

"It's the red hair." I joked. The real fact of the matter was that I still wanted to run from this thing, but since I couldn't I wanted it to go away NOW. I was like the cornered animal. I couldn't run so I was going to give it my all to survive.

"They actually had told me on the phone that this crazy woman from Fort Collins is on TV going nuts." Jay replied.

We all laughed, while I felt a little nauseated and unsure about how I was really looking to the community. My reputation, or my idea of what my reputation is, was still important to me. I didn't want to be referred to as the crazy woman.

As we circled back to the meeting with the Powertech representatives, we discussed how we were surprised to see they already had had a copy of our meeting flyer. We wondered where he had gotten it since we had only begun to distribute them that day. One of the representatives had pulled out the flyer and said he heard that people were coming from miles away. There would be 100's of people at the meeting from what he said he had heard. We figured that he was hoping to de-motivate us by scaring us about the crazies who could show up at a meeting of this nature. He talked about protestors and the dangers of these types of personalities. I can assure you that I took his words to heart and had my misgivings about what the meeting might look like, especially after the stories from my activist friend. Not to mention that, again, I was fearful about how I might come off in this scenario. How would people look at me if we had a huge newsworthy event with lots of 'hippies' and loud people? I knew we were committed but I sure was having a difficult time feeling any level of comfort as everyone was talking. My breath was getting shallower and my eyes were getting wider.

Then, Steve, began speaking quietly, "I was a little bit nervous at the end of the meeting, because everyone seemed just a little bit too happy. At least that was my first impression. They had come out and they read right out of the manual of negotiating. They complimented us on how smart we were and how good our questions were and other things. And all I could think was, ugh, this is scary. I mean, I'll take a compliment anytime, but by the same token, this is scary. Then he starts inferring that he's gonna buy property and stuff like that. I kept thinking that they were doing nothing more than stalling us. They just want to keep us quiet so we don't burn a bridge and lose a sale. That's what made me nervous.

I have been on the extreme edges of this from the beginning. One thing is that it's not my property that they are looking at, they don't own my mineral rights, though, it is right next to us. I wasn't as up in arms when I first heard about this. All I could think was, okay, science has come a long way, and I'm a science guy. Maybe it's gonna be safe and all that. So, I've been just sitting in the middle of the road. I've been listening to everyone. I was looking forward to the meeting with them. I had called the Powertech representative before the meeting to get some questions answered and get it straight from the horse's mouth. I wanted to appreciate their side of the story and what their plans are. I wanted to understand where he is coming from too.

I called Shawn to get his point of view. I spoke with him for over an hour and got an agreement from him that he would not sell to Powertech without letting us know beforehand. I feel pretty good about that.

I've been staying right in the middle and just collecting information.

Now, honestly, I'm glad to hear what I'm hearing tonight. I'm glad to hear that everyone wasn't as taken in from the meeting with Powertech as I was afraid you were. That is all I have to say."

As Steve finished, his wife chimed in about how they had talked on the way home from the meeting and she was feeling pretty good about the fact that Powertech would buy us all out. She felt relieved that we would not have to worry about it any longer. But that her husband wasn't convinced that they really would buy us all out. They had discussed the way it looked was that Powertech was doing nothing more than trying to manipulate us.

I was asked at this point what I thought of the meeting and the offer to buy us out. I said that I think the reason we were so happy at the end was because the meeting was finally over. Then I told the group that I was very aware of how we were cornered and how the landman seemed to be trying to keep Jay and me away from everyone else as he offered to buy our land.

Then Jay shared that he was able to relate to the consultant. "He is doing the same kind of thing I do. He knows how to have 'public' meetings like this without saying a whole lot." Jay went on to talk about how in his line of work he has to speak at homeowners meetings and county planning meetings.

Jay: "You give just enough information to meet the people at their level of understanding, but that's it. You never really give them details. I understand how they couldn't give a lot of details yet. They really aren't at that stage of the game yet. Though, they did seem to be sweating a bit about the questions we were asking. They were on the spot."

Jay continued by saying that he had been hoping to gather information since his previous phone calls didn't get him any. "I always had the feeling that they are just looking at the bottom line and their stock options."

Jay shared that some of the questions on our list of questions would really help him begin to dig into more detail about the way this project is supposed to proceed as well as their attention to detail. "If they'll answer those questions honestly, I can really start to look at them and do a bit more research to either feel better about the project or not. Many of those questions should be able to be answered in some way right now. They relate directly to the drilling operation itself. Basic questions. Maybe I could feel better about what their plans are."

Jay continued to say that the fact that the consultant is not working directly for Powertech made him a little uncomfortable. "He can make recommendations and take a stand about the way things should be designed and operated from a safety standpoint, but in the end, it is Powertech who makes their design and operation decisions. Generally, they go for how to increase their profit, not what is best for the public or the land. We need to get directly to the point guy to find out what their answers would be on the design and operation."

"Glad we recorded that meeting. We might have some really good stuff to use in the future. They didn't stick to just the company line at times. I could tell that these guys like what they do and believe in it.

"They admitted that there are no guarantees and that the risks are not black and white and they couldn't guarantee the lack of water contamination. That encouraged me and made me feel like we have really gotten more information than what they had planned to give."

Jay went on to talk about the details of how radionucleids scatter and move more rapidly in water. "I just have been reading everything I can find on this issue. Radioactivity in water, confined and unconfined aquifers and what the difference is...... all of this and so much more."

He had found a study done by the USGS on our aquifer and its water quality that had been done at about the same time uranium prospecting was taking place here. Rocky Mountain Energy (RME) was poking over 3000 holes within what is now where Powertech intends to do ISL mining. "So even if it was a confined aquifer before RME began poking their holes, how could it still be confined? In the late 70's these kinds of holes were never abandoned 'properly.' The regulations and inspections are much more stringent now."

Jay continued by saying he was also talking with the father of a high school/college friend who had spent 35 years studying the risks associated with radiation and radioactivity, especially associated with uranium mining projects. This professional had told Jay that we should be way more concerned about the heavy metals associated with any mining than the radiation. He encouraged us to get baselines from our own wells before Powertech begins doing anything.

We all agreed that we would begin having our wells tested. This became one of our greatest tools. Colorado Division of Mining even developed a baseline 'mining test' because of the number of requests for the same test by most of the residents in the surrounding area. When Powertech discussed how they have to pull baseline tests before they could mine, they would not be pulling those tests from the very spot from which we were drinking. It is important to have the baseline pulled from the depth and location in the aquifer that is being used. Plus, with us doing our own testing we were watching Powertech and their ethics closely. We had a chain of custody developed by asking Weld County to collect the water and then to deliver that directly to the State for testing. Powertech was using their own guys to collect and their own contracted labs to test.

Of course, we all had to pay for our own tests but it was well worth it to have those reports. Many of us had our water tested multiple times over the seasons to show the

differences and to monitor if any changes occurred because
of the drilling and testing that Powertech continued to do.

We all agreed that we didn't trust Powertech to follow through with all the
best practices that they kept talking about. They are interested in making
as much money as they can. 'Best practices' do not always coincide with
making money.

Carol had done a bit of research on the evolution of Powertech and noticed
that they had already been through at least three name changes. She
provided a timeline of information on Powertech's activities to date:

*April 16, 1986 – Incorporated as Ararat Oil and Minerals, Inc. in Vancouver,
British Columbia*

*January 20, 1992 – International Power Systems, Inc. On the Canadian
Stock Market*

June 1995 – Company changes its name to Powertech Industries, Inc.

*October 14, 2004 – Shareholders approve the sale of all company assets,
Gasmaster Industries and all intellectual property to Fama Holdings in
exchange for a partial settlement of bad debt. Powertech incorporated
Gasmasters Industries, the manufacturing arm of the company to
make boilers and water heaters.*

*February 22, 2005 – Powertech announces reorganization. Three directors
resigned and are replaced.*

March 22, 2005 – Powertech announces the settlement of more debt

*August 9, 2005 – Powertech announces its intent to acquire Denver Uranium
Corp. And Dewey Burdock Uranium Property.*

*September 27, 2005 – Powertech announces that they have secured third
party funding. The focus of this acquisition is to develop ISL mining
"initially in North America, with an eye in the future at growth
through international acquisitions of the proper character."*

*November 18, 2005 – Powertech enters into a binding property purchase
agreement with Energy Metals Corporation to acquire additional
Dewey Burdock claims.*

*November 28, 2005 – Powertech announces its "Change of Business" from
manufacturing heating equipment to mining uranium.*

January 19, 2006 – Dewey Burdock 43-101 report available for review.

January 23, 2006 – Private Placement Financing

February 8, 2006 – Private Placement Financing

March 3, 2006 – Private Placement Financing

April 12, 2006 – Change of Business and acquisition of the Dewey-Burdock Uranium Property conditionally accepted by TSX

April 28, 2006 – Private Placement Closes

May 12, 2006 – Acquisition of Dewey-Burdock property and private placement close, change of business completes.

June 2, 2006 – Powertech announces a change of name and a transfer of the head office to Centennial, Colorado

June 6, 2006 – James Bonner is appointed as the VP of exploration and Frank Lichnovisky as chief geologist.

July 19, 2006 – Richard Blubaugh, MAOA, BSC in Biology is appointed as VP of Health, Safety and Environmental Resources.

August 2, 2006 – Powertech establishes an advisory board and appoints two members.

August 10, 2006 – Powertech enters into an agreement to acquire a uranium database from R.B. Smith and Associates. This database contains information on uranium deposits in Texas, New Mexico, South Dakota, Wyoming, Arizona, Nevada and Mexico.

September 12, 2006 – Powertech acquires 6000 acres of mineral claims in Weston County, Wyoming and named it the "Dewey Terrace Exploration Property."

September 27, 2006 – Powertech receives authorization to proceed with uranium exploration and confirmation drilling at Dewey Terrace Drilling. The issued exploration and baseline study permits allow Powertech to test the extensions of the known mineralization, coring for leaching testing, and a pump test to establishing flow rates for in-situ leaching.

October 3, 2006 – Powertech purchase 5760 acres of mineral rights in Weld County, Colorado known as the Centennial Project, from Anadarko for an initial cash payment of $1,000,000, eight separate payments of $250,000 per annum, and a lump sum payment of $1,500,000 upon receipt of all regulatory permits and licenses allowing the production of uranium from the Centennial Project. Powertech agrees to a minimal *annual work commitment of $250,000 until uranium is produced from the Centennial Project and to pay a royalty of 5% to 6% of the value of uranium and byproduct mined from the Centennial Project. Uranium deposits are said to be from 120' to 620'.*

October 5, 2006 – Powertech retains Swiss company Studar Consulting to provide investor relation services for the company in Europe.

October 11, 2006 – Powertech acquires 9,299 acres for privately owned mining leases, 640 acres of state mineral rights and 710 acres of filed claim notices for a total of 10,649 acres in Crook County, Wyoming. This is designated as the Aladdin Property.

October 13, 2006 – Letters sent by Lone Tree Energy & Associates, LLC to Weld County residents introducing Powertech uranium and their intentions to mine uranium.

December 18, 2006 – Powertech enters into an agreement with Energy Metal Corp to purchase the database for Aladdin Project and Dewey Terrace Project, both in the state of Wyoming.

January 10, 2007 – Powertech announces that they have acquired 3000 acres of privately owned mining leases for a total of 13,590 acres in Crook County.

January 19, 2007 – Powertech announces that they have received an exploration permit for Dewey Burdock project. This permit will enable Powertech to conduct additional drilling of up to 155 holes and perform two 72-hour pump tests to determine the permeability and flow rates for the host formations. The objective of the drilling is to confirm and potentially expand historic in-pace resources. Including in this program will be the completion of six core holes to obtain samples on which metallurgical and leach testing will be performed.

January 26, 2007 – Applies for special warranty deed – Grantor: Anadarko S3 T8N R67W

February 26, 2007 – Request for notification form (minerals) for S9 T9N R67W; S15 T9N R67W and S35 T9N R67W

March 14, 2007 – Warranty Deed – Grantor: John Hoyt, S9 T9N R67W S2 NE4

March 22, 2007 – Powertech awarded two drilling contracts to Conquest Energy Services of Gillette, Wyoming and Tefertiller Drilling of Spearfish, South Dakota.

April 12, 2007 – Warranty Deed – Grantor: Patrick Malone, S9 T9N R67W
    E2 SE4
April 12, 2007 – Warranty Deed – Grantor: Suh Taekwang S35, T9n R67W
    W2 NW4

One of the landowners changed the subject by saying that he was hoping that by pointing out to Powertech that we had only landowners at the meeting last night it would encourage them to open up a little more honestly.

"We don't have Greenpeace involved yet," he stated, "but I have no doubt that this issue will gain that kind of attention as we share about it. This is gonna be big." He also shared his fear that going up against these guys could get more and more difficult as we have to go against bigger entities with more money and power. He went on to tell us that he was not convinced that we could really fight and win, unless we could get bigger environmental organizations to take this on.

It is this landowner's daughter and son-in-law who have the backgrounds in selenium from uranium mining and water chemistry. He proudly expressed how much Carl knows about testing water and water chemistry. Carl had already made his own list of questions for Powertech but will not be asking them until the timing is more appropriate.

Everyone agreed and had a good laugh about how the surprise will be fun, especially after our meeting with the Powertech representatives. They were so sure that they were the smartest people in the room and so invested in making sure we knew that as well. Watching them have to speak at a higher level will be really interesting.

We then started to list the things that we needed to do: a discussion with Weld County Health Department, a deeper understanding of our zoning and what it would take for Powertech to be able to create a uranium mine within an agricultural area, and monitoring the Weld County Commissioner meetings for anything with Powertech or uranium mining in case we were not notified. Powertech had assured us that they would keep us informed about any meetings but we decided that we had better be proactive.

We also wanted to put together a brochure and/or purchasing the Colorado Water Atlas to give to every elected official and their staff that we could, so we could educate them as simply and efficiently as possible. When asked if any elected officials had agreed to come to our meeting in Wellington yet, I replied that had I sent several e-mails but had not yet heard from anyone about attending the meeting. I had heard from some of the State legislators from outside of our district. They had asked to be kept on our mailing list so they could remain informed. I was still disappointed to report that our own elected officials were silent on the topic as of yet. Weld County has been pro oil and gas mining for decades and our collective interpretation of their silence was that none of these politicians wanted to upset these types of paying constituents.

A couple of the landowners said they had been attempting to contact our state Representative Jerry Sonnenberg and that they had not heard from him either. At that time there was a bill in the legislative process that might give surface owners more rights than what we currently had, but it wasn't going well so far. Representative Sonnenberg had voted against this bill so we weren't feeling too positive about his support in our issue.

We passed around the upcoming meeting fliers and everyone took a stack of them to pass out and post where ever they could. While doing this I shared how many press releases had gone out and that another letter to the editor was going to be published by the Fort Collins Coloradoan. I asked everyone to write letters to the editor as part of our education campaign.

Our Yahoo! Group was growing and becoming quite active but we needed to make sure only credible information was posted. We were seeing some inaccurate information and some emotional ramblings posted that we were not too excited about. Jay encouraged us to just moderate all postings rather than leave it as an open forum. My tension level rose as I considered the work involved. This was work that I had thought I was eliminating by forming the group in the first place. But I understood the need for concern.

We really needed to maintain credibility. Carol and I agreed to go through it as best we could in the next few days. "There are SO many e-mails in there...." she said with trepidation.

"Siiigggghhhh, I know, but that's a good thing, I guess." I replied.

The meeting closed as I reminded everyone of the meeting next Thursday to prepare for the Wellington meeting. People got up and collected in small groups as they were preparing to leave. One of the landowners stopped at the door on his way out to ask about the rumors that we were attracting anti-nuke activists from New York and protestors from other states to our Wellington meeting. Jay said he had heard the same thing, but he didn't figure it was true but he took a positive view, "If they do show up, great, we are getting recognition and the word is spreading."

We chatted about how we had all moved out here to get away from these kinds of issues and to live a peaceful lifestyle. Jay joked, "Yeah, we find out that we have a super highway going through and a uranium mine in our water. I guess we can have a peaceful life of dodging the traffic and not drinking our water." We all laughed one of those dry, inauthentic laughs one uses to cover up unbearable pain.

Another landowner thanked me for letting them know about the proposal, since they would not have known otherwise. They also thanked Jay and me for speaking out and taking on leadership with this issue. All I kept thinking was, I don't want to be the leader in this group. I'd rather be the leader of a bunch of kids excelling in horsemanship. Okay, so I see the need, but isn't there someone who is more qualified? Or someone who would enjoy this? Or someone who understands the science? I am just scared enough at this point to be dangerous by speaking up to get us noticed. That coupled with the fact that our lives and livelihood were threatened, these were the only qualifications I had for leadership in this issue.

After saying goodbye to those who were walking out the door, I walked in on a conversation Jay was having with the last straggler. This man was sharing a story about a friend of his who worked on drill rigs. This friend worked on a drill rig in his younger years, then went on to do a different type work for 25 years. He had recently found himself out of work, and thought he'd try the rigs again. He was hired readily because of his past experience. This same friend shared how things were exactly as he had remembered them 25 years prior. "So what's this about new technology that Powertech keeps talking about when it comes to drilling these wells? I am not convinced that there is new technology and my friend is proof."

Jay agreed, "Yep, a hole is a hole is a hole. I'd like to know what they plan to use as casing and how they plan to test the soils. I'm especially concerned about all of those holes that are already out here. I've heard way too many stories from people I know who work in the field. They will abandon a core hole by pulling the casing and then just kicking the surrounding dirt back in to just cover the top of the hole. 'Looks good' they'll say as they need to stay on schedule and quickly move to the next site. Especially in the late 70's and early 80's before the environmental awareness was as heightened as it is now."

"This is scary," the landowner answered.

"Oh yeah! We aren't making anything up. We don't have to. We wish it wasn't as scary as it is." Jay answered as he walked him to the door and they shook hands.

The house was now quiet as Jay began cleaning up. I stood lost in my thoughts for awhile. At this time in my life my fear tended to present more often in a frozen state. When really scared, to the bones, I would freeze, disassociate and hope that I would be overlooked, and all things will be fine once I return to my body. Only then would I be able to function again. I was really scared.

> Disassociation is what I used to deal with trauma. I'd check out and freeze until it all went away and I could come back to present again. It was how I learned how to survive the sexual abuse of my youth, as well as how I learned to forget the abuse. I got really good at being ungrounded for most of my life. That is how I got through so much of life without having to engage my deeper wounds. Fear would send me right into blissful disassociation.

"We really need to think about this whole deal," I said as I pulled myself back to the present and began puttering around the kitchen, "What if they are serious about buying us out?"

Jay didn't argue, he just jumped right into discussing what sort of value would be appropriate. He could see that I was really rattled and was willing to support me in my needs. I often wonder if he knew that in the end I would do the right thing, or if he would have called them up and offered to take a buy out if I really insisted. Thankfully, we never found out. In the meantime, we discussed how the recent appraisal for our 2nd mortgage gave us a number where we could start with Powertech. We talked about how we would be moving only because of the possible uranium mine, so at the very least Powertech should have to pay to move us, with packers and everything. We also talked about how in reality they should present us with a list of possible new homes. Let them do the research and leg work that we had just been through to find this place.

We discussed what it would take financially, for us to keep our mouths shut about the risks of ISL mining. Would we be able to sign a contract where we agreed to not speak out about ISL mining? Could we do that and still live with ourselves?

Jay brought up the fact that as the leaders of this newly formed group we had a lot of responsibility, real or perceived, in maintaining a positive attitude and belief in the fact that we could stop this mining. Standing in the truth and the facts might eventually win this war, but we had to maintain that it definitely would. Taking a buyout and shutting up could really dissolve any momentum already gained in stopping this mine.

I brought up the fact that this entire thing, the mine, the protest, all of this could potentially destroy us financially.

> Money, money, money. 'The root of all evil.' Not really, but it is what many people believe and so goes a common belief about money. What did Jay and I believe? I can't speak for him but I lived in a lack mentality and never believed that there would be enough. I had such a depth

of unworthiness that I could not step into a place that I could believe that I would be supported in doing what was put in front of me.

The true soul of money is what we have given it as a society. But at its core is that it is nothing more than a tool used to demonstrate what we value. What was put in front of me was a choice to accept money to turn away from a deeper relationship with the Whole, or stand up to the damage that would be caused by the love of it. Very interesting considering that they had used the term 'making us whole' when discussing or alluding to the possibility of buying us out. I had to really drop into my core values to turn away from this offer. Jay and I had so many discussions about this because there was a deep pattern that I had to break through here.

I wanted to take the money and run rather than accept the fact that I had to step into a place of belief that I would be supported. Finances were always a big part of our discussions. My relationship with money was a reflection of my relationship with myself.

"Where could we go?" Jay asked. "We always have to live with ourselves. How can we walk away from all of these people. Look at the young families, especially the _name kept anonymous__ (the neighboring 4-H family). Do you really think that Powertech would buy them out since they are not sitting on surface over Powertech owned minerals?"

I wanted to make sure we kept the door at least a little ajar to the idea of selling out to Powertech in case they presented us with a real figure that would make it worth moving. It had to be more than an appraised value for the property, that I was sure of. We had already put a lot of blood, sweat and tears in the move and the set up. Our move to this place was supposed to be our last.

We decided that we would cross any selling-out bridge if we really came to it. We did not have anything in writing from Powertech so we weren't even sure if they were serious.

We called it another long day and night. I went out to finalize some horse chores. Dusk as well as dawn are my favorite times of the day. Such a peaceful time that allows me perfect time to pray and generally reflect and plan. This night found me praying for God's guidance and help in this new journey as uranium mining warriors. I prayed for the strength to make good decisions. I prayed for our business. I prayed for our entire area to feel God's presence and protection.

Seeking Spiritual strength ended up being a very deep part of our strategy.

> No matter what your practices are, if you ever decide, and I pray that you do, to go up against something that offends your values, staying in touch with that core guidance is very important. Spiritual practice of any type will keep you in alignment and strengthen you throughout your journey. Going up against something that offends your values does not have to look like what we did, it can be as simple as just being willing to speak out against something to those you know well.

> A Spiritual practice is important in offering you guidance, strength, peace and connection to what is greater than the ego. A Spiritual practice will keep you Whole as you walk whatever path you are guided to walk.

I came in and went to bed so we could start another week in the morning. As I lay in bed drifting off, I remembered that I had not yet done my promised look at the Yahoo! Group. I couldn't make myself get up, so I promised myself it would be the first task in the morning.

I was awakened more than once with that disturbing nightmare of aborted fetuses and horses with no manes and tails.

CHAPTER 9

READY.... AIM...

Monday. I woke up and remembered that we had a horse study group that day. I rushed down to the horses and got them started on their morning hay so they would be done eating before students arrived, then quickly walked back up the hill with the Nunnglow Yahoo! Group on my mind. I needed to jump online and at least get started on validating the e-mails that were already on the site.

I grabbed my coffee and a peanut butter and honey sandwich to fuel my morning, then sat down and opened my e-mail account. 250 new e-mails.......... Sigghhhhhhhhhh......... I hadn't been online for the entire weekend, an obvious mistake. I knew that if I started looking at any of these I would get too distracted before really accomplishing my goals. I logged into the Yahoo! Groups right away instead. Ahhhhh, Carol had already been on and had changed the access to "moderated." Yes, that would give us a bit more breathing room, as well as make our jobs more complex. For one, we would not have to worry about any wrong information being posted, but for the other, we would have to read and validate each message before it was posted. At least we had two of us on this job.

I went back to my personal e-mail box and looked for any return e-mails from the media or any elected officials. After I read and responded to any of these priority e-mails as necessary, I scanned for 4-H or Mustang

Hollow business e-mails. Time was flying by. I had 20 minutes before 9am and when my students would be showing up and expecting me to have a plan for them and their horses today. I logged off, brushed my teeth, got dressed in more appropriate layers for the day, grabbed the book we were using as a study guide, turned the outside water on at the house in order to fill the horse tanks, and headed down the hill just in time to see a couple of students showing up. I still had to get water into the horse tanks and sort horses away from the free choice hay. I set my book at the table, waved as Sally was getting out of her van, and got busy placing the hose to the emptiest tank. Then I moved the horses into paddocks.

These things done, I was able to really think about what I wanted to address in our horsemanship journey this day. Or all of 30 seconds, that is....... When I turned around to refocus on the class I saw that Sally, Laura and Evan were already sitting at the table. Laura had brought Krispi Cream donuts and they were eating and chatting. I slid in to the picnic table bench next to Sally and accepted a donut.

They were so happily nibbling on their sweet treats while chatting, obviously enjoying the clear spring day, that I found myself getting caught up and just basking in the camaraderie without considering that I needed to present an agenda. I allowed myself to let down and join in the friendly banter until Evan asked what I'd planned for the day's lesson. Oh yeah, I was the leader here. I really was growing tired of being a leader and unfortunately it was showing up sooner in my horse business than in my activism role.

Remembering what we were there to do, I apologized and asked them all to share what they'd like to work on this day. We decided to work on round penning techniques. The round pen can either be a fabulous tool or it can ruin the confidence of both trainer and horse. The trainer (or such as in this case where the student and trainer are one and the same) must be completely authentic emotionally and have total focus on what their body language is projecting to the horse or the horse will get confused and either shut down by just running round and round or trying to escape over the fence. Or, they may stop and look at the trainer as they try to figure out what it is they want. The former is the more common reaction from the horse, who is a prey animal, and resorts to flight instincts when confused.

Evan was diligent and really wanted to move forward with his project, a young filly. The filly was a cute blue roan and one of my favorite boarders because of her striking color shifts. The filly wasn't quite sure she didn't want to accept a halter every time we presented it. Sometimes we could get the halter on her easily, and other times it was totally rejected. Today was a day for her to reject the halter. As we worked together to herd his filly into the round pen, Evan was looking for good solid advice and technique to help move him and his horse forward.

I began by attempting to demonstrate tips on body position and how we need to understand the difference between trust vs. respect vs. fear based acquiescence. Moriah's mode of shut down was to respond to the request for turns by turning to the outside. She would refuse to do what we call 'facing up' when I drew her, but instead just continue trotting around the round pen. What she was picking up on was the fact that I was not being authentic in my emotions. This caused her to respond instinctually to keep herself 'safe.' I was stuffing all my frustration while doing my best to wear a trainer hat and smile while she went about showing everyone the truth of what was really going on. It's unfortunate that I did not have the additional emotional intelligence then that I have today. Otherwise the morning may have gone much differently. If I had acknowledged to her and my students the emotional turmoil I was experiencing, this filly may have just walked right over to me in support and understanding and put her nose right into the halter. Instead, she was determined to do her best to get away from me and my scary incongruence for fear that I could act out my aggression upon her – though, I would have never done that. True to her species, she only knew how to protect herself from the uncomfortable energy presented.

After finding a place where I could reward a 'try' I stepped out of the round pen and asked Evan to see what he could get done by building on the 'try.' At this point I had hoped that the relationship that Evan had already built with this young horse would inspire different results.

While Evan worked with his horse, Sally and Laura began asking me about our weekend, the meeting with Powertech, the landowners and more details about the upcoming Wellington meeting. We three became very distracted and just talked about uranium while Evan struggled along without any good coaching. I was still tired from the very full weekend and had the many tasks that still needed done swimming in my head, so it was not easy for me to stay focused. Evan, to his credit, did get a couple of good moments, but he was rightfully frustrated. Discouraged, he asked if anyone else would like to work with his filly. Sally agreed to see what she could get done. Laura and I continued to talk more about uranium than to be focused on the activities in the round pen.

After awhile of this, Evan expressed his need to get to his office. "So do you have any advice for us before we get together next week, Robin?"

I gave him a few tips and told him that maybe we could work together the upcoming week if he'd like. I was aware that I had not been present for him at all and hoped that I might be able to address more of his needs on another day. When we compared schedules his work schedule and my uranium stuff and/or 4-H schedule would not present a time for us to meet. He reassured me that it was OK, and that he'd muddle along with his filly until the next study group. We all created a human fence and helped him get his filly back to her paddock. Evan thanked me and got in his truck and drove away, I could tell he was not happy.

Nothing else productive horsemanship wise came from this day. Laura and Sally and I talked a little about what to read out of our study guide for the next week but the topic turned to more uranium stuff before we all split up for the day. Sally and I attended and were very active at Saint Joseph Church, so we found easy comfort in our complementary viewpoints. As she was readying to leave she turned to give me a hug and said, "It's just wrong, Robin, we cannot leave polluted water for our children. How can we say we protect life if we do not protect the water?" I could never get that phrase out of my heart. How could we say we protect life if we do not protect the water?

As they both left I saw that some of that precious water had overflowed to flood the ground below the tank I had begun filling earlier. I quickly moved the hose to another tank and cursed myself for forgetting that it was running. Just one more way the distraction of the uranium mine was showing. I then walked back up the hill to head directly for my computer. I had a HUGE to do list and at least 100 new e-mails still to read that might or might not add to this list. No more horse business for this day, I had a uranium mine to stop. I did remember to turn off the water before the next tank overflowed. That simple success made me feel at least a little better about my effectiveness as a responsible horse ranch owner.

One of the e-mails I had not read before going outside for the morning was from State Representative Randy Fisher. Representative Fisher. His e-mail was the first e-mail I opened that afternoon.
I was pleased to see that Representative Fisher opened his note by telling me how thankful he was to get my emails and wished to remain in the loop. He was a member of the House Agriculture, Livestock and Natural Resources Committee, just the committee we needed to pay attention to our issue.

He recognized that he was not the representative for our area but went on to express his concerns about how close this proposed mine was to his area of representation. He attached some information that he and his staff had found and ended by saying that he would very likely attend our meeting on the 21st and how he was looking forward to meeting me and our group.

The memo included the basic information about the Powertech Centennial project as well as some historical information on uranium mining in the State and who the regulating agencies are. All stuff that we did already know, but it was nice to see that a legislator had taken some action. I was excited that Representative Fischer was so interested and would be coming to our meeting, though, I wasn't sure if it would be that helpful since he didn't represent us directly. I wondered again why I hadn't heard from Representative Sonnenberg. He was also on the House Agriculture, Livestock and Natural Resources committee with Representative Fischer.

Representative Sonnenberg is a Republican and Representative Fischer is a Democrat. I wondered if these guys just didn't talk because of party lines. Silly, I thought, especially since I knew that my e-mails to all of these guys did not hide the recipient's line. I wanted them all to know who I was contacting within the state Capitol. I was sending them every pertinent article that I could find. I started out sending them at least 2 or 3 e-mails per day, but then decided I had better slow down and send them only one per day. I had heard from a couple of the Representatives in the positive. They thanked me for my concern and asked me to continue to send them information. Representative Fischer was the first note back that really looked like he was taking a serious interest.

Representative Sonnenberg was entirely silent.

My to-do list included pulling together some information to take to the Weld County Planning and Zoning Department. They were the ones who would be meeting with Powertech in a week. Jay had recommended some pertinent pages of ISL mining violations from the www.wise_uranium. org site. I printed these pages, Dr. Mudd's paper, made copies of the letters we had received from Powertech, printed a copy of the letter with the questions we had for Powertech, the letter to the editor that Jay and I had written and then arranged all of this into a three-ring binder with dividers. In the front I placed a short cover letter thanking them for taking the time to review all of the enclosed information. I asked them to keep us informed of any public meetings that we would be able to attend regarding Powertech and uranium mining in Weld County. I closed the letter with our contact information, phone, e-mail, mailing address and our www. nunnglow.com website address.

I then drove to Greeley to drop this notebook off in person.

Wednesday

Another interesting e-mail...... A woman who watches for any uranium and nuclear issue had posted a note to our Yahoo! Group.

"Friday, April 20, the NRC is having a licensing meeting with Powertech for their proposal in South Dakota. I am going to listen in via conference call (here she gave the time of the meeting, the phone number and access code.)

Her note went on:

"Richard Blubaugh, environmental manager for Powertech, used to be the regulatory affairs manager for Atlas Mineral Corporation, the owner/operator of the Atlas Uranium Mill in Moab. He was the equivalent of environmental manager for them. Under his watch, Atlas went bankrupt. Thousands of gallons of contaminated groundwater continue to flow into the Colorado River daily."

Carol had been doing research on the Powertech players for her portion of the presentation coming up on Saturday. She kept talking about how their individual histories were not good. I had not really looked at the information she was gathering yet, but this e-mail confirmed some of what she was saying. I decided that I needed to listen in on the NRC meeting with Powertech, so I put it on my calendar with the noted phone number and access code.

Thursday

We had another landowner's meeting in our living room to plan for our big event coming up in Wellington at the Leeper Center. Our two absentee property owners did not return, though we did have a new couple join us, the woman is the daughter of a lady with whom Jay and I attend church. They found out about the issue through their mother and were able to contact us through our church directory, they have a large family of natural and adopted children and live a little over 2 miles from the proposed open pit uranium mine. Had we not been speaking up about the proposed mine, they may have never heard about it until it was too late. Weld County only notifies homeowners within 500 feet of any proposed permit.

Our established group was getting better at being a cohesive bunch and had begun to get to know one another better through our previous gatherings and the multiple phone calls and e-mails that were going back and forth. This meeting got to business much more smoothly and rapidly than any of the past meetings.

Lisa encouraged us to do our best to stay on track this evening so that we could all get home at a reasonable hour. We all agreed that we'd rather not have another 3 hour meeting, which seemed to be our normal. Lisa began running the meeting in her polite yet focused way. She could see that we really needed help with the organizing portion of our group, so she naturally jumped in with her experience in creating organizations. She wanted us to stay focused on the upcoming meeting and began by asking if the invitations we had sent out prompted any response from our elected officials.

"We have a definite yes from state Representative Randy Fisher," I replied. "I have nothing definite from any others."

David shared a letter that he had received from the Weld County Attorney. "He's advising the Weld County Commissioners to not attend any meetings that have anything to do with the uranium topic right now." At this there was an uproar of shock from many in attendance. The letter described how the public hearing process for any special use permit application by Powertech Uranium Corporation could be perceived as being partial if they attend our meeting. The integrity of the Weld County Commissioners quasi judicial role could be questioned and any commissioners who had attended any previous public gatherings regarding the uranium issue could be asked to recuse themselves from a vote on a permit.

"So they'll listen to Powertech and not us?" Was the question asked by many in the room. We already knew that Powertech had a dog and pony show set up with the county planning office. We were shocked at what appeared to us to not be a balanced approach by doing their homework on both sides of the issue.

We discussed going directly to the County officials in a professional way with a Powerpoint presentation of our own. Since they had already agreed to see Powertech's powerpoint, it was assumed they would have to agree to see ours.

I shared a conversation that I had had that day with a gentleman who used to serve on the Ault town council. He had advised us to go to the county, not with scientific data on uranium and the health threats, but with a powerpoint of photographs of the lifestyle in the area. 'Show what will be impacted directly and immediately,' he advised. I suggested that we get photos of the surrounding cattle operations, horse operations, kids on horses, dairy operations, wheat fields, kids playing in their backyards, etc.

Lisa thought this was a great idea, but focused us back to the upcoming meeting. "So that's the Weld County Commissioners, what about your state representatives? Representative Fisher is from the Fort Collins area and doesn't directly represent the area of proposed mining. What do we hear from the ones that you guys elect?"

I told her that I had nothing yet from State Representative Jerry Sonnenberg or State Senator Scott Renfroe. I had heard from many other representatives from other districts, no one who would commit to coming to this meeting, but they at least wanted to continue to get information, our local representatives were quite silent on the issue.

I then asked what we want to happen from the meeting. "What are our goals?"

Lisa brought up a petition that she had put together. "People are going to want to know that they can do something immediately. A petition fulfills this basic need as well as gives us something tangible with which to take to our elected officials."

She read the petition aloud for our comment....

To Weld and Larimer County Commissioners and State of Colorado representatives and officials:
We, the undersigned residents of northern Colorado, are deeply concerned about proposals to mine uranium in our area.

- *According to the Nuclear Regulatory Commission's 2007 report, in situ leach mining has a history of contaminating water.*
- *Uranium mining provides material used for nuclear power, and our area would benefit far more from renewable energy development, such as wind and solar energy.*
- *Uranium mining benefits out-of-state companies, not our local economies.*

We urge our representatives and public officials to:

- *Avoid providing any permits that would allow uranium mining until all questions about safety, health, and water quality are answered by those who propose to mine.*
- *Develop regulations that protect your constituents from the use of in situ leaching technology to mine uranium in Colorado.*
- *Promote economic development that provides for local people and meets local needs.*

We liked it and used that language for our petition for the duration of the fight. We decided to have a one page handout on the history of uranium mining with a bulleted list of the effects of ISL mining and a page that had a list of contact information for elected officials and media. The intent being that many voices to the media and decision makers would create a squeaky wheel effect. They couldn't NOT listen to us if we and others kept putting it in front of them.

We decided to have posters hanging on the wall so that people could spend time before and after the meeting learning more or reinforcing what they had heard in the meeting. There are several different types of learners and we wanted to address as many learning styles as we could.

The posters we created:

- A list of current violations at working ISL mines.
- The map of the aquifer with the wells located on it.
- A history of some of the Powertech players and their trail of contamination

Our goals were to educate, gain signatures on our petition and to grow our group of warriors.

I shared who the media outlets were who said they were considering coming to the meeting.

Then we walked through what Ann had already put together as our powerpoint presentation with input from Carol, Jay and Lisa. Going through the slides, we made a few edits to the look and feel and some of the content. As she got to the photos that she had found of existing ISL operations, the reality of the surface disturbance really started to hit home. We recorded all of our meetings and the voices on the recording are filled with dread and shock as these photos came up. "So they really take up that large of an area?" "Where do we place our livestock?" "How can they call that benign?" "I didn't realize they would have such large ponds and buildings?" "That many well heads?" "Whoa........" "These are where?"

The photos were of current ISL operations in Wyoming and Texas. Ann then went on to show some photos of the resin beads and talked about how even though Powertech says they are only using baking soda, they are changing the PH of the water in a very drastic direction. Base or acid is just as dangerous when the change is this drastic.

Ann's slides then turned to the selenium issue. "Powertech has told me that they are concerned about selenium in this area. I really want to talk about the risks associated with selenium. If they are admitting to it being a problem already, then it must really be an issue, so I wanted that to be emphasized. It's very difficult to get it out of the water to begin with, and then it's an issue of where will they put it if they do get it out of the water. Selenium is a required element in small doses, but too much is extremely toxic."

The slides then changed to the health risks associated with radioactivity.

The next slides were "Who is Powertech?" All of the Powertech officers had worked for previous uranium mining companies. The previous companies had track records of either going bankrupt before completing clean-up, or had a significant list of violations for which they had been fined.

We discussed how it is important to give all the facts about uranium, ISL mining, health risks and the Powertech officers and allow the public to come to the same conclusions we did. Our intent was to educate, not influence. We believed that if we treat people with respect by giving them all of the facts, they will rise to the challenge of sincerely thinking through their decisions. So we did just that, we laid out the facts without commentary or sensationalism.

We finished the slides and moved on to the issue of security at the event.

Lisa told us, "My experience with these kinds of businesses is that they sometimes create disruptions at these events. So don't be surprised if a guy from Powertech shows up and attempts to dominate the conversation. Or sometimes local people that you don't know attempt to dominate the conversation. The way the presenter should deal with this is to say that there will be a question and answer period at the end, please let me finish what I am here to talk about. If that doesn't work, the presenter should then turn to one of our assigned security detail and say, 'Could you help this person by answering their questions outside please.'

We want to think about who we want our security people to be. Having a big burly guy is actually not the best strategy. A young girl or friendly woman is better. This is more disarming."

Talk then turned to contacting the Larimer County Sheriff or the Wellington police and letting them know about our possible concerns. We decided that it would be better to project an image of trust and openness than asking for a patrol car to be available. We would not contact the police, but trust the fact that the media would be there in case an incident occurred. We agreed we would all have cell phones available to call 911 if needed.

Lisa then encouraged us all to make sure that we kept our cool and our heads level no matter what might happen. "It is very important that we project professionalism at all stages of the game. No matter what they call us, we need to make sure our skin is thick and we do not respond in kind."

Again, my mind started to reflect back upon some of the protests from the 60's and early 70's. Some of the types of frightening things my activist friend told me about were being brought up again. What was I getting into?

Our security ended up being two capable women who volunteered for this role. They were professional, charming and disarming.

This brought us to discussing how we should be more organized with a business entity of some sort for donations and to be able to hire an attorney as needed. Not knowing what kind of attorney we might need, we hoped that we might be able to tap into an attorney group already in place within other environmental groups.

The fact that the group of people sitting in the room all had something personal to lose because of our property, businesses and families, it was important that we find someone we could trust and would make every best effort in winning a battle. We agreed that any attorney coming into the issue would not have anything to lose so it might be difficult to find someone we could trust. Right then our trust for any professionals who were 'outsiders' was running very low. We were feeling threatened and that common thread bound us together. Already we had property owners who had come to some of our meetings attempting to sell their land to Powertech. Our initial conversations with them had us believing they were with us, yet they cut off communication and offered their precious land to the enemy. It was really feeling like war. We needed an attorney who would be a warrior with us.

> We were truly feeling betrayed. We were seeing that those who were supposed to offer some support, such as our elected officials, were not. We were watching how some of the people who we thought might join our opposition were unable to stand strongly alongside of us as we originally had believed they might. We were feeling unsupported by the system. This sense of betrayal turned into a deep lack of trust.

For myself, I was a lifelong Republican who believed in the system of safety regulations. I was feeling deceived by the powers that be. I thought I had a strong relationship with a system that worked. I had truly believed in property rights and that our lives would be protected by those in charge. I believed that our Founding Fathers had laid out a system that protected the life, liberty and pursuit of happiness of each American. I had followed the rules so I expected that the rules would protect me. Knowing what I know now, I was operating from a place of unconscious white privilege. I believed I was entitled to clean water, clean air and had the rights to do what I wanted to do, within the local laws of course, on my own property.

Is this really where all of us who were sitting in the room that night were coming from as well? Maybe not all of us, but I feel pretty certain that many of us might. We were a group of straight whites. We felt entitled, and felt subsequently betrayed by the fact that our government was not responding to us in our plea to keep us safe.

We also discussed what the appropriate timing might be for hiring an attorney. We didn't want to be spending money on an attorney until we really needed one.

Carol had already been contacted by an attorney. He had seen her and David when they were interviewed by Fox 31. She told us, "His group is Western.... something or other, anyway, they are supported by grants so they do work pro bono. When we spoke last night he had already been doing research on Powertech and was sharing information that I already knew, as well as a couple of tidbits that I did not yet know. That was a positive in my mind. But I haven't had a chance to check him out yet."

We discussed getting several attorneys and letting them work together. There was hesitation in working with a pro bono group, even with our lack of funds.

This was another place our entitlement showed up. Several spoke out against working with a pro bono attorney group because we had a lack of trust in their commitment. We felt like if we gave them money they would have to represent us completely without hesitation. Again, with the power/soul of money and the belief that 'he who has it is in control.'

Lisa changed the subject and asked to set a planning session so that we could have a plan with goals. "We don't want to get caught reacting, we want to be the one riding our own horse," she quipped as she looked straight at me.

"Boy, I sure would like to be able to spend time riding again. It's been a couple of weeks since I've had much time with my horses," I replied. The reality of how much time I'd need to spend fighting uranium miners was really hitting home.

I was spending a great deal of time fretting and worrying that my time management at this point was bad. I did spend a lot of time reading, posting, strategizing, meeting, reaching out, passing out flyers, and more so that was very real. Truth be known I was also very bad at delegating. The pressure I was under caused me to waste a lot of time in that ineffective frozen fear state. To be clear, there was a very real time investment, but if I had a more balanced emotional state I'm sure I would have been more effective, as well as a better time manager.

We set our planning session a week and a half away, Sunday, May 6th, again in our living room. We blocked out 4 to 5 hours to allow for in depth discussion and strategizing. We also hoped that we might have a couple of new volunteers from our upcoming meeting.

Our final agenda item was to establish a plan where we would all have our water tested. We had found a local lab who could do a thorough testing of all the metals and any radioactivity. Wanting to maintain a chain of custody on the water we would have someone from the lab come collect the water from each of our wells.

> This was our first test, before we involved both the County and the State.

Before the meeting broke up, Lisa warned everyone, "Do not share what we are talking about in these meetings outside of this group. We need to be careful about who we share candidly with from this point on. The one thing the mining industry will not hesitate to do is to plant spies."

No one knew what to say. We didn't want to take the warning too seriously, but we also didn't want to disregard her experience. So the group broke up with just a little more lack of trust for anyone who was not in this room. Especially me. I was finding it more and more difficult to trust anyone.

After the meeting, Lisa stayed to train both Jay and I how to deal with the media. I was so glad to have her expert advice. I was not too happy with some of my media experience to date, so my confidence was lagging. Lisa explained the use of 'talking points.' She encouraged us to each have a message that we would want to say at least 2 or 3 times during the interview. With a repeated message, the media is more likely to pick up what it is that you'd like to have them air or publish. Jay and I both agreed that our main message was water pollution. I added that my message included the safety of children and that we should stop at nothing to protect them.

Lisa encouraged us to come up with 10 or 15 words which clearly stated our message, write it down and practice it into both video and voice recorders. Seeing ourselves would allow us to critique our presentation. Then she reminded us that we were representing more than just ourselves at this point. She discussed our appearance and how we looked to the general public. "You want to make sure that you look professional, yet approachable. You want to look like you belong on a ranch, but aren't too rough. Make sure your hair is always neat and your clothing is clean and matches." We discussed our current looks and changes that we should make.

In Lisa's signature blunt and honest way she addressed Jay first. He has always worn his hair long and dresses very casually. Lisa encouraged him to wear more button down shirts rather than the fleece pullovers he loves. She then asked if he would consider cutting his hair. He said he'd think about it.

My turn.... Lisa told me that I needed to quit smiling so much. "This is a very serious issue and we don't want people to think that we are taking it lightly. I know that you are not, but you generally end sentences with a chuckle or a smile. People who are wondering about this issue, might see that you think this is a joke." She then encouraged me to practice on tape or on the camera and it would become easy for me to change my habits.

Jay and I felt like we had been exposed, washed and pressed into what other people would like to see us be. The uncomfortable advice was very good and we tried to take it to heart as best we could. We thanked Lisa for her honesty and I felt tons of gratitude. We really wanted to win this battle and were willing to do what it took to appeal to those who might be judging who we were.

When Lisa left, we picked up from another long night and went to bed feeling rather odd about ourselves. I was beginning to feel as though I might be living in someone else's skin. The horses were taking a back seat, my lessons were mostly ineffective and suddenly I was thrust into the limelight and having conversations with elected officials as though I had been doing it for a lifetime. Greenpeace 'babe' indeed.

Friday.............

Our letter that had been published as a letter to the editor in the Rocky Mountain News appeared on the front page of the Wellington tribune. The newspaper included the announcement regarding the public meeting the next night and our phone number. The newspaper had also published a photograph that was one of an open pit uranium mine. I got an anonymous phone call.... "Do you realize that the photo of mining is not the ISL mining that is being proposed?" "Yes, I do," I replied. "I had nothing to do with the photo." "That's all, just wanted to make sure you knew that." He hung up. Weird.

Fort Collins Weekly News had an article written by Greg Campbell.
"When the price of uranium collapsed in the 1990's, it resulted in one of the most flamboyant bankruptcy cases in state history, the liquidation of Denver uranium magnate, Oren Benton's vast empire to satisfy debts of more than $1 billion."[7]
Was how it began. After extolling the history of Mr. Benton and his personal collapse with that of uranium prices, it went on....

"But just as crashing uranium prices caused one multimillionaire's dream to implode, so too may rising prices and the scramble to fill a global demand ruin the ambitions of those with far less personal wealth at their disposal."

Mr. Campbell tells some of our story here, then continues....

"Powertech seeks to capitalize on uranium's growing demand by extracting it in the fastest way possible, through the use of a leaching technique."

The article describes the leaching process, then quotes Jay, *"I would expect the first thing of concern to be the potential for the groundwater contamination. There are any number of cases where they have groundwater contamination, surface spills.... these aren't directly from Powertech, but from the in-situ process."*

The article continues with Richard Blubaugh, Powertech's vice president of environmental health and safety resources stating that he knows of no groundwater contamination. Then continues on....

"Blubaugh adds that the mining proposal is still 'at the very early stages' – the project has not yet received mining permits from the county, state or federal regulatory agencies and it may be that after further study and exploration that in-situ leaching isn't the best option for extracting the uranium from near

---

[7]   Fort Collins Weekly News, Boom Time For Uranium by Greg Campbell, April 18-24, 2007.

where the Davis's live. If that's the case, Powertech would consider the more expensive – and intrusive – option of an open-cut mine.

'That's a possibility,' Blubaugh says, 'All options are on the table... We don't have answers yet to many of these questions that are being posed. There's still a lot of baseline work (to be done) to characterize the current environment.'

What's clear, however, is that the uranium in Powertech's new acquisition will come out of the ground one way or another, as long as it's economically feasible to do it.

'What's driving it is the need for power, the need to keep the lights glowing and the TV's on,' Blubaugh says. 'There are still two billion people in the world that don't have electricity, and there are 440 nuclear plants in the world in 30 countries, with more being planned.'

Blubaugh says it's typical for those living near a proposed mine to be concerned about something they're unfamiliar with.

'It's kind of a knee jerk reaction, it's a fear thing to radiation,' he says. 'Most people don't know much about it, but they're around it all the time. Just living in the state of Colorado gives you more radiation than living in a place like New Jersey.'

Be that as it may, the Davis's and other landowners aren't eager to risk exposure to even more radiation if it can be prevented. Jay Davis says his current priority is to learn as much as he can and to help inform neighbors and regulators about his concerns. But he admits that there may not be much he can do to stop the mine.

'Ideally, what I would like would be that everything went away, and it went back to the way it was,' he says. 'But they own the mineral rights and the mineral rights take precedence over the surface rights in Colorado. Right now our goal is to make a lot of people aware of what's going on. It's something they've not even heard of, for the most part.[8]"

---

8   Fort Collins Weekly News, Boom Time For Uranium by Greg Campbell, April 18-24, 2007.

The Loveland Reporter Herald also ran a front page article. A small map with the location of the proposed uranium mine highlighted near the Fort Collins, Wellington and Nunn area.

"A group of residents worries about a proposed uranium mine about 20 miles northeast of Fort Collins will contaminate Front Range water supplies and pollute the area with harmful amounts of radiation." [9]

Included, was a small block with the information about our meeting the following evening. Ms. Depperschmidt wrote about the technical data of the proposed project, number of acres, amount of uranium Powertech intended to extract, etc.

"After the uranium is removed, the water is cleaned and returned to the area.

Opponents of the mining operation say the water may be contaminated when it is returned to the earth, polluting the water supplies with radioactive waste.

If the water is contaminated, it will affect the people who live downstream from the project, as well as the people who eat the food produced by farmers in the mining area, Robin Davis said.

'It doesn't sit well with me to allow our water supply to be contaminated,' said Davis, who owns livestock on the land and also runs a 4-H group that rides horses near the proposed uranium mine. 'It will affect the whole surrounding community.'

Davis wants the public to understand the uranium extraction process of in-situ leaching and wants the company to explain to concerned residents the actions taken to correct past mistakes of in-situ leaching.

Powertech's vice president of health, safety and environmental resources did not return calls. But the company maintains that the in-situ uranium mining process is safe, and that the company will take proper precautions to avoid contaminating the water supplies." [10]

---

[9] Loveland Reporter-Herald, "Worry Grows, Community on Edge over uranium project." by Ann Depperschmidt, April 20, 2007

[10] Loveland Reporter-Herald, "Worry Grows, Community on Edge over uranium project." by Ann Depperschmidt, April 20, 2007

These articles all include how uranium is used for nuclear power and the statistics of the number of nuclear power plants in operation as well as proposed and under construction.

Every one of these articles ended with a for more information blurb: www. nunnglow.com and www.powertechuranium.com were both listed.

When I logged on, my e-mail account had a note from a neighbor .5 mile to the south of us. I had only briefly met these folks when I had stopped by to drop off some information regarding our 4-H club. They were a young family with 4 girls ranging from approximately 3 to 11 years of age. They had moved into their newly built home around 4 months earlier.

The note from the gentleman asked me if he could talk to us about what was going on. I invited him to stop by that evening after work. He agreed.

I called Jay to make sure he could be home in time to meet with this neighbor, then called Carol to see if she and David could be here as well.

When our neighbor arrived, I could tell that he was a professional from his business attire. He was a nice looking blonde who looked fit but not athletic, a working dad. I asked him how his kids were. He shared some of the adventures of being a dad of 4 girls. We laughed about the cross he had to bear. I could tell he really loved his daughters.

Jay, David and Carol were already sitting around our dining room table. I invited this neighbor in and offered him some lemonade. He accepted it and took an empty seat at the table.

Jay introduced himself and David and Carol. "So what the heck is going on with this uranium thing?" The neighbor asked. "I thought uranium was only on the western slope."

"Yeah, I know what you mean, I never figured we'd be fighting a uranium mine out here," Jay replied and started to share some of the information that he had been gathering about the ISL process. We pulled out a laptop and showed this neighbor the Powertech Uranium Corporation website for the graphics of the ISL process.

This neighbor shared how he worked for a local health care provider and that he already knew quite a bit about the risks associated with heavy metals and radionucleides.

We talked about how we were planning on opposing Powertech's plans. He had already briefly looked at our website so we began talking about the violations that are occurring at other operating ISL mining sites. We encouraged him to join us at the meeting the next night and to join the other neighbors from the area in our opposition.

He mentioned that he had heard that Powertech was buying land in the area and wondered if Powertech would buy his place so he could leave. He went on to talk about how they were not even entirely unpacked, and he sure didn't want to put his kids at risk. We told him that we knew about properties that had been purchased by Powertech and told him a little bit about our meeting with them. I shared that Powertech mentioned they might be willing to purchase all of the properties in the vicinity of the mine. Since his property was south of the proposed mining area, we did not know how much of the surrounding area Powertech would purchase, or if they really would purchase all of the land.

As the conversation progressed, the poor man slowly turned as white as a ghost. We could not give him the answers he was looking for. He was starting to realize just what it was he is in the middle of. As he got up to leave, he told us that he'd stay in touch and shared that he sure did not want to see this mine go in. I got up to walk him to the door and noticed that he had never touched his lemonade.

When I returned to the table, David said, "Boy, I think that is the most frightened I have ever seen a man in my life. I feel really bad for him."

"I feel really bad for all of us," I replied.

CHAPTER 10

FIRE... THE FIRST SHOT

Saturday, April 21, 2007

Another perfect Colorado Spring day with a deep cerulean sky.

Tap, tap, tap... the For Sale sign went up in the yard of the neighbor who had come over the night before.

None of my calls nor e-mails were returned.

Our group arrived at the Leeper Center an hour early to set up. We had room to set up about 60 chairs in theatre style facing a projector screen where we would be showing our Powerpoint.

On the wall we hung up a map of the Cheyenne aquifer with dots which represented all the recorded domestic and livestock wells. Plus a parcel map of the vicinity of the proposed uranium mine by Powertech. With an enlarged a bullet pointed list of many of the spills, leaks and other violations that were currently happening at other ISL mine sites.

David set out a couple of props. He wanted everyone to maintain the focus on the water, so he put out a pitcher and a large glass of water on the table right in front of the projection screen.

Our 'security' (the friendly women) showed up and we gave them bright orange mesh hunters vests so they could be spotted easily. They took a couple of our new yard signs up and placed them at some key intersections with arrows to direct people to the event.

At the entry we had a greeters table with sign-in sheets and a flier on the history of uranium mining. An adjacent table was set up with the petitions, a volunteer signup sheet and 'a can' in which folks could place any much needed donations.

Our presenters did a brief, dry run through our presentation to make sure everything was working. Once we felt good about how our set up was going, we all gathered together in a circle of prayer. We invited God to help us in this journey, knowing it was much too powerful for just us humans. It felt good to know that we were coming together in this way…"Where two or more are gathered together in my name, I will be there." We took it to heart.

A couple of reporters from KRFC came in early, Carolyn Harding and David Peterson. They asked if they could set up a microphone next to our projector. They wanted to record the entire meeting. "Can someone talk to me in a brief interview before the meeting?" Carolyn asked.

Everyone looked at me. "I can talk to you." I answered with a nervous feel in my gut. What was my message? Kids, water, uranium inherently unsafe..... Was that 15 words? How should they go together? I was nervous about remembering my opening for the presentation let alone staying on track with a reporter. I had practiced for both but speaking in public was really a challenge for me. Oh well, here we go.....

"Can we find a quiet place so I don't pick up all the background noise?" she continued.

I didn't know the building well, but I knew there was a hall that lead to the bathrooms, so we went down it. As we started to talk, someone came to use the bathroom. This kind of disruption would not do, so we tried a door that we discovered was unlocked and found an office room that was quiet and private. The privacy only served to make me more nervous because now I was entirely in the spotlight and the microphone Carolyn was holding up to my face felt even larger.

Carolyn was very nice and disarming, but my nerves were out of control. I just could not remain present. She did not ask me too many questions, I'm sure my voice sounded strained and small since I was not breathing. After just a few moments we rejoined the group in the meeting room. I spent the next several moments beating myself up for my lack of effectiveness in my new role as media contact.

> Yep, my habit of disassociating showed up here again. I had so much coming at me that night and my fear was great that I automatically escaped by disassociating. I didn't even know yet what disassociation was so I couldn't have even addressed it in an effective way. I didn't know about grounding exercises or how to do them. I didn't know about trauma first aid by breathing more deeply. I didn't know any of this. So, I was ineffective in my statements. I was out of my body so I could not rely upon the wisdom of my body to come forth through my voice.

> My lack of presence continued to show up. I was trying so hard but I just wasn't fully there.

I nervously joined Jay and Ann as they were visiting about technical/science stuff regarding uranium mining. I didn't hear a word they said as I watched the door and worried over what I might have said on tape and fidgeted with my notes for my speaking debut. I wouldn't even have known if they had spoken to me.

I stressed over the turn out for the meeting. Would we be an overflowing crowd? Would we even get 5 people? Would the meeting turn into an anti-nuke activist rally much like Powertech said it would? Would Powertech come? Would there be confrontations? Would we have to call the police? Would any more media come? Would any legislators come? All I could do was wait and try to breathe.

5:45 pm a couple of the first cars began to show up. As they came in and signed the sign in sheet, we had a total of 6 new people in the room. These few people drifted around the room and looked at our posters, I looked at the clock. Almost 6pm. Would anyone else show up?

Just then, to my delighted surprise, State Representatives Randy Fischer came in with Representative John Kefalas. Lisa was near the door and went to them immediately. She walked them towards the front of the room to introduce us all. I knew Representative Kefalas through some work we had done together through our respective churches. We were both involved in a group that pulled together the premier "Way of the Cross" event through the streets of the City of Fort Collins. This Good Friday solemnity has a social justice theme and continued for several years since we began it in 1998.

It was good to see John again. John is a rather short man, with a unique look. Thick, dark hair and a racially ambiguous face with an olive skin tone. His concern for the common man virtually emanates through his eyes. Though we differ politically, we have many of the same ideals. We hugged as we reconnected. "Good to see you, John. Congratulations on your election." I hadn't seen him since he had been elected. The 2007 legislative session was his first at the State Capitol.

"Thank you, Robin. It's good to see you. I have some concerns about this uranium mining. We are still in session, but Randy and I felt this was an important enough issue to drive down from Denver for. I'm curious about this meeting," he replied.

This was the first time I had ever met Representative Fischer. I don't know why, but I was surprised to see Lisa was so friendly with these two state legislators. My e-mailing back and forth with Representative Fischer had me very curious about him. I was happy to finally meet him. "Thank you so much for coming tonight." I shook his hand.

He seemed friendly and very approachable. Randy is a Caucasian man of average height, balding, with open and friendly eyes. "Thank you for inviting us. I'm anxious to hear what will be said tonight, but I am already concerned about this proposal for a uranium mine so close to Fort Collins." He replied.

Lisa encouraged them to sit in the front row and then sat down with them. I turned to see the door filled with people entering the venue.

Laura gave me a hug when she arrived. How I needed that bright spot of encouragement right then. I turned away from her as she went to find a seat and noticed that a line had formed and was going out to the parking lot. People just kept coming in.

As the chairs filled and a few folks were left standing at the back of the room, the clock said 6:05pm. Time to get started. I took my last deep breath before approaching the podium and called the meeting to order. "Thank you all for coming. It's really nice to see that so many people have come to listen to our concerns regarding the proposed uranium mine in the area." I spoke over the general chatter as it died down. There were a few stragglers still coming in but we had determined to stay punctual in both our start time and our ending time.

"First off, I'd like to recognize any Local, State or Federal elected officials that might be here tonight. I know that there are some here. Would you please stand so we can see who you are?" I already knew about Representatives Fischer and Kefalas, so I was hoping others might have come. We had invited all of the Larimer and Weld county elected officials. All of the City of Fort Collins, Town of Wellington, Town of Nunn, city of Greeley, our district and adjacent districts State Representatives and Senators, and our Federal Representatives and Senators. Only Randy and John had stood up. I thanked them for coming and they sat back down.

"Are there any representatives from Powertech Uranium Corporation here?" I then asked.

We all looked around. No one spoke up.

A voice from the crowd asked, "Did they know about this meeting?"

"Yes, they did," I replied.

I continued, "We are a group of concerned citizens. You are looking at a group," I waved my hands toward our presenters up front, "who are your neighbors. We're ranchers, farmers, business owners, landowners and families in the area. After finding out about the proposed uranium mining project for the area, we began doing some research. We felt the need to share with our community the risks of the in-situ leach mining process. The intention of this meeting is to educate our community about the in-situ leach mining process and the way that it contaminates. Powertech Uranium Corporation is the company who is proposing this uranium mining project.

"We are concerned about our Colorado water supplies. As you can see," I point to the map of the aquifer with the wells dotted on it, "we have a multitude of wells already that rely on the water that will be affected by this in-situ leaching process.

"So without any further ado I'd like to turn this over to the folks that you guys are really interested in listening to." I had a slide that bullet pointed our agenda for the meeting. "The folks who can talk about what the in-situ leaching process is, what the potential health and environmental impacts are, and who Powertech Uranium Corporation is. Then we will open up the floor for a short question and answer session." I was so nervous, it was difficult for me to get these few words out. I'm sure I sounded as nervous as I felt.

I breathed in a shallow breathe and continued, "Our first presenter is Dr. Ann _____."

Ann stood up as I her handed the powerpoint projector remote and sat down. Relieved to be breathing again, I began to look around the room in earnest now. This didn't look like what I had in my mind as an anti-nuke activist gathering at all. The room was filled with people who fit in the small town of Wellington. I recognized a few of our neighbors and a couple of our 4-H families. I noticed that everyone was dressed casually. Some were in cowboy hats, some in farmers implement ball caps, some were more yuppie looking. A person could not have pigeon-holed this crowd at all. Older, younger, middle aged, male, female... a diverse group.

Ann introduced herself, shared her credentials and went on to discuss what the in situ leach mining operation was and what it looked like. Ann's background as a teacher made her discussion of how the in situ leach mining worked easy to digest. She was clear without speaking over our heads in too much technical jargon. Ann was clear in letting the crowd know that the process would be happening in our aquifer. Our drinking water. Our irrigation water. Our livestock water.

"To get the mineral out in the first place you need to change the chemistry of the water under the ground within the aquifer. What they do is alter the PH. One point that the company continues to make is that they are not using acid to extract these minerals. Everyone knows what an acid is. It's a scary thing, right? The only thing that defines an acid is the particular PH. What they plan to use for this project is to make the PH basic. Which is going the other way. What they plan to use is sodium bicarbonate. Also known as baking soda. So, that doesn't sound so bad, right? But, it's still a base. A couple of examples of other basic things, and one of the most common ones you'll find is drain cleaner. Do you really want drain cleaner in your water? I don't.

Don't be fooled by the comments that this is okay because it's not an acid. A base and an acid will both burn you the same way."

When Ann had the powerpoint slide up of the multitude well heads and the material piles. An audience member broke in, "Where are these pictures from?"

"They are in-situ leach mining operations currently active in Wyoming." Ann replied.

I could hear the room shifting in their chairs. I sensed that they all understood how this was not as benign of a process and Powertech wanted us all to believe.

Ann went on to discuss more details of the uranium extraction. Then said, "They will be taking as much of the uranium as they can. The thing they won't be taking away is the other mobilized minerals. Things like arsenic, molybdenum and especially of concern in this area, selenium.

In meeting with the Powertech representatives last week, they told me that selenium is an issue in this area. I know it's an issue all along the front range, but it's not an issue in the area they propose to mine until they stir it up and bring it to the surface. It's way underground right now."

Ann closed by showing a bulleted slide and stating, "A summary of what in-situ leach mining is:

- It's in the ground where the ore body is.
- It's a process that alters the PH of the water, thereby
- Removing the minerals, and
- The leftover waste can be toxic and difficult to deal with and very difficult to remediate."

"Now I'll turn this over the Lisa." Ann then handed the floor to Lisa.

"I will add my thanks to everyone who came tonight, I'm glad to see so many people here. My background is in environmental policy and I worked as a researcher in the uranium mining industry several years back during the last uranium boom." Lisa introduced herself.

Lisa spoke about uranium and its characteristics. "Uranium begins to break down once it's exposed to oxygen." She charted its process of breakdown all the way to lead.

"Exposure to any amount of radiation can produce health threats." She shared as she spoke of the safety precautions that we are given and our care providers take during x-rays. "The highest risk is to children and seniors."

Lisa then shared the risk already presented by the prospecting holes and that it will increase with more holes being drilled during the mining process. "These holes can cause contamination between aquifers."

Lisa went on to describe the detail of how the piping systems in the ISL process are prone to leakage. "This is another way that cross contamination between aquifers can occur. Or even just contaminating the aquifer they are mining in. Retention ponds and flooding are another source of possible contamination."

"There are complex chemical reactions going on and some of those reactions are not always controllable. History shows all sorts of problems from in-situ leaching."

She then quoted the Nuclear Regulatory Commission from a report they had put out in January of the current year, "Although these in-situ leach mining techniques are considered more environmentally benign than traditional mining and milling practices, they tend to contaminate the groundwater."

As Lisa said this, I really hoped that the group was paying attention. When the very commission in place to regulated uranium mining states that the in situ leaching process tends to contaminate the groundwater, why are they even allowing this process to be permitted?!?!

> As I sit here several years later after asking that question over and over again, I don't have to ask why. The why is greed, entitlement, and a lack of respect for LIFE. The capitol letters are to signify the greater reality of life. LIFE as in the Spirit of life and all of life not just a few lives.

Lisa pulled up her summary slide: "In summary:

- The reason uranium mining companies like in-situ leach mining is it's kind of out of sight, out of mind compared to an open pit mine.
- It's inheritantly unsafe because of the uncontrollable chemical reactions.
- One of the biggest problems can be existing fractures in the layers below the ground that may not be known about."

Here, Lisa handed the floor to Carol.

"I'm going to talk about Powertech as a company," Carol began.

She had done a ton of research on all of the current Powertech officers. Each one of them had a history of working in the uranium mining industry for many years. And of course, each one had played significant roles in companies who had left behind a legacy of destruction and pollution that we tax payers were still cleaning up. Superfund sites. Carol didn't have to hyper-inflate anything, she just showed a timeline and history with each of the current officers and let that information sit in the room as the crowd took it in.

Our presentation ended with David sharing his concern as a rancher and how growing up on a farm gave him a deep understanding of the incredible value and fragility of water. He spoke from his heart as he shared how water would disappear and reappear in different places because of gopher holes and natural cracks and fissures in the land. He closed by saying how when one stirs up shit, it stinks much worse. A powerful close.

At the end of the power point presentation all of the presenters stood at the front of the room for a question answer period. One of the first questions we received was by someone who lived two miles to the west of us. He had already heard about the plans Powertech had because we had told him just a week before. He was really angry at first because he would have never heard of their plans if we had not told him. He lived outside of the 500 foot radius that Weld County uses to notify locals of any development/ permitting plans, no matter how impactful the application may be outside of that 500 feet. His was really not a question but more of a commentary: "We are being trampled upon by everyone else. First the Chronic Wasting Disease Incinerator, then the Super Slab, now a Uranium mine! I have no property rights and I'm tired of it! This stuff needs to stop! Everyone thinks they can come out here and destroy my property and I've had it! ..."

On and on, it went like this. He needed a place to voice his opinion. He needed a place to feel like he was being heard. He used this meeting to vent out as much as could. Listening to him, I felt his victimhood. I completely understood. I felt like I wanted to throw this kind of tantrum too, but.... I also felt embarrassed. Embarrassed that he was speaking the same way I felt inside, and embarrassed that adults do act in these childish ways when they feel victimized and powerless. We all feel like we want to throw that 2 year old tantrum, occasionally. We want to roll around on the floor and scream and cry until someone listens. We need someone who is in power to listen to us and to really hear us. We need to feel like someone actually cares about our humanity, about our LIFE.

> What happens too often is that this sort of emotion is made wrong. My experience now shows that emotion is not wrong, it just is. It is there as a beautiful gift to tap into in order to find how it would like to be heard. When I feel an emotion, I now ask, what is that emotion informing me? What is the message in the emotion? When we make the emotion wrong it comes out more and more in tantrums until we really listen to it. The landowner who was holding the floor so that he could vent was just spewing all of his unresolved traumas into the room. He was transferring what was really going on inside of him onto the battles that he has had to fight in order to feel like what is sacred to him was protected. While he was speaking there was a part of me that really wanted to do the same. My own history of victimhood so wanted to project and transfer all of that stuff right into this room too. I'll give credit to the prayer and the support that I had from those joining me in this fight for helping me not do that at this time.

Unfortunately, as well as fortunately, the tantrums do not work. We have to pull up our big girl and boy pants, let go of the pouty face and approach the solution as adults. We need to hear the message in the emotion and be able to act upon the solution in an effective way. Thankfully, Lisa had handled these kinds of tantrums before and was able to help him calm enough to feel heard and gain some control of the question/answer period again.

Next, we had several good questions about the technical aspects of the process. It felt like several people were really seeking to know what was really happening. Then a man who was standing at the very back of the room spoke up, he worked in the ISL uranium mines in Wyoming. He wanted us all to know that there are spills, leaks, and excursions just as we warned about in our slides. When asked his name so we could talk more to him, he would not give it. He did not wish to lose his job. His testimony at this meeting really have us a boost. We already felt sure that the dangers were very real, and this 'miner' reaffirmed our concerns. His testimony also helped many people in the room believe us.

We also heard from folks who were able to add to our information. One gentleman in particular said that he had worked at Rocky Flats in Boulder. Rocky Flats was a United States nuclear weapons production facility near Denver, Colorado that operated from 1952 to 1992. In 2000, Congress proposed transforming Rocky Flats to a wildlife refuge, setting aside 6,400 acres after cleanup and closure. The Rocky Flats National Wildlife Refuge Act passed in 2001. This gentleman worked there during the clean up and said that they discovered during the clean up that radioactivity goes in all directions. It doesn't just flow downstream the way that Powertech wanted us to believe.

Steve Tarlton with the radiation department of the Colorado Department of Public Health and Environment stood up and introduced himself. He told us that he was glad to see so many people already engaged in this issue. He assured us that the process of permitting for Powertech would give us plenty of opportunity to voice our concerns. He handed out his card to many people that day. It was nice that a state regulator took the time to show up to a grassroots public meeting on a Saturday night. He had to drive about 75 miles one way from Denver to attend so he really did go the extra mile to do his job.

The last person to speak up was a woman who had fought this exact fight before in the 1970's. She lived near New Raymer and was a lone warrior attempting to stop ISL mining for uranium in the Grover/Keota area. When she stood up to talk, her anger was palpable, she basically called us all to arms. Her journey from 40 years prior was a long and arduous one so she was not interested in seeing this happen again. As I look back on her passion, I can see how she was frustrated that we had to deal with this again, and how her ranching lifestyle was one of hard work and self-reliance. This woman had been alone in bringing awareness to the lack of respect the drillers had at the time. She was known for bringing a clay flowerpot to the state capital whenever she was there to testify or speak to legislators or the governor. The flowerpot was one she had picked up in a field where she found it covering an abandoned bore hole. "The drillers used these clay pots, hub caps, and beet pulp to do a half-assed job of closing their abandoned bore holes," she virtually yelled. The same things that Jay had been saying about the abandonment of the bore holes were being made a reality by this woman.

A few days after our first meeting I drove out to this woman's home and collected an entire box filled with photos and newspaper clippings and documents from when she had been trying to stop the mining. When I asked her to help us, she declined. She said that the way she had put her life on hold and was so obsessed about the proposed mining of that time had put a severe strain on her life and her family and her health. She shared how stopping this mining was all she could focus on at the time and how she could not go back to that person again. Unfortunately, she was not able to stop a pilot project that took place in Keota, but she did get some regulations regarding the abandonment of boreholes. Her journey and her photos as well as the information regarding some of the past practices of uranium mining companies were invaluable to us.

The only thing that had stopped the full on ISL mining for uranium at that time was the fact that it was not financially viable. Uranium prices fell dramatically at about the time they were to be starting production. No wonder she was so angry and called everyone to arms at our meeting. She said the only thing these people understand was a shotgun and a good gate! Not exactly where we were hoping to go, but my activist friend and her stories just keep showing up.

After the official meeting broke up several small groups of people remained behind to talk and to get to know one another better. I looked up to see a tall, sharp, and what looked like to be very young man walk towards me.

"Hi, I'm Jeff Parsons. I'm an attorney who works on responsible mining issues. I'd like to do whatever I can to help you guys."

My initial reaction was that this guy couldn't possibly be an attorney. He looks like he's 18 years old. Cute, without question, but not my vision of the type of attorney we would need to fight Powertech and their proposed mining.

"That's great," I replied. There were several people gathering around me and some of our core group was trying to get my attention at the time too. "Let me introduce you to some of our group." David was standing closest so I introduced Jeff to David as I was being called over to help someone find the sign-up sheets where they could volunteer to help.

I found the sign-up sheets and picked up the valuable filled out sheets. Turning around I nearly bumped into a short, blonde, woman with a stack of papers in her hand. "Are you Robin?" she asked.

"Yes." I replied as I noticed that these papers had highlights and a bunch of notes on them in multiple colors.

"I'm Andrea. I've been putting fliers up about this atrocity everywhere I can." She went on, "I have a bunch of information here that I've been finding. We just can't let this happen here. What can I do to help?" She handed the papers to me. I handed a volunteer sign-up sheet to her and while she was filling out her information, I noticed that most of what she had highlighted was information about nuclear power. Handing the papers back I thanked her for her work and told her that we were focusing on the water and not the nuclear power debate. Personally, I was still torn on the nuclear power debate so it was easy for me to hand those notes back to Andrea.

Clearly Andrea was motivated and I wanted to keep her excited so I told her, "Letters to the editor will be helpful, as well as helping us get some petitions signed."

"I can do that. I'll send you information as I find it too. I'm good at digging around and reading articles."

"Very good, I have your e-mail here. I'll send you a note right away so you have ours. Have you joined our Yahoo! Group yet?" I asked her. She shook her head. "I'll send you an invitation, so you can get on and you can post some stuff too." Now that we are moderating the posts anyone can pass along anything, it just won't get posted until we have a chance to 'vet' it. I encouraged Andrea and again expressed our need to stay focused on the issue of water contamination as we agreed to stay in touch.

The next person to approach me was a somewhat reserved, middle-age gentleman, his round glasses made me think that he was either an accountant or a musician. "Do you have a good e-mail database put together yet?" He asked.

"Well, we have a start. I've started a Yahoo! Groups where several people have already signed up and these sign in sheets will give us more," I replied.

"I was just recently involved with helping shut down the chronic waste disposal burn site. I have a pretty extensive e-mail database that I might be able to pass to you," he shared. Chronic wasting disease was epidemic in Colorado at that time and a proposal to build what was essentially a crematory for deer and elk who had been diagnosed as having this disease had been proposed and successfully opposed in northern Colorado. Public health was determined to be threatened by the smoke that would come off the burn site. "I found that the internet and e-mail are very effective in getting public involvement in an issue like this."

"Yeah, we are finding that this issue is spreading like wildfire with the help of the internet. I am finding that I just cannot keep up and could use some help. Would you be willing to help me?" I responded.

"Umh, I just finished with the chronic waste issue. I might be able to get you the e-mail addresses, but I don't want to get too involved with another issue just yet." He answered. "Besides, I don't like working with organizations. I'll be happy to help get the word out, though I do see this as a valid opposition."

"Have you signed our sign in sheet so I have your e-mail?"

"Yeah, I'm right here." He pointed to his name on the sign in sheet. "Jack." Jay had joined me by this time. I introduced Jay and Jack and got my card out for Jack.

"Thanks Jack. Here's my card with my e-mail address. We'll be in touch." I shook his hand. By this time the room was beginning to clear.

Our little core group was so energized. We actually had a professionally good and open meeting. We had shared straight up information; what we knew about ISL mining for uranium, the health hazards and Powertech. We had also learned from others and their experiences. Plus, we could tell that people were not too happy about the prospect of a uranium mine in the area. The clean up of the room went really fast as we were all on such a high.

Once home, the energy from the meeting would not allow me to sleep any time soon, so I logged onto my e-mail. I already had an e-mail from Jack. "Hi Jay and Robin. Great meeting. Thanks for putting it on. Thought you'd want to see this..." He forwarded an article that had come out that day in the Northern Colorado Business Report.

The article started out by highlighting that Powertech is a Canadian company who plans to mine for uranium in north Weld County. They reported that Powertech has contracted with a Denver firm for the environmental studies then goes on to give the information on our informational meeting in Wellington. This all felt very good since it was balanced and reiterated how a foreign-owned company planned to do toxic business here.

This article also confirmed that Powertech would begin their open-pit mine with a sand & gravel operation that would commence very soon. This information was in conflict with what the Powertech representatives had told us just a week ago.

After reading it I forwarded it to Jay's and Carol's e-mail addresses. These quotes stood out most to me:

"A rising global uranium market has spurred Powertech to develop the mineral rights it bought in October from Anadarko Petroleum Corp., the successor to the Colorado mining company that discovered the uranium deposits in the early 1980s. The company says the rights have the potential to yield more than 9 million pounds of uranium for use in the nuclear-power industry.

The company paid $4.5 million for the subsurface rights on the 5,760-acre tract, plus annual payments of $200,000 to Anadarko until uranium is produced and royalties of 6 percent of the value of the uranium extracted.

The company plans to extract uranium through a process called in-situ leaching, whereby treated water is injected into sandstone formations 120 feet to 620 feet beneath the surface. The uranium within the sandstone is dissolved into the water, which is returned to the surface, where the mineral can be recovered.

Powertech officials say the process is far less invasive, safer and cheaper than conventional surface mining techniques. But a group of area residents, led by Nunn homeowners Jay and Robin Davis, say the process poses environmental and public health risks.

The opponents say the uranium-contaminated water has the potential to spread through the aquifer, affecting water supplies far from the mining activity. They also say radiation exposure in the mine vicinity poses significant health risks.

The tract of land in question is already pock-marked with more than 3,000 drill sites where the original prospectors worked to estimate the amount of uranium in underground deposits."[11]

Up and down went the roller coaster of my emotions went:

- I was energized and excited about the meeting,
- glad to see an email for a new contact already,
- disappointed to read this sort of article that showed the business aspect of the uranium mining and the huge thing we were up against,
- challenged in trusting the gentleman who sent this to me (what was his motivation – was he promoting the mining operation?),
- happy to see that a balanced article had come out,
- excited to realize that the incredible amount of work I was putting in and the press releases I was throwing out might be making an impact,
- and sad and angry that one meeting would not make this thing just go away.

I hoped I would get some sleep at some point that night. As soon as I drifted off, the dream began again... *The black mare craned her neck downward until her whiskers touched the water inside the water tank. She drew back a little as her whiskers vibrated with the energy of knowing that they were in contact with something that is not for the highest good of the mare. But, she was thirsty, so she pushed through the vibrational warnings.*

---

[11]   April 20, 2007, Business Report Daily, *Uranium prospector secures permit help*

CHAPTER 11

WARRIORS UNITE

Monday, April 23, 2007

I woke up to a brisk breeze on a cold, yet sunny day. I had decided to not do anything with uranium until the meeting we had scheduled that night. I knew that the e-mails might get a little out of control, but I needed a break after our success on Saturday night. I also needed to be with my healthy horses after that darn reoccurring nightmare. I prayed it would not come true.

Our horsemanship study group was scheduled for the morning. I had a personal mission of helping Evan with his filly and really moving our group forward after I had messed up so badly the previous week. I sat down to write some notes about some of my observations from the past several weeks. I don't know how much of it had to do with all that we were going through with the uranium mining issue, but the underlying current seemed to be trust and respect. As I thought about how each of the students was either approaching their horses with too much pressure in an effort to demand respect, or approaching in a way that begged "please trust me," so that the horse really had nothing to respect or to trust, I felt it was time to seriously address the topic of trust and respect in horsemanship. With my notes and my study guide in one hand, I started down the hill with my cup of coffee in the other. I was focused, energized, and happy to not have uranium on the brain. I was able to get all of my horse chores done and even had time to drink a little more coffee as I reviewed my notes before anyone showed up.

I pursed my lips as I looked at my watch and noticed it was our start time, looking up I saw no one was coming down the road. Edgily, I again reviewed the lesson plan and the goals I had in mind for the day. After what felt like an eternity, I looked up in time to see Laura pulling in. Her arrival led the way for Sally and Evan to pull in shortly thereafter.

I remained seated at the table while they greeted one another after parking and waited for them to join me. They had barely sat down when I quickly began sharing the notes that I had made and drew their attention to a section of our study guide without much of a greeting. I was finally prepared, but these three seemed less than enthusiastic based upon their arrival time. It was up to me to begin leading again, or lose this part of my life that was so important to me.

I encouraged them into a group conversation about the difference between trust and respect and what it meant to each of us as we worked with our horses. This required more vulnerability than I had the skills to coach out at the time, but we had as meaningful of a discussion as we could.

Time to put our discussion into action in the round pen. It was mutually agreed upon that we would start with Sally's young gelding first. She had bought her 6 year-old son a 3 year-old Haflinger gelding with the thought that she would have the Haflinger, Winter, trained by the time her son had grown some and had become a more confident rider. Winter was to be her son's lifelong 4-H horse and friend.

As Sally released Winter into the round pen, the snap in the air along with the energies from our group, and most likely from me especially, encouraged him to take the initiative of galloping and kicking up his heels.

I watched his energy for a bit before moving to do the demonstration about trust and respect in a way that met offered him the space in which to be himself. When I opened the gate to join him, Winter stopped on the opposite side of the round pen to watch. I stepped into the middle of the round pen and he gave a little buck and continued his gallop using the fence as his guide. I watched him gallop then asked Winter to do a direction change using a small motion at first to see if I had any of his respect or trust in that moment. He was focused on playing and responding more to the commentary from my students at first, so I had to increase the pressure and apply a lot of directed energy to get him to tune into me.

With the energy that I had available to me and Winter's already heightened state of excitement he responded very quickly and emphatically. What I intuitively knew was that I needed to make a slight move back to allow Winter space. This made him feel respected enough to be allowed to move within the space of the round pen rather than driving him to want to find an exit out.

Each time I sought a response from Winter I began with a subtle ask and increased pressure based upon his level of response. I'd had a day of rest and was feeling up after our meeting on Saturday. I was present, in touch, aware and energized. Winter was young and fit and playful. We operated on high speed.

After a short while both Winter and I were breathing hard. We were in a dance of connection that felt euphoric. Winter liked to play. I met him where he was and we played together with a lot of energy. I trusted his intent, he trusted mine, I respected his being, he respected my leadership. We ended with some nice, controlled turns and a pleasant halt where, afterwards we both approached each other. I reached out my hand while he reached out his nose as we connected physically saying, 'Hello and thank you'. Trust and respect. Winter lowered his head as I pet him on the forehead and then neck.

I turned to exit the round pen and Winter attempted to follow. I smiled back to him as I asked Sally to come in and to follow my lead. As a teacher, you don't always know what your students are seeing through their own filter until you see it mirrored back to you. Sally went into the round pen with ferocity. Winter was galloping around in no time at all. She was <u>demanding</u> his attention without <u>asking</u> for it first and not giving him space when he did respond, just asking for the next transition. No question, she was getting the job done and she sure had Winter's respect, but I knew it was more from a fear place rather than a trusting place. I attempted to encourage Sally to feel what was going on so she could really tap into her own knowing of how to gain both trust and respect. She finished up with Winter stopping and looking at her as he waited in a braced state. She dropped her energy and was able to approach and pet this forgiving soul as he then dropped his head in submission.

I could tell she felt good about the experience since she'd had success in achieving Winter's submission as well as getting the direction changes and then the halt. I found myself triggered by what I had just witnessed. It felt like domination tactics after I felt that I had shown how a partnership of trust and respect is what we were really seeking. I unconsciously went to that frozen fear state and was not sure how to effectively coach her. Instead I asked Laura and Evan if they'd like to work with Winter, hoping they might be able to show a gentler feel.

Neither Laura nor Evan wanted to work with Winter, so I ended up bypassing the opportunity to be a good leader and coach by moving on.

> If my own emotional intelligence had not been so damaged at this time I could have re-entered the round pen with Winter and discussed the differences between the techniques that Sally and I each had shown. I would have done my best to not make Sally wrong, but to encourage her to be more subtle and conscious of her impact on others. I could have demonstrated how to ground into the feel of the situation by remaining grounded in our own bodies and listening to the emotions as they arose. I could have demonstrated how to intuitively listen to the horse and how to be in relationship with him rather than just dominating him using technique. Instead, I got triggered into an ungrounded state by the situation. I lost any real leadership skills because of my habit of disassociation.

I could have had a discussion about using emotion in a positive way as our messenger rather than just unconsciously projecting it onto another. For that is what Sally was doing, her own anger came out in her need to perform with perfection and to follow technique no matter how the other was responding to it. In her mind, at least she was getting the job done. Granted, it was by domination but she had achieved the understood goals. She had not looked for a willing partnership, she just went in with her ideas of what needed to be done and demanded that they get done. Winter acquiesced. Sally did not have the awareness to look at anger as the driver in the situation. She fell into the same cultural camp as I did, that anger is wrong. She would have said she was just driven and that she knew what she needed to get done. Winter needed to follow through. Period.

If Winter showed any thoughts of his own, such as not wanting to participate in this dance at this time, she demanded his attention through more forceful energy. A better way is to recognize where the energy is and to meet it there, not take it and whip it to the ground so you can remold it into your picture. What Winter and I had experienced was an energetic dance. I'm sure I used more domination techniques at that time than I would now – because that is where I was at the time. Even with this in mind, I know that I had met Winter at a much better place as a partner because of his response to me. He came to me in the end. He and I thanked each other for the dance. We had turned it more into play rather than work.

Today, this study session would have gone much different.

We switched from Winter to Magic, Laura's mare. Laura was in the spotlight as she started to ask Magic to move around the round pen. Magic pretty much ignored her and was passively moving off but not really paying attention to Laura's cues. After a few minutes Laura asked me to demonstrate what she should do. As I switched places with Laura, Magic picked up on my vibes and started trotting around the round pen right away. Horses are very sensitive to any emotions that we are telegraphing. I knew that I felt focused, but obviously there was more than that going on because I had just moved into the round pen and Magic began moving without my asking.

> Today, at this stage of my life I understand how Magic was responding to my ungrounded state and the emotional turmoil that I was attempting to keep stuffed. I was inauthentic in that I did not admit that I had this deep underlying anger from previous violation that was really coming to surface with the current violation from Powertech. Sally's domination tactics with Winter had triggered me and I didn't fully realize it. I was completely disassociated and didn't know it. Magic did. And she didn't know if she wanted to be around when I came back into my body. She knew things were off and just wanted the heck away from me.

Magic began galloping as soon as I presented what felt to me was just a slight movement to encourage a canter. She was running in fear of what I might do because she felt my incongruence. I knew I'd have to dramatically change my presentation to develop any trust from this mare. So, I began by working with the energy that both Magic and I were feeling at the time. Again, things were done at top speed. I had the energy and so did Magic. Little did I know at the time we were both working from a fear-based place. I was fearful that I'd have to honestly look at myself and what was driving me; she was fearful about who I really was in the middle of all that turmoil she could sense around me.

Thankfully, my skills allowed me to have the timing and presentation it took to gain Magic's attention. She responded to my cues in a way that achieved control of the situation, and soon Magic began to somewhat trust my leadership through the skills. After Magic and I developed a dance and a connection that worked for both of us, Laura felt good and wanted to trade places with me. Laura mirrored back to me that sometimes a person must be firm in order to get a change from a horse, but that if we begin by first asking, we can build trust rather than perpetuate fear. I was happy to see that some of what I was trying to get across in my demonstration was being picked up. To gain the respect of a horse (as well as any person), we sometimes have to insist that they listen, but if we begin by asking first, the horse (and any person) will also begin to trust.

> Trust and respect are truly gained through an acceptance and honoring of boundaries. Both your own and the other's. My boundaries were so violated at this point I really didn't know which end was up or what was mine and what was the other's. I didn't have good boundaries because I didn't yet know *how* to have good boundaries. I didn't know that having good boundaries wasn't an "either/or" but they could be fluid and reset as needed. I was teaching about trust and respect, but I didn't fully understand them yet, because I didn't fully understand what it took to respect myself.

> This is what Magic felt. She knew that I was hiding something deep and that it was beginning to demand that I look at it. In order to not look, I truly was ungrounded most of the time. When I stepped into the round pen Magic saw that I was not fully in my body and therefore not able to act from a completely congruent place. During the exercise, Magic helped me find a more grounded place, though, I was still not able to really stay there and listen to what was asking to come forward. The grounding that Magic helped me find is what allowed my skills and timing to come forward in a way that allowed Magic and I to create a dance which Laura was then able to see and mimic.

Laura led Magic from the round pen and Evan began to herd his filly, Moriah into the round pen. The last time Moriah had been worked with was the week before. She remembered that she did not have to put the halter on, so she refused again this day. She was understanding that she could control the situation because we had not yet earned her respect. Evan worked with her awhile, but was getting frustrated. I knew that my energy this day would really send this filly for a loop, so I asked Sally if she'd like to try. The difference between the way Moriah responds to our energy and the way Winter responds is night and day. I hoped that Moriah would help Sally see her way of demanding was not really fitting for a horse.

Sally did see that Moriah would shut down with much demanding, so she went to a fun way of just working with Moriah's curiosity by throwing her coat on the ground and walking away from that. Sally did have Moriah's full attention, but she would not allow Sally to touch her. This little filly was an excellent teacher in the ways of gaining trust and respect equally. She taught us all a little more that day and we had a good conversation while Moriah stood at a distance. Evan expressed his need to return to his office so we were out of time to work with her. Moriah had to be herded back to the paddock with our human fence, yet again.

Evan rushed off to work and Sally and Laura took their leave as well. As I watched them pull out of the driveway I found I was not interested in doing anything with uranium, so I decided to drive into town and spend some energy, or in this case some money.

Jay and I had an annual tradition of planting at least one tree as our Earth Day celebration. I realized that Earth Day had come and gone over the weekend and we had not even talked about planting anything. We generally would find a tree that was inexpensive but just the right fit for a location that we had picked ahead of time. We had picked a location for a tree and had dug the hole more than 2 months ago, but since the whole uranium issue had heated up we had decided not to buy a tree for that spot after all. We had wanted a fairly large shade tree to go in the middle of a square hitching rail Jay had built a few months before. We knew that the size of tree we were talking about would not be inexpensive and we were unsure of what our future at Mustang Hollow was at this point. We had learned a rough lesson by spending a great deal on the trees that we sadly left behind in Masonville, and did not want a repeat.

That day I had changed my mind. I wanted a tree. I wanted some stability. I did not tell Jay. I just got in the truck and found myself at a nursery on the southeast side of Fort Collins that had advertised a tree sale. I had a mission. I wanted a BIG tree. I wanted a statement. With the threat of the uranium mine we had become so uncertain about whether or not we would be staying at Mustang Hollow that we had stopped all projects of improvements. My dream was being shattered by Powertech. I needed something that would lend some positive energy in the direction of a belief that we would be victorious.

In the nursery office I told them what I was looking for and they gave me some suggestions for the types of trees that would do well in our area. I climbed into the golf cart with a lot worker and we started driving down the aisles of some trees.

"What do you have that's a little larger?" I asked as he was showing me some 1" and 2" caliper trees.

We ended up going towards the back of the lot where the bigger trees were. We drove down a couple of aisles and I spotted the tree I wanted. It wasn't the fullest, the prettiest, nor the most symmetric, but it was the one I had to have. "I want that one," I told him as I pointed. "Look at that big shoot going straight up to the heavens. I like the spirit of this tree. It's reaching for the sky no matter what else is going on."

Tagged, loaded and paid for, the tree and I carefully headed home. I parked the truck near the hole and then got out to admire my new friend. The tree was a 4" caliper hackberry. I named it my anti-uranium tree and didn't tell Jay about it until he saw it right before the landowners meeting that night.

His reaction was not quite what I had hoped for. He couldn't tap into my need to put down roots. He was concerned that we wouldn't be at Mustang Hollow for long and that I had just wasted several hundred dollars. He did like the tree because it was so big, but he also expressed concern about how we would get it planted. I just knew that I had to have it. The tree was a huge symbol. We were not going anywhere!

As soon as everyone was organized in the living room, Carol began to ask me if I had seen an e-mail she had sent me that day. "Nope." I said loudly. "I was checked out of uranium ALL day. I went and bought me a huge honking tree and it's sitting in the back of my truck right now. It's my anti-uranium tree."

That's exactly what I said, 'a huge honking tree.' Since we have recordings of all of our meetings, while listening to this one in preparation for writing this book I was shocked at how frenetic my voice sounded. I was feeling good because of our positive meeting on Saturday but also knew we still had a huge fight in front of us. My fear, even though I was attempting to stuff it, was palpable. My voice just could not deny the war that was going on inside of me as well as the one that I was in the middle of physically. Frenetic.

We had invited Jeff to attend this meeting since he had followed up with us and expressed his desire to help us. He shared his recent victory regarding cyanide leach mining at the Summitville gold mine and encouraged us that we could win. As I sat and listened to him I really wanted to believe in him, but he looked so young. He was articulate and confident and reassuring to us as he spoke, but he looked so young. I really wanted someone to come in and rescue us, but this guy just didn't look like what I had in mind as a hero. He looked so young.

After Jeff talked to us for quite awhile, we had decided that we needed to come up with a name for our group. A few of us threw in some ideas for names, I suggested NCAPL (Northern Colorado Aquifer Protection League), but a blind vote had us deciding on CARD (Coloradoans Against Resource Destruction). And so it was, we became CARD.

Near the end of this meeting our phone rang. I let it go to the machine, but then picked it up when I heard the voice of a gentleman who said he had been contacted by Powertech Uranium Corp. He started to describe how they were interested in leasing his minerals and added that he lived near Briggsdale, Colorado. I asked him a couple of questions about this situation. He went on to tell me that he had a contract to lease his mineral rights, a surface access agreement and a $12,000 check that they said he could cash if he signed the two other documents. It turned out that the agreement would be with Geovic Energy Corp, not Powertech, but it was for the same ISL mining process for uranium as what Powertech was proposing. He began asking me questions that I could not answer. He wanted to know where he stood if he only owned half of his mineral rights and how he was affected if his surface was already under a CRP contract with the USDA. (A CRP contract is an agreement to leave the grasses on the property in their native state for as long as the contract lasts. The USDA will pay property owners to leave their property undisturbed in an effort to study the natural way the grasses grow.)

We exchanged e-mail addresses and I told him I would keep him up to date on our efforts, but wondered if he'd like to talk to an attorney we had in the room right then. He readily agreed, so I asked Jeff if he would talk to him. Jeff took the phone and they spoke for some time.

Later that night I read an e-mail from this same gentleman that further detailed his reasons for concern. He described how he had asked the Uranium Company representative what might happen if he did not want to lease his ½ of the mineral rights on the property and the other owner did lease theirs. He was told by the representative that he would likely be forced to allow exploration due to something similar to the "law of eminent domain." He was currently making attempts to negotiate the purchase of the other ½ of the mineral rights so this would not be an issue.

He went on to describe how he had done his research on the ISL mining process and had also sent his family the information from the uranium mining company. One daughter who is a professor of wildlife biology at Washington State University and whose husband is a chemistry and biology teacher at a High School, had looked at the information and spoken to peers who were geology professors. They all had encouraged him to not lease the mineral rights because of the fears of contamination of the groundwater.

He had also sent the information to another daughter who teaches biology and chemistry. Her graduate research at Purdue University was in microbiology. She expressed a strong concern for the ISL proposal as well.

This gentleman and his wife had been living in Parachute, Colorado during the time of some of the mine clean up operations on the Western Slope. They had watched as mine tailings were used to backfill foundations for homes and other buildings in the Grand Junction area. He said that they were very knowledgeable about the danger and potential effects of exposure to uranium. His wife's father had worked for the Atomic Energy Commission in Grand Junction during the uranium boom in that area and, though not proven, they feel that his work at the lab played some part in his death in 1987.

This gentleman was passionate, precise and obviously he, his wife and his daughters were all very well educated. He wrote many letters to the editor in opposition to the uranium mining. I would include one of his letters, but would rather keep his identity anonymous here.

His call helped solidify within me just how this proposed uranium mine was not just a NIMBY issue that we and our neighbors were complaining about. I don't believe in coincidence. I believe in providence. This man came to us at a time when we all needed to be reminded how global this issue was. He helped me feel even more committed in our efforts to stop this mine. Since he had helped me see that I was not in something just for myself I was able to act more effectively. I had to really embody the fact that our fight was not personal, even though it felt very personal. It was bigger than just me.

Tuesday......

E-mails were flying regarding the attorney situation. I think everyone liked Jeff as a person, but he sure didn't look like the kind of attorney we might need to go up against the high-powered variety that Powertech would have in their budget. Carol had spoken to Jeff the most, so she was quick to support him and our use of him. Some of the landowners began talking about hiring their own attorneys as individuals. Lisa encouraged us to be wise about the way we decided to spend our money. She expressed her concern that we would not be as effective if we all went off on our own rather than coming to a consensus as a group.

In the end, we knew that we did not have any collective money to spend on an attorney at that time, so we decided to see where Jeff would take us for the time being. As it turned out, this was one of the best things that happened. Jeff is extremely intelligent and quite honestly gifted in strategy when it comes to responsible mining. It was Jeff who presented us with the idea for legislation. It was Jeff who coordinated and wrote most of the legislation and regulations that then followed the law. Jeff was a true gift. It was another way that God was showing up for us.

The other thing that was happening in my e-mail box was the receipt of a large number of e-mails from people who were involved with other environmental groups. They all had the same general tone: this uranium mining cannot happen; the individual was passionate about the issue; the group they were involved with did not have the resources to take on the issue or the issue did not fall within their mission. This was very frustrating. The advice that I repeatedly got from each group was to contact another group. Generally, the list was the very same list that I had already contacted, and many times there was an e-mail from one or more of the groups pointing me back to one of the groups pointing me to their group. Round and round we go.

> The overwhelm that environmental groups are feeling keeps them divided and scattered. Even as a concerned citizen it is often difficult to discern where we should put our energies. There is so much to care about… so much that we need to do to be in right relationship with LIFE.
>
> In reality, as we get into right relationship with ourselves we can begin to see where our efforts can be the most effective. I once heard author Andrew Harvey speak about

how the best way to decide how to focus our energies is to meditate deeply on what we truly care about. Once we have that answer we can begin to direct our energies and feel like we are making a difference in what we care most about. I will add that this can only truly be achieved once enough personal work has been done so that one knows they are in right relationship with themselves.

I did have one interesting e-mail from a woman who grew up near Standley Lake which is in the runoff drainage from Rocky Flats. She said that it was very well known that the silt in the lake bottom tested extremely high for plutonium. She went on to say that there have been many discussions regarding dredging the lake to clean it up. The decision has repeatedly been to leave it because the extra environmental risk of exposing the dredgings to the air were too great. Standley Lake is a popular recreation area where people used to swim, and continue to fish. A short blurb from a tourism site says this about the reservoir: "The reservoir is the water source for the cities of Westminster, Northglenn, and Thornton, so neither you nor your pet can swim here. The lake is used for boating and fishing and is stocked with trout, bass, catfish, and perch."

I got up to pour myself a glass of water.

As the water filled my glass, my attention was drawn to my cousins who had grown up near this lake. As children they had spent a lot of time swimming and fishing there. One of my cousins died of ovarian cancer in 1994. She was 32 years old when she died. Her husband was left alone to raise their three young children. The kids were 10, 8 and 6 years old when she passed. Since there is no family history of ovarian cancer I couldn't help but wonder if there was a connection.

The water running down my hand snapped me back. I knew this was not something that could be proven.

Drying off my hand and the outside of the glass, I felt that familiar foreboding fear and powerlessness.

My gut said that Rocky Flats and its run off of heavy metals had everything to do with my cousin's passing at such an early age. But I had no proof. It was just another anecdotal case. It was something I deeply wanted to shout about from the roof tops but knew that it would only make me look like I was the crazy lady to which they had referred. I needed to appear professional in my pursuit of success against the uranium mine. I decided to use this book to honor my cousin and her victimhood to our culture's need to ignore what is right in front of us.

As I took a deep drink of the water I wondered how long it would remain drinkable. I wondered if I would be the next cancer victim in our family.

Continuing my research, a January 2007 article in the Denver Post caught my attention. It was written by Dusty Horwitt, an energy and public lands analyst with the Environmental Working Group in Washington, D.C. The article, *Uranium Boom: New rush gains steam in the West*, said things such as:

"Late last year, the Bush administration delivered two big gifts to the nuclear power industry, signing deals to help India produce more energy from nuclear reactors and for Westinghouse to build four new reactors in China.

Those countries are half a world away from Colorado, but the worldwide resurgence of interest in nuclear power runs risk for the state's public lands, health and safety.

The nuclear industry's efforts to recast itself as a supposedly clean source of energy - a spin echoed by the administration - has helped spark a uranium boom in the American West. Interior Department records show a sharp increase in mining claims on Western public lands since 2002, driven by a seven-fold increase in the price of uranium.

As recently as 2004, no uranium interests were among the largest mineral claimholders in the West. Now, government data show that uranium interests are among the biggest claimholders across the region - in Colorado, Arizona, New Mexico, Oregon, South Dakota, Utah and Wyoming.

According to Interior records, mining interests staked just 300 claims for uranium in Colorado in fiscal year 2004. But in the two years since, uranium interests have staked almost 3,500 claims in the state. The new claims are concentrated near historic uranium towns of Nucla and Naturita in Montrose County, and in the Rio Blanco and Moffat counties in the state's northwestern corner.

The Department of Energy has begun a decade-long project to clean up 12 million tons of radioactive uranium mine waste near Moab, Utah, that have contaminated land near the Colorado River.

The waste is a threat that could pollute drinking water for millions. Cleanup estimates range between $412 million and $697 million.

In a recent series, the Los Angeles Times found that abandoned uranium mines on a Navajo reservation in the Four Corners have led to deaths from lung cancer and a degenerative disease that's come to be called Navajo neuropathy. Among other routes of exposure, the Navajo have unknowingly drank water from abandoned mine pits and had constructed some of the homes from the radioactive mine waste.

The Grand Junction Daily Sentinel recently reported that residents of Monticello, Utah, have unusually high rates of cancer they believe were caused by a now-closed uranium mill.

Residents recalled replacing their screen doors because the metal mesh would become yellow and corroded. Schools used ground-up uranium waste in kids' sandboxes.

Mining interests routinely leave behind multimillion-dollar cleanups, yet -unlike timber, oil and gas and every other extractive industry operating on public land - they pay no royalties to taxpayers. There is no federal fund to clean up abandoned metal mines.

Mining uranium is not the only concern heightened by the nuclear resurgence. We still have no answer to the problems of disposing of the waste from nuclear reactors.

Even if the government's designated national nuclear waste dumpsite at Nevada's Yucca Mountain is opened, storing waste will mean 50 years of cross-country nuclear waste shipments through major cities. We should ask if spending billions of dollars to subsidize the nuclear industry is a better choice than investing our tax dollars in clean renewable energy and energy efficiency.

Mining is a necessary part of a modern economy. But before permanently scarring some of our most treasured places to feed the nuclear industry, we should first dig deeper into the empty promise of nuclear power.[12]

Before our personal confrontation with uranium mining, I had never given much thought to the impacts of mining. How had I grown up in Colorado and not realized that we are filled with uranium mines and their toxic waste?

Nor had I given much thought to the nuclear waste from nuclear power. This theme was becoming more and more common in my readings.

It also struck me that it seemed typical that Canadian uranium mining companies were mining uranium here in the US to ship to India and China. Why is it okay for these foreign companies to pollute the water, land and soil here in the US while they ship the uranium overseas?

My conservative nature was especially riled by the statements about the number of dollars needed to clean up after these uranium mining companies finish their work and move on. Who is paying for this clean up? The taxpayer of course! Not to mention the part about no royalties being paid to the taxpayer from uranium mining.

And yes folks, it still continues today. And not with just uranium, but with oil as well. Just do a search on Canadian

---

[12]   *Denver Post,* Uranium Boom: New rush gains steam in the West by Dusty Horwitt, January 27, 2007.

oil companies who sell overseas. Make sure your search engine is a neutral one so that you get an honest search without the entrainment.

It appeared to me that this very thorough article was a synopsis of every reason why we should be so concerned about uranium mining. Foreign corporations were polluting our natural resources, especially our water, leaving us with the mess to clean up at our cost. What was the benefit to the US? I began to question the benefits of nuclear power as a sustainable solution.

Seeing the cancer statistics rattled me, especially after thinking about my cousin and Standley reservoir. I had been very close with this cousin while we grew up. I kept thinking about how I had spent many years writing letters and voting to protect the unborn and now it was looking like my government wanted to kill me with the toxic leftovers from uranium mining.

What in the world was uranium mining tailings doing in the sandboxes of school children?

My passion to stop this uranium mine was reinforced. I was feeling like I needed to do as much as I could as fast as I could. This issue had already harmed too many people. I was in rescuer mode. I had been in victim mode for most of the time so far in this issue, but now I just hopped right on over to rescuer mode as I was determined to save the world from uranium mining! My ungrounded and uncentered persona found a new source of energy from which to tap.

> The trauma/drama triangle was not something I knew about at the time, nor that I was bouncing around it, but I sure was hopping from point to point. I was most familiar with the victim and how to stay totally encamped in victimhood as I did the whole 'woe is me', 'why me', and 'I can't believe this is happening to me again' role.
>
> After reading how long the uranium industry has been perpetrating their pollution upon the US citizens and

feeling like we had a good group and an effective plan to help stop at least part of their destruction, I was becoming a rescuer. 'Let me help you out,' 'I can take care of you,' 'I'll do whatever it takes.' Not that being a rescuer is always bad, but I was doing it from a place where I was not taking care of myself first. I was not putting on my own oxygen mask before putting on the oxygen mask for the others. I was putting on the oxygen mask of the others and allowing myself to suffocate so that I could bounce back to the victim role and continue hopping around the triangle.

Of course, the perpetrator part of me showed up all over the place when I acted out with Jay, with some of my neighbors, and of course in some of the interactions I had with the Powertech professionals. 'It's your fault!' Making those that I had victimized through my perpetration feel bullied or oppressed. Again, calling folks like Powertech on their role as perpetrators is not necessarily a bad thing, but I was not doing it from a healthy place. I wanted them to feel as bad as I was.

My emotional mess was deep and the trauma/drama triangle was a common place that I invoked. The interesting thing is that as you begin to recognize this pattern you can watch someone who is in this pattern flip from position to position as they attempt to draw you into the dance. When you stand outside of the dance, they become even more erratic attempting to find that trigger that will bring you in.

We are most empowered when we don't buy into the trauma/drama triangle and own our own experience of the situation. Stepping away from the interaction will allow one to remain grounded and focused rather than drawn in, and will often make the other stop the erratic interaction so that an adult to adult relationship can be formed.

Wednesday……

My schedule was overfull between the lessons I had scheduled, our 4-H club, and now the uranium mine. The only thing I could do was to be where I had said I'd be when I said I would be there, prepared or not. I pulled into the driveway at another 4-H leaders' indoor arena where our club had been invited to participate in a saddle fit clinic. I did not feel completely present at this event at all. I was getting so sucked into the uranium issue, I just could not find balance in what truly brought me joy. Horses. Horses and kids.

Present physically, but not really mentally, I hung back rather than participating fully in the saddle fitting class. The instructors were giving many tips and offering plenty of hands on opportunities. As I was hanging back a man in a cowboy hat approached. He was the father of one of the other clubs 4-H kids. "Hey, I saw you on TV. Keep up the good work," he said. I had already had a couple more interviews by different television stations. I was always super nervous before each interview, but I was getting better at speaking and staying on point. They generally wanted to film me with the horses and, if parents allowed, with children riding. That made it easier for me. I had the support of the horses and the distraction of keeping track of the kids and the horses when that happened. I truly was becoming the 'poster child' in our efforts.

"Thanks," I replied as I shook his hand.

"These guys can't be allowed to come in here. They'll destroy our groundwater." He went on to tell me how he used to work at an ISL mine site in Wyoming. "It's a bad deal. They are always spilling, the well casings are always cracking. It's a real mess."

I asked him if he'd join our efforts and share his personal experience working in the industry.

"I really can't," he said. "I have a pension that I don't want to lose. These guys are pretty tough on anyone who opposes them. I'd rather just remain anonymous and stay away from it. But know you have my support and everything you are saying is true. It's not safe and it pollutes the groundwater."

I thanked him for sharing his experiences with me. I would soon begin to realize that this was one of many of these kinds of anonymous tips from people who work or had worked within the industry. It was a little frustrating because these people had so much fear or had much to lose in speaking out, but also motivating because these were people who were living what we were reading and also what we were speaking about. These people reinforced what we sensed and felt in our guts to be true. Each experience such as this helped to propel us forward. More providence.

Sunday, April 28, 2007.....

A few of us gathered to develop a master plan and to become more organized as a group. Lisa led us as we discussed our strengths in our message, our challenges that people would present us with and our top 5 goals in the effort to stop the mining. This meeting took 4 hours as we brain-stormed, clarified and really developed a master plan. Our goals included changing the distance of the boundary that Weld County uses for notifying area residents on public meetings for permits or land use changes. It's currently 500 feet, just far enough to reach one or two properties on each side of the property in question. This is horrifyingly inadequate. Many of our neighbors already expressed gratitude for our contacting them since they would have never known about the proposed mining if we hadn't.

Our goals also included stopping any permits along the way. We had listed all the permits that Powertech would need and discussed making sure that enough people knew about this proposal so they would speak out in opposition. Numbers in opposition were just as important as having good facts with which to oppose. Elected officials and permit granting officials truly do look at numbers of constituents who are speaking out. We needed to make sure that people were interacting with this issue.

So, gentle reader, even if you are not interested in doing activist types of things, stay involved in what you care about enough to write the letters and make comments on the permitting process. They always have a time when you can make comment online and/or in public. Use this right of our democracy to allow your voice to be heard.

What our goals of the time did not include was any type of legislation. We never even went there. We had no idea where we would really be led.

Wednesday, May 2, 2007......

We had another presentation scheduled at the Nunn Town Hall. I could not attend because of a 4-H conflict. The challenge of juggling 4-H, private lessons, and organizing and leading the opposition to the proposed uranium mine was really getting to me. I knew my butt was getting kicked and wasn't sure how I'd be able to keep it up.

Still, it was a good day since I had another letter to the editor published in the Fort Collins Coloradoan:

"The issue of proposed uranium mining in Weld County is quite serious. Not owning mineral rights, and understanding that we may have to allow access to minerals on our property, I approached the proposed uranium mining with an open mind. After hours of research into in-situ leaching, or ISL, I feel compelled to share some of the things I've learned.

ISL mining for uranium is proven to contaminate water supplies. Our Federal Government has said as much: go to www.nrc.gov or www.nunnglow.com to see government reports and scientific data. Powertech Uranium Corp continues to state that they know of no water supplies that have been contaminated by ISL. Very odd because one of the agencies from whom they must receive a permit is reporting just the opposite.

Being new to the Nunn area, my husband and I had to seriously consider taking Powertech Uranium Corps offer to buy our land and leave this issue behind. Understanding how ISL pollutes makes running from this issue a non-option. We cannot watch as water that is used to feed livestock and grow crops we eat becomes contaminated. The economic vitality of Weld County is threatened just as surely as the water supplies are threatened. Do not think that Larimer County is immune.

Do your research, understand what ISL will do. Come to our meeting at 6pm tonight at the Nunn Town Hall. Staff from Weld County will share information about the permitting process for uranium mining. Powertech Uranium Corporation is invited, but not as a presenter. They must host a public meeting of their own.

Robin Davis
Nunn"[13]

Christopher Wood who is the publisher of The Northern Colorado Business Report wrote an editorial that came out too. *"Uranium Mine Proposal Offers Plenty Of Time For Evaluation.[14]"* Mr. Wood expressed that his first reaction to the proposed uranium mine is one of opposition, but he continues the article by encouraging people to look into the issue completely. The title of his editorial was based on the fact that Powertech would take at least 1 year to apply for permits and then the time for review could also be years long.

As I read this my initial reaction was that this might give folks an excuse to not put this issue on their priority list. Our society is full of so many things that keep people busy, it would be easy to read this kind of editorial and think: "Whew, at least that is not something I have to think about right now." I didn't like that kind of thought process regarding the proposed uranium mine.

---

[13] May 2, 2007, Fort Collins Coloradoan
[14] April 27-May10, 2007, *Northern Colorado Business Report,* "Uranium Mine Proposal Offers Plenty Of Time For Evaluation by Christopher Wood, April 27-May10, 2007

Sure, Mr. Wood appeared to lean towards our side from his comments and the adjoining pencil drawing of the radioactive symbol on a sign that says "Welcome To Nunn." The drawing included farm buildings and energy windmills in the background. It clearly looked like renewable energy is preferable to a toxic area. Mr. Wood also strongly encouraged people to do their research and look at the facts. All very good.

My reaction was one of concern that people would become too complacent after reading this kind of article.

The North Forty News had an article on the front page of their May edition also:

"Uranium Mining in Works

A company's interest in mining uranium in northwest Weld County has landowners concerned because their homes are sitting atop the mineral rights that they don't own.

Powertech (USA) Inc, in October notified several Nunn area residents that the company had purchased uranium mineral rights and proposed to mine them with in-situ, or in-place leaching, which is also called solution mining."

The article went on to quote some of the Weld County regulating agents about how they encouraged Powertech to seek their State and Federal permits before applying for local permits. I felt like this was the way for Weld County to put this sticky issue off as long as they could.

This article was the first time I recall seeing Powertech adding the (USA) to their name. I like to think we had a little something to do with that since we were quick to talk about their incorporation being from Canada.

The article went on to talk about how Powertech hoped to start extracting uranium by summer 2010. It also talked more of the permitting process. Kim Ogle provided his e-mail address as a contact for questions. This encouraged me. I had already been in communication with Trevor Jiricek and now I was able to add Mr. Ogle to my list of those to be contacted on a regular basis as well. Both of these contacts were published on our list of public officials with whom to stay in contact and to express concerns. We wanted as many people to have their voices heard as we could.

After catching up on all of the press and dealing with my e-mail account, I spent some time cleaning the house and deciding what to wear. Today was the day that Tom Beardon from the Jim Lehrer show was supposed to come with a film crew. News Hour with Jim Lehrer is a nationally syndicated program. This felt like "big time" so I was pretty nervous. The woman who had arranged the interview had asked me about what we were doing and also about our 4-H club. I asked her if we could film some of the kids who come to Mustang Hollow to ride. We arranged a time that they could come shoot our land and our set up, the area for the proposed mining site, a couple of lessons, and a sit down interview with me.

As we talked more about what all we were doing, we set the date of this shoot for the date of our Nunn Town Hall meeting so they could film that as well. The plan was to interview me in the early afternoon and to interview Jay at the Town Hall meeting since he had to work until then. I hadn't asked how long the filming would take, but I figured they would be here about an hour and then I could finish my prep work for the 4-H Musical Freestyle clinic that I had that evening.

The film crew arrived about an hour earlier than I had anticipated. "We decided that the day was so nice that we would drive up and just get a feel for the area before we sat down with you," Tom explained when I answered the door. "We won't bother you too much yet, but I wondered if you have a map of the area and you could direct us to where we might be able to film some activity."

I invited him and the crew in so I could show them a map. In our reams of paperwork that we had collected we had several USGS quadrangle maps of the area, so I ran a copy of the area of interest for them. "There really isn't any activity to film yet," I explained. "We have been able to generate interest in this issue before Powertech has begun any mining." I then pointed out some of the Powertech owned property and where the open pit mine was proposed, as well as other features that I thought they might find interesting.

They asked me if it would be okay to film from the road above our property while I did some horse chores. "We like to show the real-world view of lifestyles."

I agreed and then watched as they slowly drove down the road, stopping at several locations to take in the view.

I couldn't concentrate on much else at this point. I wanted to make sure I looked presentable. Not too dressed up because I was dealing with horses, but not my normal stained sweatshirts, ratty jeans and dirty barn jacket either. I decided on a bright peach, long sleeve blouse that was a good color for me, newer jeans and a new sleeveless light blue vest I had just purchased the week before. I must have looked at the ensemble over a dozen times in the mirror. I worried that it might be too bright, look too new, might not be what people expect a horseback riding instructor to wear, etc. I worried that I might get slobbered on by a horse and these lighter colors would have a glaring green stain in no time. I worried that I might get chilled with the sleeveless vest while I worked with the kids. I worried about what Lisa would say about the presentation that my clothing said.

My hair and makeup were easy decisions. I wear my hair long and in a pony tail 90% of the time. I needed my hair out of my face, so up it went. I put on a little mascara to highlight my eyes, and a lightly colored lip gloss and called that good. But I still worried over my clothing.......

As the crew was unloading their equipment they asked me about the schedule that I had envisioned. The kids I had invited to come ride in front of the cameras were the children of both Sally and Evan, since they had horses boarded with us. The kids were at that fun and open age of 6 and 7 years old.

They were not scheduled to arrive for almost an hour.

Tom decided to do some interviewing and filming with just me until the kids arrived. We talked a bit in front of the horses, they filmed me while I filled water tanks, and it all felt like it was going pretty well. I've found that these reporters and their crews are all very good at helping people who are not used to being on television feel more comfortable.

I was very nervous about making sure I stayed "on message" and that I spoke around my 15 or more words over and over. As I was doing my best to do this, I noticed that Tom was just as expert at finding ways to draw me away from my practiced message. I'd be talking about something after he asked me several questions, then I'd begin to realize how far off "message" I was, so I'd start to stammer as I'd try to figure a way to bring the topic back to the message about water. Very stressful.

Finally, the kids arrived. Being very gregarious, they were excited about being filmed and readily agreed to having microphones attached. Neither one of these kids acted shy about being in front of the camera at all. Of course, they both had their routines already established at Mustang Hollow so they forgot about the cameras quite quickly.

First, we had to look at the chicks that I had gotten the previous week. The film crew loved the kids with the baby chicks. We spent way more time with the chicks than the horses. We did finally get everyone redirected to the horses. The kids and I got comfortable just doing what we normally do with the preparations of the horses and then a little riding. We had all forgotten about the film crew by this time.

When Tom said he thought he had gotten all that he wanted with the kids and the horses, he asked me if we could do a short interview in the house. By this time, they had been with me for almost 2 hours. I kept thinking of the final prep stuff I needed to do for my later 4-H commitment, but did not want to miss out on this opportunity for national exposure. I agreed.

Thankfully, the parents and kids knew the chores well by this time so I was able to leave them behind as I took the film crew back up to the house while they did all my evening chores for me.

At the house, the film crew discussed lighting and the best places to film as they ran their checks and tests. I showed Tom the big box of information that the woman from New Raymer had given me. We pulled out several of articles from the late 70's. The cameraman got some great shots of the headlines on the yellowing sheets.

I kept an eye on the clock, and told them of my evening commitment. Just as we were talking of wrapping up, Jay pulled into the driveway. He was home just in time to get a bite to eat and change his clothes for the Nunn Town Hall meeting.

"What a great opportunity," Tom said. "Can we get an interview with the both of you before we break up here?"

"Of course," I agreed as I watched the clock. Jay came in wondering whose vehicle was in our driveway. I introduced him to the crew and he was immediately wired with a microphone and put in front of the camera.

As the clock ticked on, I knew I had to get going. We finished up the interview and I encouraged them to quickly take off the wired microphone, so I could leave.

I was running late. The News Hour film crew had been with me for 4 hours. As they were still packing up their equipment and chatting about getting a bite to eat, I grabbed my stuff and jumped into the truck to head towards the Larimer County Fairgrounds for the 4-H Musical Freestyle Prepare for Fair clinic. I was supposed to have been there early to meet our County Horse Project Leader so I could have the space prepared and learn how to use the sound system.

The drive was one of the longest 40-minute drives of my life. I was excited by the fact that we were beginning to gain the attention of national news organizations. I was feeling the rush of what I had just been through during the interview and filming. I was also feeling the let-down of reviewing what I had said in the interview and of course castigating myself for not saying certain things, or how I should have said other things differently.

Intermingled with all of these internal voices were the voices of worry about being late to something that I really wanted to be a part of. I had looked forward to being a part of this group of people who were influential in the

Larimer County horse world. I was excited to bring Musical Freestyle to the Larimer County Fair and wanted to do a great job for the kids and for my own achievement. I had been hosting musical freestyles with the kids who had been riding for me for several years by that point. We always did a Spring and a Fall event. It was my way to present a 'show' to the parents so they could invite other family members and the kids could show off what they had been learning. We all loved it. When I was approached to become a 4-H leader I shared how the musical freestyles were exceptionally good for the kids I'd been working with and asked if we could bring them to Larimer County Fair. I was supported in the idea almost immediately. This was a big deal for me.

I had tried to call the County Leader's cell phone but she did not answer. I was worried about her reaction when I finally did arrive.

I had my notes and the information that I wanted to pass out to the kids and their parents along with some music CD's, but for the life of me, I could not remember what all I was bringing with me or the way things were organized. I had not had an opportunity to review it all. I worried about all of that on the drive.

By the time I arrived at the indoor arena I was barely breathing and I had worked myself into an internal frenzy about my lack of organization. I had not eaten since early that morning, but at least I had water with me. I gathered my stuff and headed into the arena with a feeling of dread in my stomach. I continued to fight it off, because in reality I was still excited about what I was here to do. I hoped my lack of organization would not show through.

Several kids and their horses were already arriving. Some were just unloading their horses and some were already walking into the arena. I waved and chatted with a few as I walked in with a family that I knew. The Horse Project Leader was set up at a table and surrounded by kids and parents when I approached. I caught her eye and she finished taking to the families before she turned to me. It felt like forever since I realized how much I still had to do.

"Sorry I'm late. We had a news crew at our place all day." She knew a little about what we were involved in but didn't ask any questions.

"Let's get going," she said.

We walked to the sound system and she gave me directions on how to use it. She then began sharing what she had already told the families about how the clinic would go. As I listened to the agenda for the clinic, it did not follow my agenda at all. I knew that she and I had not had much chance to fully connect on the agenda, but I was also of the understanding that I would be planning and running the clinic. It felt like the rug was being pulled out from under me. I took a deep breath and rearranged my thought processes to follow her agenda.

I decided that the best thing to do was to work with her rather than make any issue. The clinic was really overdue to start already, and I knew that by being late and not taking the time to sit down with her before the clinic that she was only doing her job by making sure the clinic ran smoothly.

"Here's the microphone. Make sure you hold it close or it doesn't pick up your voice. The on/off button is here. I have a bunch of stuff to take care of, but I'll be close by if you need anything. Have Fun!" She handed me the microphone and exited the sound booth.

I took the microphone and just started playing music. I did what I could to pull off a helpful, fun and educational experience for the kids. The clinic proceeded with me flying by the seat of my pants because I was attempting to drop into the new agenda. I kept losing focus as I really tried my best to do as instructed rather than what I had planned.

As our evening of music, horses, and kids wrapped up, the County Horse Project Leader came over and asked me if she could have the microphone. As she took the microphone, I wondered what I had not covered and what might happen now. I felt like a kid who had not done her homework completely and was preparing for a public shaming. She proceeded to enunciate the rules for the competition that I had already covered but she wanted to make sure were clear. Then she thanked me for the clinic and encouraged all of the kids to have fun creating their musical freestyles.

I breathed a sigh of relief, Whew! I did okay.

My sense from the evening was one of chaos. How much of it was real and how much of it was just internal chaos, I'm still not clear. I can say that I had many parents come up and thank me for the help. The evening was at least somewhat helpful from what I was hearing. I was glad of that.

As the last kids were leaving the Horse Project Leader asked me if I'd like to go with her to get something to eat.

I was hungry since I hadn't eaten all day, but I really was too far gone mentally and emotionally at this point to be social. I just wanted to go home and have some quiet time. "Thanks, but I really need to get home. I'd like to hear how the Town Hall meeting in Nunn went. Jay should be getting home at about the same time as me."

My drive home was not much better than my drive to the fairgrounds. At this point I was trying to turn off the internal voices that were speaking about the job I had just done. AND, I was switching back and forth between 4-H leader and uranium warrior. AND, I was hungry. I fixed that with a stop through a drive through. I had no energy to get creative with food at home. In my self-absorption I didn't even think about getting anything for Jay.

I got home well before Jay. I had plenty of time to relax and check my e-mail. By the time he pulled into the driveway I was really curious about the meeting, especially since he was getting home so late.

"We were all talking in the parking lot about the night. Everyone was also really curious about the film crew," he said as he pulled together a sandwich. He had not eaten yet either.

"Did they film the entire meeting?" I asked.

"Most of it, but I noticed that they left before the question and answer period. They must have gotten what they wanted. Powertech was there."

"They WERE?!?! Interesting. How did that go?"

"Well, I was asked about selling again. I told him that I wouldn't sell unless we could continue to fight them from across the street."

"How did he react to that? Did you have the little recorder in your pocket? We need to record everything they say."

"I did have the recorder in my hand, but I had turned it off. I don't think we can record if the other person isn't aware of the recording."

"I'm sure you're right, but it still might have been interesting to at least have his words recorded." I agreed.

"I didn't even think of it. I had picked up the recorder and turned it off after the meeting broke up." Jay went on. "Ann had a strong reaction though. You should call her and talk to her tomorrow."

Jay then shared about how representation from the Weld County Planning Department was there and how glad he was that they showed up. "They gave a short presentation before our group. Mainly just talking about the permitting process and how much public input would be available. The Weld County attorney spoke on how the commissioners could not attend these types of meetings. I just don't know what to think of that, but I'm glad we had some Weld County representation at the meeting."

We talked for a few more minutes, but I was exhausted so I went to bed and fell promptly to sleep.

Jay was energized from the event so he stayed up to e-mail the group about his take on the meeting.

I had fallen asleep to an empty space next to me and then awoke with an empty space next to me. Jay had had an early meeting to attend at work. I even wondered if he had come to bed because I never heard his alarm go off either. I guess I needed that sleep.

CHAPTER 12

MEDIA COVERAGE RAMPS UP

May 3, 2007.......

We are on the front page of the Fort Collins Coloradoan. Kevin Duggan wrote an article after attending the town hall meeting in Nunn:

"Uranium Critics Speak to Crowd in Nunn"
Opponents of a proposal to mine uranium beneath the prairie east of Wellington took their message Wednesday to farmers and ranchers of Weld County.

Speaking to a crowd of about 200 people gathered at the Nunn Municipal Building, critics said the process Powertech Uranium Corp. plans to use in extracting millions of pounds of uranium from deeply buried ore deposits could contaminate local groundwater as well as a vast underground aquifer with radiation and heavy metals.[15]"

The article goes on to describe the ISL process and then quotes Lisa:

---

[15] May 3, 2007, Fort Collins Coloradoan, "Uranium critics speak to crowd in Nunn" by Kevin Duggan

"It is inherently unsafe, just like nuclear power, just like chemical manufacturing, because of all the chemical interactions that can't fully be predicted.[16]"

Then the article turns to some information about Powertech and their plans to have permits in place so they may be mining by the end of 2009. Richard Blubaugh is interviewed for this article again and claims that the ISL *"process is less polluting than traditional uranium mining techniques.[17]"*

At least he wasn't blatantly claiming that there are no places that the ISL process contaminated aquifers. Every time he was quoted in an article with that quote, my hackles went up. Even the NRC says the process tends to contaminate the aquifers.

One of our neighbors was quoted too:

"I believe in science, and I do believe someday in-situ leaching will be safe," he said. *"It's not today, it's not in the next five years and it's not in the next 20 years[18]".*

Mr. Duggan also interviewed a person who said he was a supporter of the mine. He claimed to be a local landowner but when we attempted to find him in the Weld County parcel map records, we never could. We also spent a lot of time knocking on doors for miles around us and we never met this person. In fact we never met anyone who was as pro uranium mine as he came across in the article.

This person was quoted to say: *"mining process is not understood and opposition to Powertech's plan is being driven by 'hysteria.'"[19]*

Since I was unable to attend this meeting, the only sense I had about it was from Jay. It was good to be able to read a little more by Mr. Duggan. This had been our second meeting, so I was really curious about the entire event. I searched the online edition of the Greeley Tribune. We were on the front page again:

[16, 17, 18, 19] May 3, 2007, Fort Collins Coloradoan, *"Uranium critics speak to crowd in Nunn"* by Kevin Duggan

Nunn residents express health concerns from uranium drilling by Vanessa Delgado

This article was shorter but it started pretty much the same as the Fort Collins Coloradoan article. What did catch my eye were these paragraphs:

"Richard Blubaugh, president of environment, health and safety for Powertech said the mining process the company will be using at the Centennial site is called in-situ recovery, a process that is used for surface-mining techniques. The process is done by injecting a bicarbonate solution that will mobilize the uranium. He said he does not believe the site would cause danger to people living nearby, but he can understand their fears.

"We are going to be particularly careful to be protective of human health," Blubaugh said.

He said if the company decides to drill at the site, it would begin operations by late 2009. The process would take about 10 to 12 years to collect the uranium and then another four to five years to restore the land.

According to the company's web site, the Centennial project includes 5,760 acres of uranium mineral rights in Weld County with more than 3,000 drill holes totaling approximately 1 million feet of drilling already completed.[20]"

It's always interesting to read quotes by Powertech. My cynicism by this point overruled any belief in what they had to say. The Tribune article was concise, but covered our basic concerns. Mr. Blubaugh mentions restoring the land, but says nothing about the water.

My taste for the drama was fueled by the media reports but I still wanted more...... I called Ann.

---

[20] May 3, 2007, Greeley Tribune, *"Nunn residents express health concerns from uranium drilling"* by Vanessa Delgado

"Oh Robin, you should have been there. The people who live in the area are not happy about a proposed uranium mine. I was glad to see so many attendees. Over 200........"

She went on about how the guys from Powertech had really gotten to her by talking about buying her dad's land. Ann was not impressed with how she was told that they could help her leave the issue behind with the purchase. In fact, she felt like all of her family's dreams were being destroyed. Her dad had put everything into the building of the new house. He was so excited about the prospect of having a place where the entire family could live. Her dad had given his all and she did not wish to see him go through that again in another location.

"He made me so mad that it made me cry," Ann said with frustration. "I don't want to cry in front of these guys."

Ann said that Powertech was handing out glossy brochures in the parking lot. "Everyone was taking one, Robin. I didn't get one, I wonder what they have in them. I hope people see through their pretty pictures and marketing jive."

After talking a bit more about the crowd, their reactions and the Powertech presence, we moved on to planning our next Town Hall meeting. Ann was energized and ready to really take on Powertech after this meeting and how it had impacted her.

Sunday, May 6, 2007........

State House Representatives Randy Fischer and John Kefalas asked if they could come out and see where Powertech wanted to mine. We invited them for a tour of the area that would start at our house. By now we were getting pretty good at putting out press releases and FOX 31 and the Fort Collins Coloradoan sent reporters for this auspicious occasion. We showed Representatives Fischer and Kefalas the old newspaper clippings from the 1970's and discussed how the quotes and information that Powertech was putting out looked exactly like what had been said then.

The day had a chilly, strong wind so we stayed in our house for the press interviews before a driving tour of the area. Knowing that we had a couple of legislators interested enough to physically come discuss and really understand what was going on inspired us.

We had also invited our own State Representative Jerry Sonnenberg. In fact several of us had sent him an email or called to invite him. He had indicated that he might attend, and I looked for him all day, but he never showed up. I still wonder if he wouldn't come because Representatives Fischer and Kefalas were Democrats and Representative Sonnenberg was a Republican. By this time I was getting very angry with our lack of local representation. The very title of the position 'representative' describes exactly what he was not doing. He works for us. WE voted him in. What did he think he was doing by not responding to our invitations to learn more about what was going on in his own district?!? Especially when we were getting representation from those outside of our district.

While talking with Representative Kefalas about our concerns I said to him at one point, "You know, I've spent the last several years speaking out for and praying for protection of life. I've been doing what I can to protect the lives of babies, and now our government wants to kill me." This is how I felt to the depth of my core. Not only was our livelihood threatened but so were our lives and the lives of future generations.

May 7, 2007

Another front page article in the Fort Collins Coloradoan. This article had a photo of Representative Randy Fischer and me talking in our kitchen.

"Residents Voice Concern About Uranium Mining - Lawmakers listen to their worries about Canadian company's plan"[21]

---

[21]   May 7, 2007, Fort Collins Coloradoan, "Residents Voice Concern About Uranium Mining" by Megan Read

"Rep. John Kefalas, D-Fort Collins, and Rep. Randy Fischer, D-Fort Collins, met with concerned residents who say the uranium mining will contaminate the area's groundwater and, as a result, negatively affect the health of livestock.

Kefalas, who is against the Canadian company's plan to mine in the area, said he's most concerned about the quality of the area's groundwater.

"Personally, I think the risks far outweigh the benefits. I'm here to stop this," he said.

Kefalas also said he admires the way local citizens have banded together to show their disapproval of the mining.

"It's important to see how people organize themselves," Kefalas said. "They're going to put up a good fight."

Fischer also said he disapproves of the company's plans to mine, and also shares Kefalas' fear that the groundwater will be contaminated.

"To me, protection of water resources is one of the biggest concerns," Fischer said.[22] "

I was really glad to see this as a front-page article. The understanding that Representatives Fischer and Kefalas had of how this proposed uranium mine could really impact the entire Northern Colorado area was very insightful.

I rubbed my bleary eyes. I needed a break, I had decided to give myself some down time. I had already canceled our horsemanship study group for the day the night before. I needed some time to just regroup. I planned to spend the day puttering around the house and cleaning.

---

[22]   May 7, 2007, Fort Collins Coloradoan, "Residents Voice Concern About Uranium Mining" by Megan Read

I turned on the Weather Channel as a nice background noise. My attention was immediately drawn to the destruction caused by an F5 tornado that had torn through Greensburg, Kansas the day before.

I sat down and absorbed the feeling of shock at what I was seeing of a town which I had driven through earlier that spring to pick up my friend's horse. While soaking it all in, the phone rang.

"Hello."

"Hi Robin, it's Sally. Great article in the Coloradoan today. You got your picture on the front page. Congrats."

"Pretty cool, huh."

"Yeah, Representatives Fischer and Kefalas really need to act. They need to do something about what they see as wrong. We need to make sure everyone is still contacting them." She rallied.

I knew these things, but I also just wanted a little peace this day, so I changed the topic. "So how are things with you?"

"Actually, that is part of why I'm calling........ I just heard from the Doctors office. The results of the biopsy are in. I have breast cancer. It's malignant. I have an appointment for an MRI to confirm and get more information."

"Oh Sally. I'm so sorry."

"I'm leaning towards just getting a mastectomy right now. Maybe even a double mastectomy as prevention for the future. I just want this stuff OUT of ME." Sally's voice quaked.

"Whoa. Are you sure you want to do that? Think about it. I just can't believe you have cancer. I don't know what to think. I guess we are both battling cancer now. You with it in your body. Me trying to be the first line of defense. Wow! What can I do?"

"Nothing yet. We don't really know what we are dealing with yet. The MRI will help. I have a lot of decisions to make. I have some more research to do."

"I'll pray for you." I told her with tears in my eyes.

We hung up as my attention was drawn back to the weather channel. The drama of the destroyed town in front of me, Sally's diagnosis of cancer, the potential of uranium mining in my backyard. I sat down and cried. I felt like I was in a spinning vortex. An internal F5 tornado had just wiped me out. I wanted to run away from it all, but I had nowhere to run. I asked God, "What is happening? Why all of this? What is becoming of our world?" I felt that God would not hand a person more than they could deal with. I questioned His faith in my capacity.

The rest of the day was spent in and out of tears and in a general fog. I didn't answer the phone any more that day. I didn't log onto e-mail. I can't even say what I did other than just ramble around.

Jay got home long after I had gone to bed that night. When I heard him come in I got up to tell him about Sally's news. He looked as shocked as I felt. We embraced. Later in bed I held onto him for dear life all night long. I was feeling under siege and really wanted to just be rescued. I was the little girl who needed someone to comfort her and tell her everything was going to be okay. Jay just held me but didn't have any comforting words to say.

After a long night of despair and being awoken several times by my now familiar reoccurring nightmare, I started into an upright position with the realization that I had an appointment for another television interview.

I was so spent emotionally that I never really felt nervous for this one. I was angry and tired and over this whole thing. I wanted it to just go away. My voice was strong in the recording when I watched the news later that day:

"It's a public health disaster waiting to happen," said Robin Davis, one of the concerned residents. "It's purely profit driven and they're going to contaminate our water supply for it. So we're very concerned."

And of course this was juxtaposed with our perpetrators speaking:

"There's a risk of everything," said Richard Blubaugh of Powertech Uranium. "The risk is relatively small. With good engineering and good management, the possibility of any kind release or contamination is highly unlikely."

May 10, 2007........

Mishie Daknis of the Wellington Tribune wrote a small blurb on her experience at our April 21 meeting in Wellington. *"I attended the meeting April 21ˢᵗ, regarding the Uranium mining that is proposed for Weld/Larimer County. It was very informative. This is something that will affect all of us and should be watched closely! What got my attention was the comment that it's not a matter of "IF" something goes wrong, it's When![23]"*

Very encouraging to read this kind of comment since Ms. Daknis was also a Trustee for the Town of Wellington. We needed public politicians to be on our side and it appeared that they were showing up.

May 13, 2007........

Reading the paper I noted how many articles were published on the importance of water here in Colorado and how we need to develop a plan to keep more of what we get off the mountains rather than sending it to other states. There were also many articles on energy and how we should and could go about creating sources of clean energy.

I was encouraged that we were doing the right thing. What I didn't realize was that they were a lead-in for what I was about to see the following day in the paper.

-----

[23]   May 10, 2007, Wellington Tribune

May 14, 2007........

The front page of the newspaper had a bold headline: *"Weld County gives uranium drilling firm a less-than-glowing welcome."* News page 6[24]

I open up the Denver Rocky Mountain News to page 6, there I am in a half page sized photo with my mare Auris Cordis. Her head is dropped to the ground as she looks for bits of grass to eat. I'm petting her neck while standing near some of fencing. I'm wearing my 4-H club t-shirt and a cowboy hat and I have a worried look on my face. At least I'm not smiling about uranium mining in this photo.

"Uranium worries in the wide-open spaces of Weld County, residents fear a company's plans to use a mining technique called 'in-situ' to pull uranium from beneath their land will pollute the aquifer."[25]

This was a two page article with a detailed diagram of the in-situ leach mining process and a fairly large map of the area. Mr. Hartman had called me the previous week and a photographer had been out shortly thereafter. I was getting pretty used to media types calling and taking photos of me by this time. The thing that was disappointing was how they never seemed to do a really informative article. Most of the articles were news briefs that hit the emotions of the issue without detail. I was thrilled to finally see a more in-depth article on the issue. Mr. Hartman had done his homework and was ready to educate the public right alongside of us.

I recognized many of the things we were linking to from our website. He even quoted directly from our website in a few places.

From the article:
"I think the bigger issue is that there was, over the last 25 years, a stockpile of uranium that has now been exhausted," Said Ron Cattany, director of the state's mining division. *"And the (2005) energy bill (passed by Congress)*

[24, 25] May 14, 2007, Denver Rocky Mountain News, *"Uranium Worries"* by Todd Hartman

provides some incentives for nuclear power. I think it's a combination.... that has created the renewed interest in Colorado uranium stores."

Newly formed Powertech boarded the uranium train in 2005 and, according to its website, has two "advanced stage" projects with uranium resources of more than 17 million pounds.

One of those is in South Dakota. The other is the Weld County site, known as the Centennial project. The company said it also has two "exploration" projects, both in Wyoming.

Richard Blubaugh, the company's vice president for environmental health and safety, has called the chances of contamination "vanishingly small."

He said the company believes it can do the work safely "because it's been done safely, and we have people in the company who have done it and know what it takes."

Blubaugh concedes there have been problems internationally with the technique, but he blames those on the use of acids to liberate the uranium, which also mobilizes other contaminants. His firm, he said, would use far more benign chemistry to free the uranium.

"Forget (problems around the world). Look at the United States and what is allowed here," Blubaugh said. "The technology we're talking about, to my knowledge, hasn't created a problem with any known drinking water supply.

"It's been used in this country for 30 years. The regulatory agencies wouldn't be licensing these things if groundwater contamination was inevitable."[26]

My blood began to boil as I thought of all the violations we continued to post on our website. Large spills of toxic heavy metals and radioactive elements. We continued to cite many recorded excursions of these same contaminants from within "the contained" mining location towards the

---

[26] May 14, 2007, Denver Rocky Mountain News, *"Uranium Worries"* by Todd Hartman

rest of the aquifer. These violations were generally in Wyoming and Texas. Mr. Blubaugh could say what he did because the water was not yet being used for drinking water. There were no homes as close to those sites.

Back to the article:

But "in-situ" uranium mining in the U.S. hasn't been without controversy.

Southeast of San Antonio, the Uranium Energy Corp. Has drawn scrutiny from residents who complain that drilling activities have left dirt and sand in their water.

The state also has cited the company for numerous instances of failing to follow its permit process, news reports show.

A company official said the firm is working to correct the problems and is "dedicated" to doing it right. The company also has told the media that there has been no mixing of uranium with drinking water.[27]

I thought about how lucky we were getting baseline water quality tests done. These people in Texas had not done a baseline test, so the company can say that they 'haven't polluted the water, the water was bad to begin with.' This is typical rhetoric. They do their own 'baseline' tests without state or federal oversight and present the regulating agencies with reports that show the water is already undrinkable.

When the company said they are "dedicated" to doing it right, I nearly laughed out loud. If they are so dedicated and so moral why are they already in violation to the State of Texas?

In 2005, the Navajo Nation, which covers parts of Arizona, New Mexico and Utah, voted to ban all uranium mining, including in-situ. The region's 17 million acres contains enormous stores of uranium, but Navajos blame decades of mining for a legacy of radiation sickness and other mining-related illnesses.

---

[27]   May 14, 2007, Denver Rocky Mountain News, *"Uranium Worries"* by Todd Hartman

Though the federal Nuclear Regulatory Commission agrees that in-situ mining is less damaging than conventional mining, the technique "still tends to contaminate the groundwater," according to an abstract of an NRC report on the issue published in January.

Because of that, the report said, the NRC – or its designated regulator at the state level – requires that companies set aside sufficient funds to cover any cleanup necessary.[28]

Unfortunately, Mr. Hartman did not delve into the real costs associated with the cleanup. Many of these companies would post bonds well under the dollar amount required to fully restore a mine site, then they would go out of business to avoid paying any additional clean-up costs. Mr. Blubaugh himself was directly associated with the Atlas mine near the Colorado River in Utah. The restoration of this site is still costing the tax payers millions and it may never be fully cleaned up.

In Colorado, Powertech has yet to submit an application to regulators, but Blubaugh said it likely will do so by the end of 2008, with the hope it could begin work by sometime in 2009.

But Government environmental officials, aware of the project already are gearing up to handle its review. So complex is the web of regulatory agencies involved that officials at the State Department of Public Health and Environment met this week with officials within the Division of Reclamation, Mining and Safety to sort out who is responsible for what.[29]

Looks to me like our calls and e-mails were paying off.

In all, at least two divisions of the health department, the State's mining office and the Federal Environmental Protection Agency will have a role. County planners and Weld County health officials also will have a say.

---

[28] May 14, 2007, Denver Rocky Mountain News, *"Uranium Worries"* by Todd Hartman

[29] May 14, 2007, Denver Rocky Mountain News, *"Uranium Worries"* by Todd Hartman

Blubaugh said the many agencies involved is more evidence the company plans to do things properly.

"We believe with all those agencies, all those people telling us how to do it right, we're going to do it right," he said."[30]

This article hit the entire issue from our angle, the company angle, the Federal angle and the State angle. Our arguments for why the risks associated with this project outweigh the benefits seemed to be justified through Mr. Hartman's research into ISL mining for uranium. This remains one of my favorite articles by a local reporter. Nice job Todd Hartman. I shout out a big thank you to the *Denver Rocky Mountain News* for seeing the value in running such a big and well written article.

---

[30] May 14, 2007, Denver Rocky Mountain News, *"Uranium Worries"* by Todd Hartman

CHAPTER 13

ROLLER COASTERS

Though we were already hitting the ground running we could all see how much we needed help. We had our list of those who had signed up at our Town Hall meetings and it was time to find out just how serious those who had indicated they wanted to help were. We decided to host a volunteer meeting.

We identified the areas in which we really needed assistance and chose committee names. Our core group members each took the committee in which they were already strong. We had Research, Outreach, Fundraising, and Communications. I was strung out doing Communications and Outreach. Though Steve had volunteered to create a new website he hadn't put one up yet so I was still updating our red and yellow site on a nearly daily basis with new information and links, plus helping maintain the Yahoo! Group and creating a database of contacts. I was also still communicating with elected officials regularly. I was putting out press releases and doing the interviews that those press releases generated. I was really looking forward to finding people who would help and/or just take over. I still yearned someone to take over the whole effort so I could go back to doing what I loved. My frustration and internal conflict was constant.

Everyday I'd make the choice to fight the uranium mine by making the calls, writing the e-mails, reading the information and distributing it, distributing fliers, updating the website, etc. Every day I'd feel bad about not doing what I needed with the horses and clients and the 4-H club. Every day I'd get mad and feel victimized by Powertech which drove me harder to fight them so they'd just go away. Every day.

The volunteer meeting ended up a bright spot in our efforts. It was a huge success. We ran it like a job fair with each of us presenting our needs and asking those who attended if they felt like they could help with those specific needs. We met several people who were really committed to helping. We had people joining us from all walks of life. One lady who said 'yes' to being my co-chair in the Outreach Committee, made my day. It turned out that this particular woman became a key player in CARD. What a powerhouse!

We also met many of our other key players at this meeting. We were grateful to attract a local Realtor who was elemental in organizing many of the meetings that we did in front of those involved with real estate. She was so energetic it was tough to keep up with her at times.

A middle-aged couple who already dedicated their lives to activism had found this issue to be the one to trump all the others. When not working at their regular employment, they focused completely on CARD activities. They were first to volunteer for nearly every activity we did. They were also the ones who committed to setting up, personing and tearing down the booths we had at events. This was no small effort to be available for 2, 3 or 4 days of talking with people and then re-organizing the booth for the next event.

There was a German couple who stepped right in with their skills of organization and website hosting. The technical skills we found in these two helped create and maintain all of the information we were gathering. They were instrumental in hosting and helping to create the more professional website that you can still visit today at nunnglow.com.

This is just a few examples of talented folks who stepped up and offered their skills in such a huge way to help us defeat this proposed uranium mine.

I felt so much support and relief after that meeting. Now that we had people whom we really did not know, we decided that our planning meetings needed to be moved from our living room. From then on out we scheduled all CARD meetings to a basement meeting room in a Fort Collins coffee house. Our first one was scheduled with our new group of lead volunteers for one week from the initial volunteer meeting. Things were looking organized and ready to really roll.

> Standing up for the water turned out to be a huge victory for me and my psyche. My soul needed me to be present and available for Truth. Because of the fact that throughout most of this endeavor I was either attempting to look the other way or give the responsibility for it to someone else, staying involved and present for the protection of the water and for our lives was a huge victory for me. I had to step into a place where I could not look away any longer. I could not give the fight to someone else.

> The lesson for me was that I needed to reset some boundaries. Standing up to Powertech presented the opportunity to learn how to set those boundaries.

By this time I was turning into a fully armored uranium warrior. I was stuffing my emotions and just plugging along with the lists of tasks that I had in front of me on a day to day basis. I had horse chores interspersed with uranium tasks, interspersed with 4-H leadership tasks, interspersed with horse training, lessons and other business tasks. There was not much room for anything that was just for me.

> When I say armored, I can say that I was developing some good skills through my personal growth during this time, but I was still not fully honoring the emotions that were roiling within. I continued to make the emotions wrong rather than befriending them in a functional way. I was stronger in my convictions as I was learning all that I was

learning, but the head smarts were not truly helping me
be a whole person.

Laura encouraged me to go to a yoga class that we had signed up for several
months before. I had not been in several weeks. I agreed because I also
thought it might be a good way to continue to spread the no uranium
mining word, so I went armed with fliers and petitions. Laura showed up
with her armloads as well. We laughed about how 'of course we were both
thinking the same thing.'

As we changed into our yoga clothes, we chatted with a few of the other
ladies about the proposed uranium mine and got several signatures on our
petitions. The instructor even asked for a copy of the petition to leave in
the studio along with some fliers.

As the time fell away, our instructor had to break up the lively conversation
that had ensued so the class could start. I love yoga and the way it releases
tension and in the same way allows for a better flow of energy throughout
the body.

About half way through class, I felt my body start trembling. I kept
attempting to regain control over the constant shaking.

I tried to find a place in each pose that might relieve any strain causing
this shake. No help.

Tears began streaming down my face and the trembling would not cease. I
grabbed some nearby tissues, wiped away some of the tears, and continued
to do the poses as best I could. Thankfully, everyone was focused on their
own experience and didn't notice my struggle.

Finally we got to the last pose of Savasana - the pose used to relax and
refresh the body and mind, and to relieve stress and anxiety, as we quiet
the mind while we lie flat on our backs. The trembling slowed down long
enough for me to regain a little composure.

Class ended and as I stood up, the emotions began flooding again. I stood carefully, kept myself turned away from the rest of the class and I rolled up my mat.

I was moving in slow motion walking into the changing room, remaining separate as I changed back into my street clothes.

Laura was busy talking with the group, so it was easy for me to remove myself until I felt like I could engage.

As we walked out with a few classmates, our instructor sidled up next to me and asked how I was holding up during all of this. My sense is that she had been monitoring me but didn't want to speak in front of the class.

"Interesting you should ask that." I then shared how the emotions had just shown up. "All I could think was, how dare they!" I said as tears began to flow again.

"HOW DARE THEY," I said loudly and emphatically with nose and eyes running, "What gives them the right to come in and do whatever they want to us. How DARE they....."

I found an already used tissue in my pocket and mopped up the mess of my face.

"This is really something, Robin. It's going to be a long hard battle. I agree, how is it fair? I want to really encourage you to take good care of yourself." She hugged me. "Make sure you come back next week. This is what you need to do for yourself. Make sure you are eating right and get plenty of rest. This is some really deep emotion brewing."

We parted and then Laura gave me a hug with tears in her eyes. "Let's go get some lunch." She encouraged.

A part of me didn't see how I had the time to enjoy a leisurely lunch with a friend. Instead I set that aside and justified it by acknowledging the fact that Laura was already invaluable to me and someone who I could really talk to about the uranium issue. Laura is often quick to point out the humor of any situation so she also really helped me maintain balance with laughter. I eventually agreed and we got in our vehicles to drive across town.

As we arrived at the restaurant, I was feeling pretty close to being in control again. "Boy, that was weird." I shared as Laura got out of her car and we walked inside.

"No worries, Robin. I'm sure there will be other times when it just gets to you like that. You just can't be emotional in front of the people that matter. Like the media, our legislators, or Powertech. Let them only see the logical part of you."

I was not ready for this kind of advice so recently after such a raw and powerful release, but let it slide as we approached the counter to order our meal. We had chosen a locally owned and operated Mexican restaurant for our lunch. They do lunch in cafeteria style. Order your meal at one end, grab your plastic tray and get your chips and drinks, then pay at the other end before you go sit down. Laura knew the owners of this restaurant from her many years of frequenting, so she chatted easily with everyone behind the counter as we got our meals and paid. Her chatting allowed me to stay in my much-needed quiet place.

The restaurant was nearly full so we headed towards a table near the back of the room. As we passed a couple of tables, Laura recognized and connected with a few other people she knew. I was following and the room was crowded so I had to wait as she visited. I'd offer lame smiles as she introduced me while discussing the uranium issue. All I wanted was to sit down, eat and continue to process my morning.

We finally reached our table with Laura talking about the uranium issue and all that still needed to be done. Laura was doing a lot by helping me see some of the many angles we could take with this issue, but she was also very hesitant about getting directly involved. This day was no different in her approach to the topic, "You need to do _____, (fill in the blank with any number of things from adding things to the website, to making contacts, to talking to media)" each sentence began. Being solution oriented and a logical thinker, she hadn't liked seeing how my emotions had taken over earlier in the day. I know she was trying to help me recognize some actions I could take to keep things moving.

All I was hearing was my list getting longer and longer. My fork shook as I attempted to place another bite in my mouth.

A restaurant patron stopped by our table. He was an old friend of Laura's that she had not seen in many years. As they caught up, Laura introduced me and told him about the proposed uranium mining issue. He was interested in finding out more so Laura gave him the website address and encouraged him to get a hold of me since I was the best one to talk to.

I had been keeping my head low while searching for emotional balance and seeking to stop the now reoccurring full body trembling. I looked up when Laura introduced me.

"You look familiar," he said.

Laura told him that he had probably seen me on the news. I stuffed another bite into my mouth.

He turned back to Laura as he agreed to look at the website as he made his exit. Mouth full, I offered a small wave while Laura and he expressed how good it was to see one another after so many years.

Alone again, I changed the topic to horses. As most horse lovers, Laura and I could talk horses for hours. We had a good long distraction before the topic of uranium came up again.

I told Laura about some of the things that were happening with Legislators with whom I was talking. Then we began talking about our newly formed action groups within CARD. Laura started expressing her concerns about the new website that had just begun to post. "The information that you had on your red and yellow site is not all there, Robin. If you want people to join you in the fight you need to make sure that website is tip top."

I just looked at her. She went on to talk about all of the information that was not there and all of the information that she had found lately that needed to be added. "You've GOT to get that website up and running in a useful way. The website is what is really driving this thing. Talk to Steve, help him see how important it is to really spend as much time as he can on it."

I noticed the trembling returning. "I'm so tired of having to motivate and direct people. Steve has just as much to lose as we do. He's doing as much as he possibly can to stop this proposed mining already. Remember, he has a young family and a full-time job too."

Laura would not hear of it. "Then you should go back to the red and yellow site until he has time to put up more information. You've got to get all the information out there."

I started to feel the tears. I did not want to start crying again. Instead I yelled, "I CAN'T DO IT ALL!"

I went on to speak very loudly about how all of these tasks were just too much. I needed to stay focused on our business and get that running too. I couldn't be locked into uranium 24-7. Not to mention that even if I could, there was way too much for me to even get it all done if I WAS doing uranium 24-7. I was worried about the kids and their horses. Worried about losing students that I currently had. Worried about losing our property. Worried that our water would become contaminated. Worried about Sally. Worried about Jay's business because of the time he was taking away from it to fight uranium miners. I began crying in earnest as I continued to express how I was sick and tired of it all already.

Laura tried to calm me down, "Robin, you don't want people to think you are a lunatic. Please keep your voice down. People are beginning to recognize you from the paper and the news. You can't be so emotional. You need to keep it together."

"I'M TIRED OF KEEPING IT TOGETHER. I can't express any of my true feelings anymore because I have to be so politically correct. I don't give a FUCK about what people think of me! They can all Fuck Off as far as I'm concerned. Let them live in the middle of a fucking uranium mine and see how they like it. Let them see if they can maintain emotional control. I'm emotional. I'm mad," I cried and as my rant petered, "I'm so tired."

Embarrassed I looked around the room to see how many people had been watching. I noted that when we had come in the room was full and now the room was nearly empty.

"Alright, alright, I'll help, just lower your voice. Tell me what you want me to do, what would help YOU. I'll help you. You're right. You can't do it all. You really need my help and as much other help as you can get. Just do your best to keep your emotions in check."

"I need safe places to allow my emotions out. I am not a rock. I'm an emotional wreck." I sobbed.

"Don't worry, we'll do this together. You can be emotional with me, but you HAVE to maintain in front of those who matter."

I was calming down finally. Still trembling, but at least not sobbing any longer I lowered my voice several notches, "Thank you, Laura. I'm sorry. This is so hard and so unfair. I just can't believe we are in the middle of this thing."

We sat in silence for a little while as I continued to pull myself together. I could tell that Laura felt horrible for me. I felt horrible for the fact that she felt sorry for me. I hate for people to feel sorry for me. I like to consider myself a strong and self-sufficient kind of person. It was becoming more and more apparent that I needed people way more than I had ever needed them in the past.

"Sorry about the F-bombs. I must really be stressed." I apologized.

"I know that's not who you really are, Robin. I've never heard you say such words before. You just needed to really let some stuff out. Now, let's get busy driving uranium miners away. What shall I do first?" Laura replied.

We got up to leave and I told her about the upcoming meeting that our website design group was having. She agreed to attend and see what she could do.

We hugged in the parking lot as we parted. We also agreed to make sure we were doing at least *something* with our horses once a week and to make sure we attended this yoga class *every* week.

> Can you recognize the trauma/drama triangle in the interaction between Laura and me? I really was trying to find that place where I could be on stable ground but my emotional build up would not allow it. This is NOT to make the emotions wrong but it is to notice that I did not have a solid relationship with my emotions. I did not allow them to flow in a healthy way. So they came out in a really unhealthy way.
>
> The yoga allowed my body to begin to speak. I still wasn't listening. I didn't know how to listen at the time. I had deep anger welling up. Old, repressed anger that had not been directed as it should have been. Anger is the emotion that tells us that a boundary has been violated and needs to be restored. I had spent my life feeling anger on some level because I had such a huge boundary violation that had not been allowed to even be recognized, let alone to be restored. How dare they - indeed!
>
> Instead of going home and working with the emotions while they were up, I chose to stuff them. I wanted them to go away so that I would not have to look at the message behind them. At this time, I didn't even know there might be a message within them. They were just an annoyance, something to make me look weak. What I didn't understand is that they are truly my strength and needed to be honored.

My lunch with Laura was set up for failure at the moment I made that decision to stuff those emotions. Then, they just wouldn't stay stuffed. They had to come out in some way. So they came out as a projection onto Laura. She did not get outwardly angry right back at me which would have resulted in turning our lunch into a screaming match, which I was well worked up into creating. Her control in this situation allowed me to continue to seek equilibrium even while I was twirling. She was an effective human trainer in that situation. Just allow the human (horse) to express how they need to until you can redirect the energy.

So, emotions properly stuffed as per our cultural expectations, I moved onward with an even deeper set up for emotional and/or physical unwellness in the future. If I had not been blessed to do the amount of work that I did following this continued pattern, I may well not be with us today, or with us but deeply physically or mentally unwell.

CHAPTER 14

CARD STARTS TO PLAY

Time for our first CARD Board meeting, where we would step into titles and begin the process of integrating our new volunteers by delegating some of the tasks. As was becoming too normal for me those days I walked into the basement of the coffee shop a little later than I had intended. Everyone was already seated at the table and a spot at the head of the table was open. I pulled up an additional chair on a long end rather than taking the spot at the head. Lisa asked me to lead the meeting. I told her that I was expecting that she would since she had the experience.

"I don't want to lead this group," she replied, "I don't have the time. Besides, you have already begun leading. Go ahead and get us started. You know what needs to be done."

"No," I replied. "I cannot. I have too much on my plate, there is no way I'm going to Chair this group."

I sat quietly and expectantly as everyone looked at me. After what felt like a forever pause Lisa turned to Carol, "She's not going to do it, so will you?"

Carol moved to the head of the table, pulled out a sheet of paper and began our first official CARD meeting.

I was in overwhelm. There was just no way I could pull my emotional mess together enough to be effective as the official leader of this organization. I knew it. I knew that I would continue doing everything that I was already doing, but I was not going to carry the title of Chair. I did agree to be a Co-Chair of the Coordinating Committee (that is what we called this main group) and to Chair the Outreach Committee.

In all honesty the leadership of our Coordinating Committee changed quite a bit in that first year. I did not remain Co-Chair for long and did not even remain Chair of the Outreach Committee for long. Those of us who began CARD were the landowners within the proposed mining area. We were certainly motivated to drive Powertech away. But the leadership shifted and changed until those who were really best suited for each role fell into place. I am very grateful that this happened, but I can say that it did not always happen with ease. We had arguments. We had drama. We almost completely lost some of our new found relationships as we disagreed about how certain things should be done.

We even had a couple splinter off to form their own group since they were very frustrated with the way things were going. Their group never did gain as much momentum as CARD. If we all would have had a greater emotional intelligence we could have remained one cohesive group and possibly been much more effective united together. A big threat like this was is likely to create divisions. It was important that we all remained focused on the big picture to avoid getting caught in such dramas. We could disagree and still remain allies and keep a strong group together. In fact, by listening we could make a bigger group even stronger through the disagreements. We all deserve a voice, so if we would have listened better – on both accounts, we could have been stronger.

Lisa, with her experience as an organizer, had warned us that this would happen. We just couldn't believe it when she told us this since we all had the same goal. But having the same goal does not mean that everyone can see the same steps or the value in all the steps. Those of us who lived in the middle of the proposed mining zone were under an incredible amount of stress. We felt like we were at war. Any unresolved trauma that we had became our greatest weakness. Feeling victimized and powerless makes one respond in unpredictable ways when one has not done the personal work it takes to resolve past traumas. The blessing was in our total commitment to stop the mine. This is how we were able to be successful in the long run. The people who showed up to help us and the power they wielded made this infinitely clear.

Each of the subcommittees made good use of the volunteers who had attended our first volunteer coordinating meeting. As the Outreach Chair I had some highly intelligent and motivated people. The woman who started out as my Co-Chair became the Chair only a few months after we began meeting. I asked if she would like that position and offered to remain as Co-Chair so that I could attempt to develop a little more balance in my life. Setting agendas, coordinating volunteers and just the general responsibilities of Chair was something I was glad to pass off so that I could continue to do the work I was doing with the legislators and the media. This shift in responsibility helped relieve much of my stress.

CARD was putting on at least four Town Hall meetings per month, and sometimes many more. We presented at surrounding towns, county commissioner hearings, and in front of as many professional organizations as we could. We continued to use the first PowerPoint presentation with very few minor changes. We were sticking to just the facts. Professional groups were open to hearing from us because of our professional presentation. We developed a very effective marketing strategy and it was apparent that Powertech was aware and attempting to catch up. Often, one of their members would show up at these meetings. Sometimes, they attempted to co-opt the meeting by standing up and rebutting what we were saying. Our speakers got very good at letting them know that they could have their own meeting if they wished to have the floor. Some of the best lines we heard from these guys are:

When discussing the safety of the mining operation and that there is no guarantee that the water will not be contaminated they stated, "The guarantee question is not really a fair question."

And once it was said, "Uranium is the heaviest of metals. So, it sinks to the bottom of the river."

They really did not help themselves when they spoke. They appeared to be so self-assured that they could just come in and mine because they held the power. Might (and money) makes right! This 'might makes right' attitude had them responding in a condescending way that implied that the rest of us clearly had no intelligence so therefore no valid concerns. With this 'might makes right' attitude they often just spoke without thinking or even considering the impact of what they were saying. We had many a chuckle with their ridiculous one-liners. We even began creating some commentary comics for our website to keep things light. These lighter moments helped us stay balanced with all the anger and grief we were already feeling.

Speaking of the website, boy did it blossom with the right people focusing on it. The informative originally written articles, along with the links used as reference in writing these articles, were very popular. Yes, I got something up and just starting blasting things out to the public, but the new website is professional and organized and readily accessible to everyone. The guy who was in charge of the hosting of the site would monitor who was visiting and often saw government agencies spending a lot of time exploring. We had the United Stated Department of Defense and the White House visit often. We even had the FBI and CIA monitoring us. It's a good thing we kept it professional and all completely above board.

CARD was in every parade we could find with a float, or horses, or bicycle riders or motorcycle riders, but always with walkers who were carrying petitions for people to sign and fliers to pass out when anyone wanted more information. We had fun with this as we'd design floats that were simple but fit into the theme of the parade. Walking through the crowds lining the streets with petitions was always interesting. If we had someone who was really negative we'd hand them a flier and ask them to just check us out. When we had someone who was positive and wanted to sign the petition we'd ask them if they had more friends who would sign and gave them the website where they could sign digitally as well. We passed out a ton of informative fliers.

We'd set up ironing boards on a sidewalk in Old Town Fort Collins, Greeley or in Wellington and use those as tables where we'd collect petition signatures and pass out information. The ironing boards were brilliant. Easy to set up, a nice table and easy to carry off when we were done.

When we had a town hall meeting scheduled in a town, we would do door to door canvassing the weekend before the meeting to collect petition signatures and to invite people to attend. And we always used the newspaper free event calendars to publish the dates and times and locations of each town hall meeting in all of the surrounding towns.

Booths were purchased at as many local events as we could find: 4th of July, Earth Day, Farmer's Markets, New West Fest, County Fairs, Sustainable Living Fair, etc. We had t-shirts to sell and collected donations as well as petition signatures all while we educated people on the threat of the mine. We really stuck to the fact that it is the water that we need to protect.

Often people would wish to get into a debate about nuclear power and how we need it as a 'green' solution. We did our best to not engage this debate and to keep the issue to the water. As you all know by now, I had started with the idea that nuclear power is our solution. As my research evolved, I can firmly say that I no longer agree with nuclear power as a solution at all for the many reasons that I will not go into here. While addressing the uranium mining issue we got really good at keeping the focus on water. We need clean water to live. Water is life! There is no argument to that.

We wrote letters to the editor and encouraged others to do the same. Whenever someone asked what they could do, we always asked them to write a letter to the editor, to the elected officials, and to join our ranks of volunteers. We developed a really good following because of our professionalism. People were quick to claim membership in CARD regardless of their level of participation. They were proud to be a part of something bigger than themselves and we were happy to accept any help offered.

While our Outreach Committee was busy, our Research Committee continued to look for any information they could that would help stop the mining from happening. Jay was part of a small group who was working very closely with Jeff Parsons, Rep. John Kefalas and Rep. Randy Fischer on writing legislation that would protect our water supplies. Jeff was very experienced in protecting resources from destruction caused by mining through his work with Western Mining Action Project. He proposed legislation right away, and began working with Representatives Kefalas and Fischer and asked CARD to support it and to pave the way for getting that information out when it was time.

Jeff may have looked young, but that guy was brilliant when it came to writing the legislation that would readily pass. I believe he is an old soul channeling the brilliance of those who have walked before him.

So, even though legislation was not part of our planning session goals, it took priority as soon as it was proposed. It did not take long for the legislation to become a reality because of the efforts of Jeff, and the willingness of Representatives Kefalas and Fischer to step up to the plate right away.

With all of the activity and the help from the many volunteers my emotional meltdowns were becoming more infrequent. Laura and I kept our promise to ride our horses once a week in order to just get away from everything. We had some great times and covered a lot of territory. It was good to spend time with someone with whom I could be completely authentic (or at least as much as I was to myself) and could discuss CARD, uranium, politics, horses and just plain laugh together. I attribute her support for keeping me sane. Some weeks we would be in a celebration mode because we had successes to discuss, such as a signed resolution opposing the uranium mine from the Colorado Medical Association. Or other weeks we might be attempting to find a way to combat a move that Powertech made or respond to things they had said to the press. The horses showed up and supported our efforts by being ready to just go wherever we had decided to ride. I was usually on Auris and Laura rode her gelding, Sun. These two got along great and enjoyed galloping together, as well as encouraging each other when we got into tricky terrain. We really couldn't have asked for a better match.

CARD was working to maintain a professional standard so that we could readily approach and maintain the support of our elected officials and other professional organizations. It was not always easy because our emotions were strong and we would want to lash out at Powertech and some of their nonsensical remarks. One of the ways we were able to maintain a strictly fact based, no drama approach was knowing that there were some of our supporters who went 'rogue.' One such person created a website dedicated to exposing everything he could find on Powertech and its players. His website: powertechexposed.com was one that we linked to from our site: nunnglow.com. We talked to him quite a bit about strategy and the value of comic relief. He never would join CARD because he wanted to remain rogue and didn't wish to have his need to write what he needed to for his own release reviewed by our group.

Here is a sample of what he had posted:

Mr. Blubaugh promoted a plan calling for the company to simply cover the tailings pile with sand and rock, even though a 1998 report by the Oak Ridge National Laboratory concluded that uranium discharges into the Colorado River would "persist indefinitely".

Atlas was required to prepare an Environmental Impact Statement to assess the plan's potential impacts, but the company filed for bankruptcy before the EIS could be completed. Upon filing for bankruptcy, Atlas was released from all future liability with respect to the uranium mill facilities and tailings pile.

Under the Uranium Mill Tailings Radiation Control Act, the U.S Dept. of Energy is responsible for cleaning up the Moab site. On October 25, 2001, legal title to the site was transferred to the DOE. In September 2005, the

DOE issued its decision to move the tailings pile to a disposal site at Crescent Junction, Utah, and clean up and reclaim the mill site property.

Disposal of the tailings pile and clean up of the site is expected to take 20 years and cost taxpayers over $600 million. According to a recent email from the DOE contractor hired to do the work, $60 million has been spent through fiscal year 2007. FY 2008 costs are expected to be $23 million."[31]

He really called them out on their previous actions. He worked hard to keep all of his accusations factual and was even threatened with a lawsuit by Powertech, but once he had attorney's review and respond to their threat, they did not follow through. This showed just how much integrity powertechexposed.com had while pointing out the truth in a very bold way. His site and our discussions helped me channel my anger so that I could remain effective with CARD.

Another consistent and helpful rogue supporter was a man who went by the title Rad Man. Rad Man would dress up in a complete hazmat suit and stand on street corners with one of our signs, or walk around Old Town Fort Collins to pass out information. His radical approach gained a lot of attention. When Powertech hosted the one and only open house format meeting in Nunn, Rad Man was there and stood right next to Richard Clement, the Powertech CEO, the entire time. Not really saying anything, just being a presence that no one could miss. Nor could they miss the implications. He is a poet and wrote this one to give to anyone who would take information from him.

Prairie Woes
By Rad Man

I have uranium, in my cranium
What's in my head, could make me dead
What's in my water, really scares my daughter
What's in my well, must be from hell
What's in the wind, could spell the end

---

[31]   www.powertechexposed.com

I don't wash with tide, I use radionuclide
Contracting cancer, is not the answer
It's Powertech, done caused this wreck
Colorado's our State, we control our fate
Let's stop them now, we'll show you how
This site's the bomb, nunnglow.com

Rad Man provided me with great satirical relief. We all have our gifts and we all stepped up in our best ways to do what we could to stop the uranium mine from happening.

One guy put on a No Glow Concert as a fundraiser for CARD with several local musicians playing at a local bar/restaurant. Russ Hopkins wrote a song for it and printed CD's which when sold the proceeds went to CARD. His song The No Uranium Song has some powerful lyrics that are worth checking out. You can find him and this song on YouTube.

Looking back we really brought a lot of energy to the area with our efforts and all those who helped. I really cannot thank everyone that helped defeat the proposed mining operation enough.

CHAPTER 15

FOCUSING ON LEGISLATION

August 2007

While CARD was keeping me busy and things felt like they were at least somewhat manageable, I was still struggling with being effective in our horse business. The 4-H club was doing well and I felt like I was responding effectively to that group, several of the kids had projects in the upcoming Larimer County Fair and I was at the Fairgrounds when I received a phone call.

"Hi Robin, it's Evan. It's difficult for me to say this, but we are going to move the horses to a different facility."

I was taken aback but not totally surprised. We were really not making much progress with his filly. Between his busy schedule and my overwhelm we had difficulty connecting on a consistent basis.

"I'm sorry to hear that, but I understand. Sorry I am not able to be there for you as much as you need right now."

"You need to focus on stopping this uranium mine, that much is clear. I need to be where I can have the complete focus on Moriah. It's just not the right timing for you. We'll stay in touch and I'll do all I can to help you with your efforts."

I thanked him and we made plans for moving his horses. At this point he had 3 boarded with us. This would be a big financial hit. I really didn't have that many boarders yet. I had not put a lot of effort into building my training/boarding business. I had a few ads out but I wasn't networking like I needed to, nor keeping our Mustang Hollow website up to date. I should have been offering clinics, hosting events, writing articles to post and sending out e-newsletters. Any time that I might have for that was taken up by CARD or 4-H. This loss did not feel good at all, but I knew there was not much I could do until the uranium mine was stopped.

I still was uncertain about the protection of our land and water. I didn't feel right committing to bringing in too many boarders when I couldn't say how long our water would remain drinkable. While we were doing our town hall meetings and raising awareness Powertech was drilling testing wells and installing air monitoring stations, all right next to us. They even put signs on the properties they had purchased that touted nuclear power as the green option. We had one sign pointed right at us from the neighboring plot. Every time I'd see one of their trucks drive by I'd want to scream. I'd film their activities and then double down on my efforts to make them go away.

I wasn't truly spending quality time with my own horses let alone the few horses I had in training, even though my weekly rides with Laura did often involve my ponying of another horse. At least I was working with two horses on those days. Sometimes both were mine, sometimes one or both were horses in training. I generally spent my mornings working with the horses, but I was never fully present because I was so in my head about the uranium mine. I was ungrounded and incongruent with my emotions when I was around them. Thankfully, I was not badly hurt because of the skills that I had garnered by this point in my horsemanship journey. But as I look back in all honesty, I was ineffective as a partner in the relationship training that I wished to build. It was really a different kind of domination forced on the horses by me because I was living in so much fear. It makes me so sad when I think about it now.

The training techniques I was using were all techniques gathered through a variety of Natural Horsemanship training. On the outside they look like they take the horse into deep consideration, but much like a technically skilled violinist vs a virtuoso, I was not tapping into the heart. I was not pausing to really ask the horse if they really *wanted* to be in relationship on a certain day. I was not pausing to seek deep conversation that helps a horse feel empowered and successful in a partnership. I was listening through body language but I was not listening at the soul level. This type of domination is difficult to see by the observer, but the horse knows it and quite honestly so does the aware trainer.

Knowing what I know now has me in a much deeper relationship with my horses because I know how to listen at the soul level and I take the time to do so. This is also why I cannot just train a horse and send it back to their partner without the opportunity to develop the relationship between the two. I will never just train a horse and send it home again unless the owner/partner is interested in being a part of the training process the entire way through. In my current work I am just a coach helping the two develop authentic communication which creates a working relationship.

The domination paradigm is evident in all disciplines of horsemanship. There is also the opportunity for a beautiful relationship in all disciplines of horsemanship. When I am able to watch a performance of two beings who truly love and respect one another my heart sings. When I watch the same level of technical skills performed on a horse who is respected to a degree but not really allowed a voice in the relationship, I feel a bitter feeling in my throat and a lump in my stomach. The soul knows what it is watching and also knows in what it is participating.

I hate to admit that I was basically ineffective with my riding students at that time. We just didn't get anywhere. I lacked presence. The 4-H kids were gaining some skills because of the covering of the 4-H organization and the great manuals. I just was not effective in helping them truly meet their goals of being ready to show their horses. I was fully locked into being an activist and stuffing all those bad ol' emotions so that I could function competently as a leader in the other areas of my life. At the time I didn't realize that I wasn't fully functional and that I could have been so much better if I would have allowed myself to express emotional intelligence. My past traumas had me in a frozen state when it came to this emotional intelligence. I was just not able to tap into it on my own even if I had wanted to.

So, now my horse business was declining rather than growing. I felt trapped again. I felt fear which quickly morphed into anger which fueled my unbalanced lifestyle of focusing totally on uranium miners and what felt like a rape of me and my dreams. I couldn't give up now. Through the fear and frustration, 'Onward' was my consistent rallying cry.

Evan moved his horses out. Sally was focusing on healing from cancer. Laura and I had shifted into peers more than instructor and student, so our study group was disbanded. Well, one more thing off my plate, but it sure didn't feel like the right thing.

Still 'onward' we went as we continued to have town hall meetings, collect petition signatures and work on legislation which we hoped to have passed.

Since I was involved with maintaining the relationships with our elected officials I noticed a weekend that Congresswoman Marilyn Musgrave was going to be in Loveland. I made an appointment and invited a few other people to join Jay and I to discuss this proposed uranium mine with her. Being that lifelong Republican I had great respect for Representative Musgrave and was looking forward to meeting her. As we shook hands in our initial meeting I thanked her for her work to protect the life of the unborn. She and I immediately connected and as we all sat down I did most of the talking. I told her about how in-situ leach mining contaminated water and that we needed water for life. I discussed how we are not truly protecting the sanctity of life if we are willing to sacrifice clean water. I ended by telling her just how much I felt my own life was being threatened.

She asked several detailed questions, which Jay was able to then answer. On the way out she told her closest aide to get my information and to give me his direct contact information. She stated that she wanted to stay informed about this mining proposal. She gave me a hug and encouraged me to stay strong. It felt like we had found a very heartfelt connection. From that day forward I stayed in touch with her aide on an almost daily basis as he tracked our efforts and became more educated on what in-situ leach mining for uranium really is.

With what felt like more national support, I felt energized to continue the steps we still had to take. While in the process, the legislations we were working on felt uncomfortably intense and lengthy to me. Looking back now I can see that it really went well. Being in it, living it, knowing that it could save our dreams, made it feel like eternity. Jay spent many hours working on the wording with Jeff and Representatives Kefalas and Fischer. He was putting in long days working at his civil engineering business and long nights and weekends working for CARD. I felt tired and overwhelmed and I could see the same in Jay. Near the end of 2007 Jay decided to sell his half of the engineering business to his partner. The truth is that the economic down turn for 2008 was beginning to hit, though we had no idea how bad it was to really get, and his 'selling' of the business at that point was a small buy out. Jay really needed to get away from this partnership as it was no longer working. The added benefit was that this would allow him to focus on the legislation. We figured we could last a few months without him working until the legislation was nailed down and hopefully passed. He was well networked in the industry so we thought he'd find a job rather easily. That was BEFORE the reality of 2008 really hit.

We stepped out on faith and quite honestly needed to find ways to regain our footing. We were both so exhausted, stressed, and deeply unsure as to our future. Jay's move of getting out of his business was likely a really good thing in the long run, but he was out of work for quite some time before finding any work in his field. Out of necessity, he took a job as a magazine delivery driver nearly a year later. The blessing was that his being out of work really allowed him to focus on CARD.

Jay became the go-to guy when it came to doing presentations to professional organizations around the State. He presented to Realtors, chamber of commerce groups, professional networks and to the Colorado Medical Association. His work with the Colorado Medical Association resulted in getting a resolution written and passed by them in opposition to in situ leach mining for uranium based upon the health risks associated with its implementation. His time was really effective. He did not do all of these presentations on his own. There were many others who helped, but he became the one who was always available no matter who else was or was not because of work conflicts.

Republican State Senator Steve Johnson asked to be a co-sponsor of the legislation. With his support we now had a bi-partisan bill. With a bi-partisan bill, a showing of good faith by meeting several times with Powertech and the Colorado Mining Commission and taking to heart their input on the wording, we finally had what we considered to be the final draft of the bill. We had our scheduled hearing in front of the Agriculture, Natural Resources and Energy Committee. The week before the hearing we scheduled a rally on the Capitol steps to bring awareness and support for the bill. We put out press releases and encouraged everyone to show up. I was to bring a couple of horses and we had some kids who would be there to hold the horses. It was a powerful photo op situation with speeches and everything.

I had been asked to speak. Me… asked to speak on the Capitol steps. WOW! I was so excited and motivated and really didn't feel as fearful as I would have just one year before. I wrote some notes but in the end decided it was best to just speak from my heart.

That same week/weekend U.S. Representative Marilyn Musgrave had a town hall meeting scheduled in Nunn. Plus, I had an opportunity to be a student in a 4-day clinic with an international horsewoman. My close relationship with Congresswoman Musgrave's top aide had me feeling really good about how our work was paying off. I was ready to give myself some real 'me' time with the upcoming clinic.

The morning of the first day of the clinic I was feeling good about spending some quality time with my horses. I was excited about the town hall meeting that night and the rally scheduled for Sunday. I was on a rare high about all the work I had put in so far. My plan was to clinic that day, attend the Musgrave meeting that night, then to immerse myself in the clinic for the next two full days and then leave early on Sunday to take the horses to Denver for the rally.

As I was driving the truck with my mare in the trailer behind me I got a phone call.

"Robin, we have an email from a reporter who wants to talk to you about the rally this weekend," said our newest member of the Outreach Committee. He came with credentials and a list of the many environmental groups with whom he had been deeply involved. We had originally been excited about adding his experience to our team, but right away we all were feeling the stress of how he jumped right in and began telling us all exactly how and what we should be doing in every turn. By the time of this phone call we had all already been talking about how best to handle him and his desire to help.

"Great," I replied as I let my foot off the gas, "I can get back to them around noon when I take a lunch break today."

"You need to get back to him right away. The rally is only a few days away."

"I will call him later, I'm on my way to a horse clinic and will have a break at midday."

"WHAT?!?!? What are you doing at a horse clinic when you should be getting back with this guy as well as what I'm sure will be the many other reporters who will want to talk to you right away."

"Listen," I said with anger in my voice. I punched the gas. My mare stomped as she sought balance. "The horse business is my real job and I've been letting that go for a long time now. I need to be at this clinic. I will call this guy during a break and deal with whomever else comes along as they do."

Off he went on a tangent about commitment and his frustration about our group and how unprofessional we all were, etc, etc.

Noticing that the truck was veering off the road, I quickly turned the wheel to course correct. My mare shifted as the whole truck moved. I remembered what was most important in that moment and got off the phone quickly.

Feeling the ire of the conversation and the resultant difficult trip I was creating for my mare, I quickly made a few phone calls to other CARD members. This drama was unproductive.

That was the last I ever heard from him.

> One thing about an activist organization is that it attracts all kinds of people for different reasons, and we had our fair share of difficult personalities and emotionally damaged folks. All I could think was how I didn't need the added stress of these people who were projecting their own stuff on our mission. I could do that well enough on my own, even though I didn't realize how much I was doing that at the time and was quick to judge these people for the drama they brought to us. Drama was all around me - inside, outside, created, stepped in – you name it, we had drama.

Amazingly enough, the drama never totally derailed us on our mission. We were so committed to stopping this uranium mine we just couldn't get derailed. Our very lives were threatened. Jay always was calmly steadfast and just wouldn't buy into the drama. He'd just say, "That is 'so and so'." I never really understood what he meant but I also heard that as the end of any conversation, even though I my addiction to drama really wanted to entertain the drama more thoroughly. Jay kept me balanced.

I enjoyed immersing myself as a student, forgetting the stress and drama. At the end of the day, I quickly loaded Auris and we rushed home, I showered and moved into the activist role. I was still on a high, feeling really good about the pivotal role I had in making this Town Hall meeting happen. After several emails sharing information about the real possibility of groundwater contamination, Rep. Musgrave had offered to come to Nunn and take part in a panel discussion which would include Powertech and CARD.

I walked into the town gymnasium/theatre and slid into a seat saved by a neighbor. The panel sat slightly elevated with Representative Musgrave sitting in the middle flanked by CARD and Powertech.

Jay was on the panel with Jeff and a couple of other CARD members. The audience was asked to come to a microphone and ask questions. Both CARD and Powertech were given the opportunity to respond while Rep. Musgrave moderated. Both opponents and supporters of the mine were present. A lively conversation ensued!

U.S. Senator Scott Renfroe was in the audience and after listening for some time, he stood up and said that he had come from Washington because he had heard that the opposition to the proposed uranium mine was being backed by a large environmental group. He asked if that was true.

Jay stood up, reached into his pocket, pulled out his empty wallet and said, "This is what is backing us, what we have in our back pockets."

David stood up in the audience at the same time and added, "Hey, we wish we had financial backing. We are doing this all on our own."

Senator Renfroe and Representative Musgrave were both a little surprised by the passion with which both Jay and David had responded. We were fully committed financially, physically and emotionally. This came through loud and clear when both Jay and David spoke.

This town hall went on for a couple of hours. At the end Representative Musgrave thanked everyone who had attended and publicly expressed her own opposition to the uranium mine. This was a huge win for us. Now we had a sitting Republican House member supporting our efforts to stop this mine as well! I have a feeling that her support went a long way towards helping the legislation get passed. Thank you Representative Musgrave!

After that successful evening I deeply felt the permission to fully immerse myself in real horsey time. I didn't feel pulled in two directions for a few days. I remained present to myself and my mare. What a treat!

By Sunday, refueled by the weekend, I was ready to do as I needed and leave the clinic early. I only stayed a couple of hours. I had to bring my best school horse, Cherry, along with my mare Auris that morning so I could go to Denver directly from the clinic. I wanted to stay as long as possible at what had become a sort of vacation for me. When the time came to leave I loaded both horses while telling them they would both be famous. From that day I began calling my mare 'Auris the Famous Horis.' I think she liked the new nick name.

The rally day was a wet day so we all had our raincoats and umbrellas out. I had to cover the saddles on the horses with rain slickers, but the rain did not deter us one bit. Everyone was on a high. I absolutely loved having my horses on the steps of the Capitol in downtown Denver. The kids were thrilled with all of the attention they were getting as they took official charge of the horses so I could be free to do my job.

I was the first speaker and it was my honor to introduce the bill and to publicly thank each of the sponsors. By this time I had a gotten to know

Representatives Kefalas and Fischer pretty well. I had developed a good rapport with Senator Steve Johnson through e-mail and felt really comfortable with these gentlemen. I held a deep regard for their part in the writing and sponsoring of this bill. This talk was easy for me. Even today, though, I cannot believe that I spoke at a rally on the Capitol steps. Pretty cool.

We got a lot of great pictures and had good press coverage. It was a great way to kick off what was to be the more grueling part of the process.

The first bill that was presented to committee was sent back for changes. We were asked to work more directly with the Colorado Mining Association and Powertech so that we were not doing what they call 'taking'. Taking would mean that we were making it impossible for them to access their minerals through legislation. We had to have legislation that protected health and the environment without making it too strong, and to do that, we now had to include those we wished to legislate in the process more deeply. Yup, that's how it works. I'd cuss about the fact that they shouldn't have any say because they just wanted to take what they wanted without any regard for health or the environment. Jay would just say, "That's how it works. We have to work with these guys to get something done." I had very little trust for the process.

On one notable morning Jay was asked to go to the capitol building to meet with everyone who was engaged in rewriting the bill. We were raiding the change jar to scrape enough money together for parking in one of the downtown lots.

"Why can't this meeting be done up here somewhere?" I asked.

"Because people are coming from all over the State," he replied. By this time we had a group from southwest Colorado who were heavily involved with this bill too. They had in-situ leach mining proposed within their exclusive mountain community. The meeting was to include all stakeholders, which was anyone who had a stake in the proposed legislation. Powertech would be there as well as representatives from the Colorado Mining Association, along with our allies.

"We can't keep driving to Denver. We just don't have the money for this," I said.

"I know, but we have to make this happen," Jay responded. He was getting frustrated with me because I was walking in fear rather than faith. I saw myself as being pragmatic. We had lots of money going out and very little coming in. We were still boarding a few horses and I was still giving some lessons, but the cost of keeping the horses ate up a good portion of that. Our bank account was dwindling fast as we drove all over the State to attend meetings and keep the ball rolling in whatever way we could. We were truly scrounging pennies at this point.

As he prepared to leave, I kissed him good bye with a 'Good luck' wish. All I could think of was our bills and how in the world we were going to pay them. I remember spending that day wandering aimlessly. I just couldn't focus on much because now I was overwhelmed by the stress of money. My survival mechanism was in full fear mode and I was frozen. How would we survive? If we lost everything because of this whole effort would it be worth it? Would the legislation go through? And if it did would it stop them from contaminating our ground water? Would we be able to keep the ranch even if we do win and stop the mining? How could we keep going at this pace? What could I even do anymore? I felt ineffective in my chosen dream career, I was losing the respect of my students and the 4-H club, and I was tired of fighting for my life. I was a mess.

Thankfully, I had a huge list of things to do with CARD. The phone calls and e-mails would not stop coming in so they snapped me back to effectiveness the next day after my full day of a self-indulgent pity party. This wasn't the only pity party, I had and by the Grace of God I was continually snapped back by the work still to be done. Once the ball was rolling it really took on a life of its own.

Since Jay was the more logical one he was really good at looking at just the facts and staying steady. His input in the bill was priceless. My role was more of the motivational force. In fact, Jeff would tell Jay to have me 'call out the dogs' when they needed voices to shake up the elected officials during this whole process. It became my goal to hear those lovely words: "Tell Robin to call out the dogs." Jay would share what was happening as the process proceeded and I'd get pissed off and threaten to tell everyone what was happening. Jay would have to say to me, "No, keep the dogs at bay right now, we need to work this through."

I'd walk off completely dissatisfied because I couldn't share what was really happening with anyone for fear that it would get out and the dogs would turn loose on their own. We had a lot of people at the ready who, with just a call and/or an e-mail, would show up at a moments' notice. The biggest blessing in this whole thing was the commitment level of members and supporters.

I really don't remember how many committee hearings we attended once the legislation was ready to present to committee again, but I remember how it felt. I remember lingering in the waiting area until our bill was read, and how sometimes we would have to come back the next day because the day's business ran too long for our bill to be heard. I remember waiting all day and even into the night. I remember testifying with my stacks of notebooks full of signed petitions and resolutions. I remember legislators eating at their desk. I remember testifying to empty chairs where many of the committee members should have been sitting and hearing what I had so diligently prepared for them.

I remember riding the elevators with Powertech attorneys and board members. I'd stand with firmness in my spot and as tall as possible, never up against a wall unless I had to because of a crowd. I was there to do battle and these creeps were not going to see any weakness in me at all. I was a warrior and had 1000's of people behind me. I harbored hate against the Powertech guys, and yes, they were all men. I'd judge their hair, their smarminess, their entire presence. I blamed them for my losing business. I blamed them for our being broke. I blamed them for everything bad that was happening in my life up to that moment. I could not be friendly at all. If our eyes met I'm sure they saw all of my hatred peering back quite clearly.

In fact, I'd revel in the opportunity to shoot those angry eyes at them if they'd dare look at me. Generally they would keep their eyes down. I was fine with that as well.

Jay on the other hand would walk up and shake their hands. "How you doing today?" he'd say. They'd banter about the weather and other banalities. I'd generally walk off if I could. I just couldn't stomach it. In fact, I got pretty angry with Jay for being able to treat these guys with any respect at all. I was at war and I wanted nothing more than bloodshed – not real blood, mind you (though in my anger I'm sure I wouldn't have even minded that) - but I wanted these guys gone as far away from me as I could get them after I had beaten them at their own game! Jay always said he got good information by maintaining pleasantries. I tried to understand but I was far too angry and far too damaged internally to be able to rise to his level of peacefulness. So, I'd just continue to shoot daggers whenever I had the opportunity.

My energy must have been powerful because I'd notice any Powertech goons walking around me in a different way whenever possible if I was standing where they were approaching. Yep, I took pleasure in that as well. I had passive aggressiveness down to an art with these guys.

The committee hearings were a whole new experience for me. We all came prepared with our testimonies and followed Robert's Rules of Order in how we addressed the Committee Chair, but I was astounded at how often committee members would not be present for the entire testimony. It was apparent that these elected officials all had very busy schedules, but so did I. So did the doctors, engineers and other professionals who were taking time off work to testify. Jay and I were scrounging our penny jar for gas and parking money and these public servants couldn't sit and listen to the entire testimony?!?

My lifetime of being a Republican was completely rattled when it came to some of our State representatives. Representative Gardner never responded to my emails and appeared to pay more attention to the testimony in opposition to our bill. In fact he was rarely present during testimony in favor of the bill and almost always present during the Colorado Mining Association input.

Our own House Representative Jerry Sonnenberg and I spent one evening in a long email exchange. After noticing what seemed like resistance to the information I was sharing, I asked him if he had read the bill. He replied no, but asked what was in it. I shared some of the talking points we had on the bill, such as the protection of water and that we wrote the legislation from the promises given by Powertech. He basically told me he was not inclined to vote for the bill because he was concerned about its effect on future mining in Weld County and the Oil & Gas industry. I asked him to read the bill, offering that if he did so he might feel different. We went back and forth for quite some time into the evening, and if I remember right I reminded him that he works for us, the people in his district. I rather rudely expressed my wonderment about how he could look himself in the mirror after some of the things he said about his lack of desire to even take time to read the bill. Not one of my best moments of lobbying, but I was extremely frustrated by his lack of response to us as constituents thus far.

After this conversation with Rep. Sonnenberg I stopped any more email conversations with him. I was embarrassed by the fact that I had lost my professionalism in my dealings with him. He had totally triggered me. Not to mention, I was profoundly challenged in finding any respect for him in his role as public servant.

Even though I and many others were doing all we could to rally support, it was not enough. We soon learned that we really needed to hire a professional lobbyist. Many of us in CARD were opposed to lobbying because of its reputation of buying votes, but we became convinced that it was the only way we could get this bill through. Part of our decision to become a 501c4 rather than a 501c3 in the beginning was so that we could have the option of lobbying available to us. I am so thankful to Lisa for her advice on this. The lobbyist knew how to talk with the officials and had already built relationships where they could have an in-depth conversation within the confines of these relationships. They were quite effective.

Our bill was put through the ringer. We had several re-writes and stakeholder meetings in order to finally have a bill that was as tight as we could get. We basically held Powertech to what they said they could and would do with baseline data and clean up. The one thing we continually would not give on was that in order to mine, a company would have to show documentation of 5 sites that had been restored to baseline data. This is what Powertech kept telling us they could readily do and had already been done in many areas. They swore there would be no change to the water quality. So, we held their feet to the fire.

The fun thing with all their testimony was that we kept stating that they were promising exactly what the bill required. They were on record with these statements through the media and during the process of writing the bill. They could not testify that they could not restore the water quality to baseline.

We knew that it has never been done. We had proactive legislation. This was historical and precedent setting legislation. Colorado is the only state to require that uranium miner's toe the line and do good baseline testing and prove that they can restore the mining site to that baseline data before they are done.

I'm so proud of Jay, Jeff and Representatives Fischer and Kefalas and Senator Steve Johnson. Thank you gentlemen!

Here is a synopsis of the bill from the Digest of Bills Enacted at the Second Regular Session Of the Sixty-sixth General Assembly June 2008 Prepared by the Office of Legislative Legal Services

HB 08-1161

Mined land reclamation - in situ leach mining – permit requirements – protection of ground water quality - appropriation.

Defines "in-situ leach mining" as the in-situ leach mining of uranium.

Requires the reclamation of lands affected by in-situ leach mining.

Specifies that uranium mining is a type of designated mining operation. Requires all in-situ leach mining to restore all affected ground water to its pre-mining quality for all water quality parameters that are specifically identified in the baseline site characterization in the water quality control commission's regulations. Requires applicants for in-situ leach mining permits to notify the owners of record of lands within 3 miles of the affected land and to describe in their application at last 5 similar mining operations that did not result in ground water contamination and the applicants' compliance history. In the case of in-situ leach mining, requires determined land reclamation board (board) to:

- Require the restoration of ground water to begin immediately upon any cessation of extraction or production or the detection of contaminated ground water outside of the affected land.
- Require, as a condition of permit issuance, that the applicant for an in-situ leach mining operation pay for an initial site characterization and ongoing monitoring of the affected land and affected surface and ground water;
- Deny a permit if the applicant fails to demonstrate that reclamation will be accomplished; and
- Act on permit applications within 240 days.

Authorizes the board to deny a permit:

- Based on scientific or technical uncertainty about the feasibility of reclamation:
- If the existing or reasonably foreseeable potential future uses of the affected ground water include domestic or agricultural uses and the mining will adversely affect the suitability of the ground water for such uses;
- If the applicant has previously violated the reclamation laws and any violation remains unabated; or
- If the applicant has demonstrated a pattern of willful violations of environmental protection requirements.
- Requires notification to the office of mined land reclamation of any failure or imminent failure of certain listed mining structures

within 24 hours after such failure or the discovery of imminent failure.

- Expands the list of such mining structures.

Appropriates $42,540 to the department of natural resources for the implementation of the act, of which $14,406 is reappropriated to the department of law.

APPROVED by Governor May 20, 2008 EFFECTIVE May 20, 2008

May 2008. The bill had passed with strong bi-partisan support. Some of the committee votes were in unanimous support! We did it! Now it was time for Governor Ritter to sign it into law.

A couple of weeks before the signing ceremony Laura and I went for a ride. The day was clear, calm and warm. We were feeling really good. I was riding a horse named Senator with whom I was working on developing a solid partnership. As we rode out I didn't have a thing weighing me down. Laura and I were talking and laughing and quite frankly I wasn't really paying attention to any warning signs Senator might have given me. I just wanted to have fun and relax. Laura said something that really cracked me up, I don't know what signal I may have given during the laughter but Senator went into a big buck, launched into a quick turn and as I hit the ground he galloped home. Laura, riding in front, heard the commotion and turned around just in time to see me on the ground and the dust flying off of Senators hooves. "What happened?!?"

I had come off hard. I couldn't stand up let alone walk. I had a bad hip injury and my hand looked funny when I looked down at it. We were three miles from home and I wasn't sure how I was going to get back.

Laura dismounted and attempted to help me up onto her horse to lead me home. After much painful effort I was finally up in the saddle.

One step, two steps, oh the pain, three steps, four steps. "Stop! I can't do this," I cried.

The pain was intense. Instead we decided I would wait where I was and she would ride back to our place, get a vehicle and come back to get me.

Laura took off at a gallop and I lay just off the trail while I cried in pain, anger and frustration. I wasn't mad at Senator... he had a ton of past trauma that we were working through. I was mad at myself. I kept trying to replay what had happened in my head so I could figure out what triggered him that big way. I'm sure I shifted, or jumped, or both, in a way that startled him as I went into that big laugh. He just felt like he needed to get the heck out of there and did just what he needed to get that done. All I wanted was to get back home and reassure him.

> What Senator was reacting to was my own unresolved trauma as it was stuffed. I had been asking him to release his trauma and trust me, but he couldn't truly trust me because he could sense my own incongruence. He was always on edge because he knew I really was like that shut down horse of which I spoke earlier. His trauma involved mishandling by previous humans who did things that offended his soul. My trauma was similar. We both had deep traumas that were caused by domination and we both had trust issues because of this.

> Just when I was feeling like I had overcome a huge hurdle of beating back dominators, Senator knew that I wasn't really dealing with the past frozen and shut down emotions that needed to be moved. He was trying his best to overcome his own issues, so when I scared him through a boisterous laugh, he decided to just get the heck out of there before who knew what additional energies were going to come out of me. He was teaching me that I needed to get a handle on the Whole picture before I could truly be trusted. Of course, I knew none of this at

the time. I was just confused about the fact that we had made big progress and suddenly it disappeared.

This injury was me busy manifesting what I needed to dig deeper into my past trauma's in order to release what needed to be released before I could truly continue on in a healthy way.

Jay had seen Senator gallop in without me. He let Senator into the pasture and jumped in the truck and headed in the direction he had seen us go. He hadn't gotten far when Laura met up with him. She told him what happened and then led the way back to where I was still laying and sulking.

Now I had two helpers to boost me into the truck. OUCH! Not quite as painful as getting onto Laura's horse, but it still hurt. I asked Jay to drive me to Senator, I needed to talk with him and let him know that I was not angry. Of course, I still could not stand on my own but I just had to get as close to him as I could. Jay and Laura helped me out of the truck and to the ground where Senator could come over. Jay untacked him and brought me some carrots. Senator came over and I told him that I was not angry but didn't understand what happened. I apologized for scaring him into a flight response. After I had my talk with Senator, Laura began telling me that I needed to get to a doctor. I said "No, I'll give it a little while and see how I'm doing in the morning."

"Do you guys have insurance," she asked? "Is that why you won't go?"

"Yeah, no insurance. I'll lie down and do some of my own doctoring and see how it is in the morning. Maybe I just need to rest it."

By this time Jay and I were in really bad shape financially. We were behind on every bill and barely keeping food on the table. I couldn't see how I could go to the doctor. Plus, I had a lot of trust in the alternative remedies I use. I had homeopathics, essential oils, herbs and Faith on my side.

Laura left but not before extracting a promise from me that if things worsened, I'd go to the doctor. I think I sort of promised, but knew things would have to be much worse before I'd go in.

I had Jay put me to bed and rub my hip with a blend of oils. I then had him mix up a few herbs to take internally. He taped my fingers together and I rested.

Oh my how it hurt the next day. I stayed on my regimen of homeopathics, oils and herbs all day. Luckily I had some crutches from a previous injury a couple of years before so that, with Jay's help, I could get to the bathroom.

By day three I ended up calling a chiropractor that I used to go to on a regular basis, hoping he could help my healing process. I was pretty sure I had a broken finger, and wasn't sure what exactly was going on in the hip.

He worked on my low back and hip for a few days in a row. I also did go to a cash-only clinic and had my finger x-rayed – yup broken. But between what I was doing with my remedies, the chiropractor and the finger taping I was healing.

By the time of the signing ceremony I was able to hobble using one crutch. I could stand when I had just that one crutch in front of me in case I needed it. My fingers were still taped together, but in all my wounded glory, I was ready to meet the Governor and have our bill signed into law!

Again, I was asked to speak at the Capitol. I never felt nervous, just grateful! I felt empowered. I was an injured warrior who was ready to accept honor for a battle well fought. I felt like we had just won a very significant part of the war.

CHAPTER 16

LESSONS LEARNED

Hobbling out of the capitol building with my new pen (Governor Ritter handed me the first pen from his signature on the bill) I wasn't sure what would happen next. I wasn't sure if the legislation would really stop Powertech from mining. I wasn't sure if the regulators would truly protect our water. I felt relief and a hope of a future, but I also knew that by this time things were beginning to look pretty grim for us financially.

We had made sure the legislation was written in a way to allow Powertech to mine if they could meet the criteria that they had set through their own promises. I wondered if Powertech would be able to meet those criteria, and if they could, how I felt about that. Of course, I was relieved and excited that we had won this huge victory I just wondered how real it was.

The next year was spent developing the regulations that fulfilled our new law. It was also spent watching Powertech continue to make moves that indicated they intended to move forward, law or no law. Jay kept saying they couldn't show five sites that had been restored to baseline, so there was no way they could mine. I went back to work in the horse world and eventually Powertech just went away. They still contend that they could mine here, but they've since sold their rights to the minerals in Northern Colorado and there has been no activity for several years now by them or the new owners.

Jay and I struggled for several years financially. It was extremely difficult. We were in foreclosure twice, but, by the Grace of God, we are still at Mustang Hollow.

> And this financial struggle was just another way that I was manifesting, or rather not manifesting. Even though not long after we really drove Powertech away, I began looking at myself, I had spent several years already manifesting in an unhealthy way. It would take some time for the Universe to catch up to my more healthy state of being. This struggle for survival was a big part of the lesson that I needed in order to go deep enough to find all that needed to be cleared.

> I spent years doing my personal work with the help of equine assisted therapy, somatic archeology, workshops that taught about emotional intelligence and more. I am so glad that I found the way to go inside and heal my past traumas. I truly feel that it is only because of this deep connection to my body through this work that I am still here today in a way that allows me to write this book.

I originally titled this book: "What I learned from Nunn" because this experience was a very deep learning experience for me. So what did I learn?

1. How to work with elected officials:
    a. I learned that partisan politics are ineffective. We have to stop looking at each of the two major political parties as being what we are told their ideologies within the party are and find the human who was elected and is truly serving. This is our job as constituents and I pray that the people who are serving continue to remember that they are there to truly serve us, the people, not just a political party.
    b. Remember to keep all of your communications with the opposition professional. I had one of those unprofessional

conversations, and boy did I feel bad afterwards. I blew a relationship that I had been building for months.

c.   Don't give up after just one or two communications in which you receive a form letter response back. Keep attempting to generate a real conversation. Eventually you will get a real response.

d.   Call their office, and again remain professional. Develop a relationship with whomever answers the phone the day you call. If that person answers the phone often they will begin to remember you. This can lead to them having a real conversation with the elected official you are calling.

e.   When you notice that an elected official will be in town, go to them. Set up a time to talk with them in person and compliment them on anything in which you can find common ground. I believe they got into politics because they truly do wish to make a difference for their constituents. Build upon that.

f.   Always remember to thank them for any effort they make in your direction, no matter how much your ideology might disagree with theirs.

2.   Working with the media:

a.   Press releases are your friend. Do a press release as often as you are able with any new information you have found and/or any activities you are doing with your effort.

b.   Have a few talking points that you stick to. Reporters are very good at asking questions that might lead you on a tangent. Drama sells and they may edit in a way to show the drama which may or may not work in your favor. Keep those talking points present in the conversation and redirect back to them whenever you can. Remember that everything you say to a reporter is on the record.

c.   Be available for the media given their tight schedule. Always ask what their deadline is as you attempt to find the right time to talk with them. This helps you get your message into the next publication.

3. Working with the public:
   a. Talking points are your friend. People walk around with their own idea of what you are attempting to say even before you speak. Keep to your talking points and don't allow them to draw you into a different angle on your issue. We all know that you have likely done a ton of research about your issue and know a lot of different reasons why you have decided to become active in your opposition.

   Attempting to share your wealth of information in the few moments you have to convince a person to sign your petition or attend an informative meeting will generally cause that person to either become combative or to glaze over without any desire to learn more. Stick to the few talking points that you have agreed to target. For us it was clean water. We have no life without water.

   b. Don't get drawn into an argument. Some people will see you and decide to debate you just *because*. We would have people often wishing to debate the issue of nuclear power. It took me a couple of times of having these debates to realize that debating in a public venue is ineffective for both the person to whom you are speaking and those who might be listening on the sidelines. People begin to see you as an anti-nuc activist or whatever 'anti' label they wish to give you. Instead, lean on your talking points. When someone would say, "So you must not see nuclear power as a good option." I would reply, "What I know is that we need clean water to live and that this mining process is shown to contaminate the water. We just want them to do the mining in a responsible way. We need them to protect the water." Deep down I knew that there was likely no way for them to mine and to protect the water. The person I'm speaking to did not know that and would see me as a reasonable person who will allow this mining to happen if they are able to protect the finite resource of water in the process. No argument available here, sign the petition and move on.

I had several pro-nuclear power people sign my petitions because of the way I got good at not arguing with them. In the end we really were and are about protecting the water so it was easy for me to have this conversation. My opinions about nuclear power had nothing to do with what we were attempting to accomplish.

4. Always, always, always have a petition for people to sign. When you speak to elected officials and the public you can point to the number of people who support you. Every person you speak to and do not have a petition available for them to sign is a missed opportunity. Always have a petition even if you don't know your ultimate goal just have them sign something that expresses their concern. Always have the petition available for download off of your website so that others can collect signatures and mail it to you. This doubles and triples your efforts without even trying. Before we had our first town hall meeting in Wellington, we had a simply worded petition:

> *To Weld and Larimer County Commissioners and State of Colorado representatives and officials:*
>
> *We, the undersigned residents of northern Colorado, are deeply concerned about proposals to mine uranium in our area.*
>
> - *According to the Nuclear Regulatory Commission's 2007 report, in situ leach mining has a history of contaminating water.*
> - *Uranium mining provides material used for nuclear power, and our area would benefit far more from renewable energy development, such as wind and solar energy.*
> - *Uranium mining benefits out-of-state companies, not our local economies.*

We urge our representatives and public officials to:

- *Avoid providing any permits that would allow uranium mining until all questions about safety, health, and water quality are answered by those who propose to mine.*
- *Develop regulations that protect your constituents from the use of in situ leaching technology to mine uranium in Colorado.*
- *Promote economic development that provides for local people and meets local needs.*

5. Get resolutions from local towns, chambers of commerce, businesses, associations, any organized group. We would do our informative meeting at town meetings, county commissioner meetings, real estate agent gatherings, schools, professional networking groups, etc, etc. Any place they would listen to us. These resolutions created momentum for the next resolution. If we were speaking to a group of professionals, we could point to a signed resolution from either their competition or their peers and this would generally at least get us in the door.

6. An activist endeavor is at its very core a marketing campaign. I often say that we embarked on the biggest marketing campaign I never thought I wanted to do. Flyers, websites, t-shirts, bumper stickers, yard signs, magnetic signs for the sides of our vehicles, balloons, promoting at every event we could find, walking and/or riding in every parade we could, engaging people who were willing to help us and then talking our elected officials into stepping up for their constituents. Marketing your ideas to everyone is the key.

7. I learned that you don't really have to know what you are doing, just do something. Keep doing things and pray for guidance. Eventually, more people who have good ideas will begin to show up to help. Good ideas will build upon more good ideas and things will begin to click in a functional way.

8. I learned that making the inevitable emotions wrong was ineffective. We needed the emotional appeal as well as the logical appeal. A good balance is the most effective. If people tell you that you should never be emotional don't listen. When I cried on the first interview, it got the attention of several people. Emotion is your informer. Listen to the messages given then you will be more capable of making good decisions. Of course, don't use emotion as manipulation.

> Develop a strong relationship with your emotions so that they come out in a congruent way that does not make the person to whom you are speaking feel wronged by them. I had a lot to learn in this arena and can honestly say it is a lifetime endeavor. But do some work with the emotional message charts that are available and become the fully functional emotional human that is your Divine right. I learned that it is okay to weep for the waters of our planet. I learned that it is okay to develop strong boundaries by presenting a sharp word or clear message when required.

> When our emotion is honored as the messenger that it is, we get good at not projecting that emotion onto others. This is how we can be more effective. Honor the emotions and listen to their message and make good decisions and take good actions with that information.

9. One of the biggest lessons that came out of this journey was that I had a lot of personal work to do. I didn't realize how judgmental I was, nor how truly emotionally shut down I was, even though I believed myself to be compassionate and overly emotional. I had to step out of a box of labels in which I had placed myself to be an effective activist. I learned a lot about myself and then had to learn how to not be a victim any longer. This journey brought me into a place where I had to take a deep look at myself and my past traumas. I had some extensive inner healing to do and this journey

helped me open up to that. So, I learned it was okay to look at myself and to love myself.

I met an EPONAquest Worldwide instructor and we discussed the work she was doing to enable deeper relationships with our horses. After my experience with my horse, Senator, I knew that I needed to dive deeper into what my relationships really looked like. I asked her if she would work with me. We began the session by discussing how to develop intuition and really listen to the messages that one feels from the body.

She guided me through a body scan meditation. Following the full scan I was invited to focus on that place in my body that was speaking the loudest. My solar plexus spoke to me about a deep feeling of unworthiness. I knew this in my head already and had gotten very good at stuffing these feelings because I had to put on a confident public persona. Now I was hearing it in my heart since I was in my body.

She taught me about using the emotions that we feel as the message giver. She taught me how to listen to my body speak so that I could feel the emotion in order to hear the message. She then invited me to ask my herd of horses who would like to work with me on this feeling of unworthiness.

Cherry had her head over the fence and I felt so clearly that it was to be her that day. We took Cherry into the round pen and then I did something completely different than I had ever before done in a relationship building exercise with a horse. She and I stood together in the middle of the round pen and after I asked her if she could help me. I felt the urge to walk around the round pen while she stood in the middle and observed. I felt myself checking out my body language in the walk. I noticed her watching me with love and support. I felt tears of grief rolling down my cheeks as I recognized how I had painful loss to integrate. I continued to walk as I heard very clearly that I am worthy of love.

After walking a few times around the round pen as I embodied these messages, I slowed my walk to a stop. Cherry approached me and dropped her head into my chest. I reached over and hugged her and stroked her and cried my gratitude to her. Cherry has always been my best school horse and she had chosen this day to begin teaching me more than I ever knew I needed to learn. And boy did I have a lot to learn about myself. My walk of worthiness of self-love and self-awareness was just beginning.

I believe that that is the biggest gift from this journey of fighting the uranium miners. I had a new opportunity to look within and to grow stronger and more courageous.

CARD continued on......

After we had the legislation passed, we still had a lot of work to do to get the rules written and to keep Powertech accountable. We continued to have Town Hall meetings and we made a lot of interesting connections. Our success with the legislation made activist organizations begin to come closer together and we hosted a regional meeting of these groups at Mustang Hollow.

We also had the gift of hosting Dr. Gavin Mudd from Australia. Dr. Mudd is the author of the research paper we printed out and sent to many, many people. We thrilled when he told us that he would make Colorado a part of his scheduled trip to the United States. While he was here we hosted a meet & greet at Mustang Hollow with those same surrounding regional activist groups so everyone could speak more deeply with him.

We presented a town hall meeting in Fort Collins with Dr. Mudd as the featured speaker. His talk was a powerful one and I was grateful that we had several media outlets present that day. I believe that his words had a lasting impact on the opinions about the in-situ leaching process for uranium.

One of the days he was with us, a few of us CARD horseback riders took him on a horseback riding tour of our area. He got a real kick out of an authentic western style tour.

To have someone with his credentials come talk with us and as many others we could get in front of him was really powerful for all of us. He also spoke of remaining safe as an environmental activist. He urged those of us who were most active to remain in the spotlight as much as possible, this, he felt, is what keeps us safe.

> When I look back at our journey, I do remember a few times that I felt like something was off – as in maybe I had been followed, or someone was watching our house, but I never felt really unsafe. Jay and I just chose safety and I feel that our strong spiritual connections were part of what kept us safe.

Of course, Powertech continued to attempt to get their previously applied for injection well permit from the EPA. Their public commentary period allowed us to speak both in person and online. The EPA hosted a public meeting in Nunn where many people spoke in opposition to them granting the permit.

Here is what I submitted as my comment both in person and via e-mail:

"Thank you for the opportunity to publicly comment on Powertech Uranium Corporation's application for a Class V injection well permit.

As I was considering what I would like to say about this permit, I decided to go to the EPA's website to look up the mission statement. The EPA's mission statement is: "The mission of the EPA is to protect human health and to safeguard the natural environment – air, water and land – upon which life depends."

While continuing to read about what the EPA's purpose is (which I will not take the time to read here) I began considering all that we have been experiencing during our time of guarding our lives and livelihood against potential water contamination from the ISL mining process.

You will likely be already hearing from or may have already heard from several people regarding the potential physical health impacts and the environmental impacts associated with this proposed operation.

I would like to take just a moment to discuss the psychological impacts that have occurred and continue to occur. More and more scientific data is proving that to be truly physically healthy, one must have a healthy mind, body and spirit.

Neither a healthy mind nor a healthy spirit are a part of a person when they have a lack of trust. I am operating from a state of a lack of trust. This lack of trust is justified by the fact that Powertech has admitted to performing two previous pump tests. Should EPA permitting have been done before they did these previous tests? Have they already reinjected fluids into our drinking water aquifer? If this is the case how can we trust them to operate using proper safeguards when they have already shown a disregard for regulations that are already in place?

I have also witnessed Powertech Uranium's disregard for protecting the current state of underground water supplies through improper well capping. The state of Colorado has issued at least two warnings to encourage Powertech to protect our life and safety by protecting our source of water by properly capping open holes. Something as simple as opening a water faucet in order to pour a drink of water should not generate fear.

Every time I see a drill rig in the area within which I live, I feel anxiety. I do not know if that particular drill rig will be the one which will contaminate my drinking water supplies just enough to disallow me to use our domestic water well. I will likely NOT know if my water supplies are contaminated with toxic heavy metals or radioactivity until after I, my husband, my animals and/or my family, friends or clients have consumed quite a bit of it. How many times are we expected to have to absorb the cost of testing our own water quality because of the activities of our 'neighbors?'

Since, our property lies directly downstream from Powertech owned property I feel anxiety every time I watch a major thunderstorm move in. I feel anxiety when I then watch the flood waters course through our property and collect in our ponds carrying who knows what from the tailings that are created from their drilled holes. Or the water carrying who knows what out of the now overfilled mud pits. Our livestock drinks from this water, the kids we host as family, friends and clients play in the ponds, and our dogs regularly swim in and drink this water.

Living in this kind of state of fear and anxiety and operating from a place of mistrust does not promote nor protect health. In fact, just the opposite.

I encourage the EPA to reject Powertech Uranium Corporations application for a Class V injection well permit under the guise that they may have already shown a lack of regard for the EPA's regulations and rules. I encourage the EPA to reject Powertech Uranium Corporations application for a Class V injection well permit because of the lack of safeguards surrounding the drill hole tailings and their migration with the flood waters from the multiple major thunderstorms that happen each year.

I cannot begin to fathom how the EPA could justify permitting this kind of threat to human health and environmental safety. I encourage the EPA to remember its mission of protecting human health and safeguarding the natural environment – air, water, and land – upon which life depends. I encourage the EPA to act upon this mission by rejecting the Powertech Uranium Corporation application.

Again, thank you for your time and this opportunity to comment on this permit application."

It felt good to speak from the heart.

Their application was denied on technicalities and they never did reapply for this permit. I can honestly say that I continue to urge the EPA to act upon their mission: "…. *to protect human health and to safeguard the natural environment – air, water and land – upon which life depends."* As I write this many standards are being reduced, as the reductions support growth and business. This is at the cost of human health and the health of the natural environment. It is important that we all continue to speak for LIFE.

So… what did I learned from Nunn? Oh so many things! But mostly, the power of ONE *is…*

EPILOGUE

The journey of personal growth through this process is in the story, but I wanted to reflect a little more upon what that personal growth really looked like. I started out in the capacity of what I thought was a relatively independent woman. I was a 4-H leader and a business owner. As an intelligent woman I have a strong respect for what the mind brings forward. Stepping into the role of activist really helped me see where I had many preconceived notions and beliefs that were not truly serving me.

I had to grow into a stronger leader by stepping more and more out of my comfort zone and talk to people that I never thought I wanted to speak to. I had to grow in my confidence in speaking in public. I had to learn a lot of skills that have continued to serve me well. This journey was very good for me as I grew in these skills.

The thing that I missed in my growth during this journey was the evolvement that made me more grounded, more human and more loving. I had to do my personal work to get there and this journey only helped show me that this is something that I needed to do.

When I met the Eponaquest instructor, I was on a spiral downward. Even though we had won a monumental victory for the water of Colorado, I wasn't finding a place of peace or joy within. I couldn't truly own that I had done something worthwhile because I still had that place of self-loathing. What the work that I began to do with her did for me was to find those places that were stuck because of past traumas that had not been allowed to speak.

I spoke earlier of my experience with endometriosis and the intense pain associated with it. I did a lot of work finding solutions to this pain through alternative therapies. I made dietary changes, used essential oils, homeopathy, acupuncture, chiropractic, herbal remedies and yoga to help. Yes, all of these things were beneficial, but there were still days that I had a lot of pain and/or heavy menstrual bleeding.

I had replaced allopathic remedies with more natural remedies as a way to treat symptoms rather than finding the true source of the dis-ease. Once I began diving into the emotions and learning that my body was holding things that needed to be released, that was when I truly began a deeper journey of personal growth and healing.

Going into the body with somatic work was the key to unlocking the past trauma, being able to really look at it, get the gift in it so that then it could be alchemized into the gold that I now truly embody and hold. It was not an easy process… *that is for sure.* I had to commit. I had to be vulnerable. I had to speak my new found truth to those I love dearly and who I feared would judge me and this process of self-awareness and self-love.

The reality is that the body does not lie. It doesn't know how to lie. Our ego can come in and create stories and lies that cover up what the body holds until the body has its final say. That is why I call it dis-ease. That is why I insist that one must do their personal work in order to walk this lifetime in a healthy way. The body will always show those experiences at which one needs to look.

During the process, I shed a lot of tears and sometimes wondered if I would find my way back out of that sadness to peace. I can assure you that I did. I used the tools given to me and the support of those who truly helped me become more whole. I found my way back to peace and wholeness without enabling my unwellness through distraction and addiction. It was truly a process and a deep commitment to myself, but a worthy one indeed.

My relationship with horses has completely transformed. I now recognize them to be very wise souls. Horses helped me during many sessions with an Eponaquest guide, but also in the quiet times I spent with them. They helped me develop my intuition through the many gifts they freely gave me. They helped me find a deep self-love. Oftentimes they gave me the messages that I could not truly hear because I was so imbedded in the lie that I was telling myself.

There are stories within this text that are some of those moments when the horses were trying their best to tell me something. They were teaching me all along. I just did not have the capacity to truly hear what they were saying until developing a different relationship with myself and in turn with them. Today, my horses and I are partners in coaching others. This feels much better to me and I know it feels much better to them. I am so grateful for horses in my life.

What is really cool about this story is how Powertech came at us just as a schoolyard bully comes at their victim. 'Might is right' – they proclaimed. They had the power and the law behind them. What they didn't have was what is truly moral. They had the money but we had soul. We tapped into our spiritual guidance from the beginning and I really feel that remaining in that place of faith – even though rattled deeply from time to time – is what helped us with our success.

Our world is full of those who continue to shout 'might makes right' as they dominate and destroy LIFE. Don't let them win. Remember your soul.

Blessings,
Robin